Protecting Human Rights

Other titles in the series

Protecting Human Rights

A Comparative Study

Todd Landman

Georgetown University Press
Washington, D.C.

Georgetown University Press, Washington, D.C.
© 2005 by Georgetown University Press. All rights reserved.
Printed in the United States of America

10   9   8   7   6   5   4   3   2   1   2005

This book is printed on acid-free paper meeting
the requirements of the American National Standard
for Permanence in Paper for Printed Library Materials.

Library of Congress Cataloging-in-Publication Data

Landman, Todd.
    Protecting human rights : a comparative study / Todd Landman.
        p. cm. — (Advancing human rights series)
    Includes bibliographical references and index.
    ISBN 1-58901-064-7 (cloth : alk. paper) — ISBN 1-58901-063-9
(pbk. : alk. paper)
    1. Human rights—Cross-cultural studies.   I. Title.   II. Series.
    JC571.L247 2005
    323'.09'045—dc22

                                                          2005008368

Contents

Figures

Tables

Acknowledgments

This book was conceived and written primarily at the University of Essex over a three-year period. My long-standing interest in human rights dates from my study of Latin American politics as an undergraduate at the University of Pennsylvania. The application of quantitative political science methods to the study of rights protection began at the University of Essex and has continued throughout my time working in the Department of Government and at the Human Rights Centre. The inspiration for the book came from my interaction with colleagues at Essex and during the time I spent working on an interdisciplinary European Master's Degree in Human Rights and Democratization in Venice.

The Department and the Centre at Essex as well as the Venice program provided the intellectual space to consider the relationship between law and politics at the domestic and international levels, which led to a series of questions about how to test the effectiveness of the international human rights regime with the use of dominant theories and methods of international law, international relations, and comparative politics. Without that intellectual space, this book would not have been possible, and the people in these different venues have made a crucial difference in the way in which this study has been carried out. While I must pay tribute to them for their inspiration and assistance in the preparation of the book, the questions, methods, findings, conclusions, and remaining errors are entirely my own.

At Essex, I wish to thank Hugh Ward for regular discussions on regime effectiveness, data analysis, international relations theory, and general support for the study. David Sanders has offered unwavering support and methodological advice. Geoff Gilbert offered human rights legal theory advice. Paul Hunt has been a close friend and colleague with whom I shared much time running the Human Rights

Centre and who has continually pressed me on issues of human rights measurement and impact assessment. Nigel Rodley has supported the study and asked difficult questions regarding my tests of regime effectiveness. Françoise Hampson was instrumental in helping me identify possible spurious explanations and in the consideration of reservations in the overall analysis. David Howarth provided helpful comments on early drafts of the theory chapter. Eric Tanenbaum provided assistance in data transfers and advice on the weighting of treaty variables to take reservations into account.

In addition to these colleagues at Essex, I had a series of researchers who helped with various aspects of the project. Gabriela Gonzalez-Rivas assembled the treaty information that helped build the data set. Meghna Abraham offered legal theory reading suggestions and was a valuable sounding board for my ideas. Sebastian Dellepiane collated the extant literature on human rights measurement and has been a valuable colleague. Gemma Mackman assisted in collating the data on international nongovernmental organizations. Noam Lubell helped code the reservations for the main international treaty variables.

My work at the Human Rights Centre would not be possible without Anne Slowgrove, who has been a strong base of administrative support and has encouraged my work. Finally, thanks to the University of Essex for my sabbatical leave to work on the study during the 2002–2003 academic year.

In the United States, I wish to thank Oona Hathaway and Linda Camp Keith for discussing their work on human rights regime effectiveness. Thanks to Bruce Russett and Susan Hennigan for providing data on international governmental organization membership. Bert Lockwood has continually supported my attempts to bring human rights further into mainstream political science. Zehra Arat has been a big supporter and was instrumental in establishing the Human Rights Section of the American Political Science Association, of which I am an active member. I have had the good fortune of presenting sections of this study over the last three years at the APSA meetings in San Francisco (2001), Boston (2002), and Philadelphia (2003). John Wallach has encouraged and supported my work. Richard Steinberg encouraged work on the data models in chapter 6 during our time teaching at the University of Coimbra's summer school in human rights. Andrew Moravcsik supported the nonrecursive modeling and the general set of arguments advanced throughout the study. Sumner Twiss encouraged submission of the book proposal to Georgetown

University Press and supported the idea during its early stages. Thanks to Richard Brown at Georgetown University Press for guiding the publication of the manuscript.

In Europe, I wish to thank Markku Suksi, who has been a friend and colleague in the Venice program and gave me the first encouragement to look at the correlation between ratification and protection. Horst Fischer has been an inspiration in testing the effectiveness of the international human rights regime. Attracta Ingram has been a dear friend and colleague who has supported my work and kindly invited me to present my theoretical ideas in chapter 2 as part of the seminar series at University College Dublin in April 2003. I wish to thank the European Commission for funding the project Mapping the Main International Initiatives on Developing Indicators on Democracy and Good Governance (EU Contract no. 200221200005). Many of the methodological discussions on measurement in chapter 3 draw on research conducted on this project. The Ministry of Foreign Affairs of the Netherlands funded a project on Human Rights Assessment and Performance Evaluation, which allowed me to learn more about the human rights movement from the lessons of nine human rights NGOs engaged in standard setting, monitoring, and advocacy activities.

At a personal level, I wish to thank Elmer van der Hoek, Paul and Gemma Mackman, Malcolm Latchman, Dave Smith, Leigh Amos, and Lily Amos-Smith, who have been great friends in the United Kingdom. Thanks to Drew, Kate, Hank, and Laura Landman for their continued support for my endeavors. Special thanks to Melissa Collier and Oliver Heginbotham, whose charm, wit, good graces, support, and companionship have been most welcome during the completion of the manuscript.

Finally, I wish to dedicate this book to Sophia Laura Landman, who, more than anyone, is teaching me the value of human dignity.

1

Norms and Rights at the Turn of the Century

The turn of the new century offers an opportunity for reflection and critical assessment of both the achievements and setbacks in the global human rights project. The post–World War II era has seen the establishment and subsequent growth of the international law of human rights, a turn away from authoritarianism with the global spread of democratic forms of rule, and an increasing number of international interventions carried out on behalf of human rights. The international law of human rights includes major international and regional treaties, institutions, and organizations. By the year 2000, between 95 and 191 countries had become signatories to the main international legal instruments, which many have argued comprise an international regime for the promotion and protection of human rights (Henkin 1979; Donnelly 1989; Hathaway 2002). This regime has grown in both breadth and depth. An increasing number of human rights have been given express legal protection, including civil, political, economic, social, and cultural rights. And an increasing number of countries have formally committed themselves to the human rights norms and values originally found in the 1948 UN Universal Declaration of Human Rights. Similar such regimes (albeit of different strength and capacity) have been established in Europe, the Americas, and Africa.

Alongside this evolution in the international law of human rights, the world has seen a dramatic turn away from authoritarian forms of

1

rule to nascent forms of democracy. Since the Portuguese transition to democracy in 1974, the global spread and pace of democratization have led to a world in which over 60 percent of the countries are now at least nominally democratic (Diamond 1999). Global comparative studies on the tangible benefits of democratic rule have demonstrated a decrease in international violent conflict (see Weede 1992; Ward and Gleditsch 1998; Russett and O'Neal 2001), lower levels of violation of personal integrity rights (Poe and Tate 1994; Poe, Tate, and Keith 1999; Zanger 2000a), and levels of economic development and performance that are no worse than those found under authoritarian regimes (Ersson and Lane 1996; Przeworski et al. 2000).

In addition to the development of human rights law and processes of democratization, the world has witnessed an increasing number of foreign interventions carried out ostensibly on behalf of human rights or on humanitarian grounds, such as those in East Timor and Kosovo. Moreover, the tradition of human rights tribunals first established in Nuremberg has been renewed with tribunals for Rwanda and the former Yugoslavia. Variants of such tribunals have appeared at the domestic level with the formation of numerous truth and reconciliation commissions (TRCs) in Latin America, Africa, and Eastern Europe, whose remit has been to collect information on past crimes against humanity and to offer some form of reconciliation to deeply torn societies (De Brito 1997; Roniger and Sznajder 1999; Hayner 1994, 2002). Arguably, this proliferation of tribunals has culminated in the establishment of the International Criminal Court (ICC), a process that has been described as the international "institutionalisation of criminal liability" (Falk 2000, 4).

Scholars and commentators have seen this evolution in the protection of human rights as progressing through four phases: the normative foundation of human rights, the process of institution building, implementation of rights protection in the post–cold war era, and the further development of individual criminal responsibility, minority rights protection, and collective humanitarian responsibility (Buergenthal 1997). Such observations have led some to argue that the world has now entered the "age of rights" (Henkin 1990; Bobbio 1996; Loughlin 2000, 199–214) and that it has undergone a "juridical revolution" (Ignatieff 2001), a process of international "legalization" (Abbott et al. 2000), "judicialization" (Stone Sweet 1999; Shapiro and Stone Sweet 2002), and "constitutionalisation" (Petersmann 2002; Alston 2002), in which human rights have become the normative framework for "human conduct in the world of states" (Jackson 2000) and a "moral plateau that is unique in international affairs" (Mutua 2001, 255).

This development of international and regional human rights systems, coupled with democratization and "ethically" oriented foreign relations, suggests that nation-states formally participating in the international legal mechanisms for human rights protection are increasingly embedded in larger institutional structures that seek to constrain and limit their behavior to protect the sanctity of the rights of individuals and certain collectivities.[1] Even those states that have not signed or ratified the various human rights instruments find themselves under increased international pressure from intergovernmental and nongovernmental organizations to join these regimes and to change their practices in conformity with normative global human rights values (Risse, Ropp, and Sikkink 1999; Welch 2001; Hawkins 2002).

These developments may lead to the sanguine conclusion that human rights have finally triumphed and now provide the normative framework for the future of global politics, echoing earlier claims about the "end of ideology" (Bell 1960) and the "end of history" (Fukuyama 1992). In contrast, based on an assessment of human rights failures and the continuation of state violence against citizens throughout the twentieth century, Watson (1999, 4) argues that "the international regime of human rights, if such a thing is to exist, is notable for its consistent lack of effective enforcement." For others, the rights agenda is certainly on the table, but it has "yet to realize the rudiments of its full political potential" (Foweraker and Landman 1997, 243), in which the language of rights challenges authoritarian regimes and the mobilization for rights is accompanied by democratic transitions. But a consistent gap between the formal institutions of democracy and the full protection of rights has led to the emergence of so-called hollow and illiberal democracy (Diamond 1999; O'Donnell 1999; Foweraker and Krznaric 2000; Zakaria 2003; Foweraker, Landman, and Harvey 2003). Moreover, in response to the threat of terrorism, advanced democracies such as the United States, Britain, and Germany have passed new legislation that undermines basic human rights norms, including strictures on arbitrary detention, privacy, and communication (see, e.g., Dworkin 2002, 273–75).

In addition to the emergence of hollow democracy and the new national security legislation in liberal democracies compromising long-held human rights norms, human rights interventions by the "international community" have indeed been selective. Beyond the interventions in Kosovo and East Timor, the military interventions in Haiti, Somalia, Iraq, and Bosnia have all been cast as humanitarian efforts legitimized by the language of rights (Ignatieff 2001, 37). Yet the international community failed to respond to the atrocities committed in Rwanda when in 1994 close to 800,000 people were killed in the short space of four months (Ignatieff 2001, 41). Historically, the United States has been willing to support rights-abusing governments ranging from China to Chile, partly in the hope that encouraging stability and economic freedom will ultimately lead to an improvement in human rights (Forsythe 2000, 147; Kornbluh 2003; Dinges 2004). Other liberal democracies, despite having an elective affinity for human rights, have also been selective in the use of military intervention on behalf of human rights.

Such a double standard in international interventionism is often driven by a human rights foreign policy based on geostrategic interest and "pragmatic internationalism" and is not necessarily based on "moral internationalism" (Forsythe 2000, 143). It is thus more accurate to argue that the world has witnessed a "precarious triumph of human rights" (Reiff 1999). It is a triumph, since even the most optimistic observers in 1948 could not have imagined the subsequent growth and influence of human rights discourse and doctrine (see also Steiner and Alston 1996, v; Loughlin 2000, 229–35). But it is precarious, since these same achievements can easily be reversed, where politics and power have shaped the different ways in which such gains have been achieved. Wilson (2001, xxi) notes that "the new 'culture of human rights' is very thin indeed" and that "we may need to temper celebrations of another seeming *triumph* for the model of liberal human rights" (emphasis mine).

Moreover, the world is still a place in which "there are more countries . . . where fundamental rights and civil liberties are regularly violated than countries where they are effectively protected" (Robertson and Merrills 1996, 2). In 1990, Amnesty International noted that of 179 UN member states, 104 states had committed acts of torture against their citizens, and, in their 2002 report, that 111 of 194 member states continued such practices (Amnesty International 1990, 2002). These numbers indicate only a 1 percent drop in the number of states practicing torture (58 percent in 1990 and 57 percent in 2002) over the last decade of the twentieth century. These figures suggest that there is a significant and persistent gap between rights in principle (i.e., those formally protected by international law) and rights in practice (i.e., those rights actually protected by states and enjoyed by individuals and groups) (Foweraker and Landman 1997). For international lawyers, such a gap comprises the difference between the *de jure* protection and *de facto* realization of human rights, or a gap between the "theory and reality of human rights" (Watson 1999, 1–16).

This book is concerned precisely with this significant and persistent gap between principle and practice in human rights protection. Such a gap suggests that there has thus far been an unfulfilled expectation that the growth and sophistication in the international regime of human rights will lead to a greater protection of those rights. The fact that rights protection continues to be precarious despite the increasing participation of states in the various systems for their protection raises fundamental questions for empirical research. What explains the growth of the international law of human rights? What is the nature of the relationship between the international law of human rights and the actual protection of human rights? Does the international law of human rights make a difference for their protection? What other important factors help account for the global variation in rights protection?

This book seeks to answer these questions through the application of theories and methods drawn from international law, international relations, and comparative politics. Theoretically, the book sees a "double convergence" in explanatory accounts of the relationship between politics and law, which centers on the complementary notions of the "socially embedded unit act" (Lichbach 1997) at the domestic level and "embedded liberalism" (Ruggie 1982) at the international level. At both levels of analysis, these complementary notions see individual and state behavior as being constrained by institutions, norms, rules, and expectations. Such constraints, it is argued, ought to have an impact in the long run on the ways in which states organize their domestic political arrangements and the ways in which they interact at the global level. In this way, the protection of human rights serves as an important nexus for these accounts, since the international law of human rights seeks to limit what states may or may not do to their own citizens by providing legal norms, rules, and expectations in line with a particular set of values that uphold the sanctity of the human being. The book thus examines the double convergence in empirical theories that provide possible explanations for the growth and effectiveness of the international human rights regime.

Methodologically, the book is a systematic global comparative and quantitative analysis of the growth and effectiveness of the international human rights regime. It is founded on the ontological and epistemological assumption that the content of human rights can be "read" from the international law of human rights, and that state practices with respect to human rights can be measured in some degree (Landman 2002a, 2003, 204–6). Following extant work on international regimes, the legal rules constraining state behavior in the field of human rights are induced through examination of "treaties, charters and codes" (Puchala and Hopkins 1983, 64), and actual state behavior with respect to the protection of human rights is measured with the use of observations collected by disparate organizations and long-term data research projects. This book thus operationalizes the international regime by using a series of treaty ratification, human rights protection, and other important control variables. Multiple measures of human rights protection allow for more robust descriptive and second-order analysis of empirical relationships. Using the different variables, the study maps and explains the evolution of the international human rights regime and the global variation in human rights protection and tests the two-way relationship between the international regime and the protection of human rights. The study is therefore a theory-driven empirical analysis of the growth and effectiveness of the international human rights regime, the main findings of which should be of interest to scholars and practitioners in the field of human rights, as well as those working in international relations and comparative politics. There are five such main findings.

First, the analysis shows that there is strong empirical support for the limited effect of the international law of human rights on state practice, after controlling for the level of democracy, wealth, international interdependence, intra- and interstate conflict, size, and regional differentiation. Such a result suggests that the proliferation of the international human rights regime has begun to have an impact on state practices, but that this impact should be seen as part of a larger set of socioeconomic changes that have taken place over the latter part of the twentieth century. This main inference differs from those made by Keith (1999) and Hathaway (2002), who find bivariate effects but not multivariate effects between the human rights regime and human rights protection. A different model specification, a different method of estimation, and a differently constructed cross-national time-series data set, which includes more rights measures with greater time-series coverage, account for this difference in result. The inference here also differs from the main arguments of Watson (1999, 1–16), who uses R. J. Rummel's "democide" figures to portray a picture of zero progress and failure of the human rights regime. His cursory analysis focuses on "outliers" in the world (i.e., states that have committed particular atrocities), and many of his figures on state violence cover the whole twentieth century rather than the recent period in which the regime has become more institutionalized and achieved greater international salience.

Second, the results show that democracies are more likely to ratify the instruments that comprise the international human rights regime and are better at protecting human rights than nondemocracies. This result is further differentiated across types of democracy. On the one hand, so-called fourth-wave democracies (i.e., those that experienced democratic transition during the period 1990–1994) have a greater tendency to ratify more human rights treaties with fewer reservations than third-wave democracies (i.e., those that made transitions between 1974 and 1990) and "old" democracies (i.e., those that have been democratic before 1974).[2] These results lend further empirical support to the theory of "liberal republicanism," which argues that "newer" democracies would have a greater tendency to ratify international human rights treaties in order to "lock in" future generations of political actors and limit their ability to undermine or overthrow democratic institutions (Moravcsik 1997, 2000). On the other hand, fourth-wave democracies are worse at protecting human rights than either third-wave democracies or old democracies, suggesting that despite the immediate rights improvement associated with the first year of a democratic transition (Zanger 2000a), it takes time for real reductions in human rights violations to occur, thereby lending further evidence for the existence of hollow democracies.

Third, the difference or gap between the mean ratification of human rights treaties and the mean protection of human rights has narrowed during the period of this study, suggesting a general level of convergence between the expectations of international law and state practice. Regionally, however, this difference is greatest for the Middle East and North Africa, followed by sub-Saharan Africa, Communist Europe (up to 1989), South Asia, and East Asia and the Pacific.

Politically, the difference is greatest for all nondemocracies, followed by fourth-wave, third-wave, and old democracies. Again, democratic longevity appears to mediate the relationship between the international law of human rights and state protection of human rights such that the norms-rights relationship is different across regions and types of democracy.

Fourth, global interdependence makes a difference for regime proliferation and rights practice. Higher levels of International Nongovernmental Organization (INGO) presence are consistently related to ratification of human rights treaties, and higher levels of Inter-Governmental Organization (IGO) membership are consistently related to greater protection of human rights, whereas increased levels of trade do not have a consistent effect on regime participation or rights protection. The results for INGOs and IGOs suggest that these forms of interdependence and greater embeddedness make states more likely to participate in the international human rights regime and to improve the protection of human rights. The finding for INGOs complements the results of small-N comparative studies on the impact of human rights advocacy networks on state practice (Risse, Ropp, and Sikkink 1999; Hawkins 2002). The finding for IGOs complements the larger international relations research on one leg of the Kantian "tripod," which sees a strong relationship between IGO membership and democracy (Russett and O'Neal 2001).

Finally, neither external nor internal conflict has a consistent relationship with the formal participation of states in the international human rights regime, but internal conflict is shown to have a consistently negative impact on the protection of human rights. States in conflict, it appears, do not seek increased international credibility through ratification of human rights treaties, but the strong relationship between involvement in civil war and the violation of human rights is consistent with the extant literature on the global variation in human rights protection (Poe and Tate 1994; Poe et al. 1999; Keith 1999; Hathaway 2002).

The general finding of a limited impact of international human rights law on human rights protection should be of interest to scholars and practitioners in the field of human rights. It is a finding that builds on other work examining the role of norms and institutions in international affairs and shows that over time the proliferation of human rights norms has begun to have an impact on the human rights practices of states. But such an effect is limited, since it is modeled in this study as a larger function of underlying social processes, including democratization, economic development, and greater global interdependence. In public policy terms, the results of the analysis suggest that the promotion of democracy, economic development, international institutionalization, and conflict resolution can have tangible benefits in reducing the violation of human rights.

The theories, methods, empirical analysis, and substantive discussion of the results that make up this study are divided into six chapters. Chapter 2 shows how human rights form an important nexus for empirical theories in international law, international relations, and comparative politics. The chapter shows that at the international level, there has been a convergence in the traditional "polarity of law and power" (Slaughter-Burley 1993, 207), which centers on theories of legal proceduralism (Higgins 1994), neoliberal institutionalism (Keohane 1984, 2001), and liberal republicanism (Moravcsik 1997, 2000). At the domestic level, there has been a convergence among rationalist, structuralist, and culturalist perspectives, which centers on varieties of new-institutionalism (March and Olsen 1984), where individual rational action is seen to be constrained by institutions, ideas, and norms (Lichbach 1997). This double convergence is brought to bear on the international human rights regime and is used to specify an empirical model of human rights protection that is operationalized and tested in the subsequent chapters.

Chapter 3 outlines the main data and methods employed in the study. The study uses a pooled cross-sectional time-series data set comprising 193 countries over 25 years (1976–2000), yielding a total of 4,825 observations. The period covers the years in which the International Covenant on Civil and Political Rights (ICCPR) and the International Covenant on Economic, Social, and Cultural Rights came into force, followed by the subsequent proliferation of human rights instruments. The period also includes the end of the cold war and the third and fourth waves of democracy. Given the use of the pooled cross-sectional time-series data set, the chapter reviews the advantages and disadvantages associated with this type of global comparative analysis and discusses the kinds of questions that the research design can and cannot answer. This is then followed by a discussion of the different ways in which human rights protection can be measured, in principle (*de jure*) and in practice (*de facto*). The chapter concludes with a discussion of the main variables used in the study, including their temporal and spatial coverage.

Chapters 4, 5, and 6 provide the empirical analyses that map and explain the growth and effectiveness of the international human rights regime. Chapter 4 uses descriptive and analytical statistical techniques to examine the growth of the international human rights regime, including regional differentiation and plausible political explanations for the global variation in state participation in the regime. In similar fashion, chapter 5 uses descriptive and analytical techniques to examine and explain the global variation in human rights protection. Chapter 6 brings the concerns of these two chapters together to examine the bivariate and multivariate relationships between the international regime and human rights protection, including nonrecursive parameter estimation with the use of two-stage least-squares regression techniques. The quantitative results are complemented throughout with explanatory passages and graphical figures to help clarify the main relationships that are uncovered.

Chapter 7 concludes the study by reviewing its main findings, drawing the important lessons and inferences that arise from the empirical analysis conducted in chapters 4, 5, and 6, and then discusses the implications and preliminary policy prescriptions that flow from the results for those working in the field of human rights. Taken as a whole, the book represents an attempt to apply mainstream political science theories and methods to the protection of human rights, while remaining cognizant of the importance of international law. It is not a legal history that tracks the evolution of human rights norms, and it is not a series of illustrative or comparative case studies, but a systematic attempt to gauge the growth and relative effectiveness of the international human rights regime. It is hoped that this book advances our understanding of how the international human rights regime has evolved, how (and whether) it has had an impact on human rights practices, and how the scholarly and practical human rights community can continue to struggle for the increased protection of human rights.

2

Empirical Theories and Human Rights

As the previous chapter argued, grand claims have been made over the years about the increasing importance of human rights, not only as the subject of a moral discourse, but also as a new set of constraints on state behavior that both limits the degree to which states can intervene in the lives of citizens and prescribes minimum requirements for the promotion of human dignity. An empirical investigation that tests such claims must first consider why an international legal regime for the protection of human rights would receive increasing support from states through their formal participation, and why the existence of such a regime would necessarily make a difference in the protection of human rights. Such an investigation rests on the assumptions, descriptions, and analysis that characterize dominant paradigms found in the fields of international law, international relations, and comparative politics. This chapter argues that at the international level human rights challenge the polarity between law and power, which characterizes the extreme ends of a continuum ranging from legal positivism to realism. At the domestic level, it argues that human rights challenge the traditional divisions between rationalist, structuralist, and culturalist accounts of politics and the relations between states and citizens. It argues further that any account of human rights protection must examine the overlap between the domestic and international spheres of politics, law, institutions, and norms to see how states and individuals are constrained in actions that may or may not lead to the violation of human rights.

A Nexus for Empirical Theories

Human rights represent an important nexus for empirical theories, which provide useful propositions about the likely associations and relationships between law, power, and norms, which can then be tested by global comparative statistical analysis. Public international lawyers speak of the problems of compliance, implementation, and enforcement of international law (e.g., Chayes and Chayes 1993; Slaughter-Burley 1993; Higgins 1994; Koh 1997; Watson 1999; Hathaway 2002). International relations scholars speak of problems of regime creation, effectiveness, and enforcement (e.g., Keohane 1984; Rittberger 1997; Young 1992, 1999a). Comparativists focus on the ways in which differences across domestic systems of governance affect regime participation and rights protection (Moravcsik 1997, 2000; Poe and Tate 1994; Keith 1999; Landman 2002a, 2003; Donnelly 1986, 1999) and on the linkages between international politics, domestic politics, and transnational political actors (Keck and Sikkink 1998; Smith et al. 1998; Risse et al. 1999; Hawkins 2002).

Traditionally, these three families of theory and research have had very little to do with each other (Raustiala and Slaughter 2002). But since the 1980s there appears to have been a convergence of work around the general topic of regimes to examine the degree to which international law, norms, and principles shape state behavior (Donnelly 1986, 640). The consideration of human rights has increasingly been included in regime analysis, a process that has brought international law and international relations closer together (see Donnelly 1986; Keith 1999; Krasner 1997, 1999; Hathaway 2002; Schmitz and Sikkink 2002). These concerns at the international level have also transcended the study of domestic forms of state-citizen relations, the traditional domain of comparative politics. Certain strands of international relations theory focus on how domestic actors, collective domestic preferences, and national institutional arrangements influence international action (Henkin 1979, 60–68; Putnam 1993; Moravcsik 1997, 2000; Slaughter-Burley 1993, 227–28). In a similar fashion, within comparative politics, there have been attempts to move beyond the "messy center" of theorizing to synthesize rationalist, structuralist, and culturalist approaches in an effort to show how actors within domestic political arrangements are similarly constrained to states in the international sphere (Kohli et al. 1995; Lichbach 1997; Landman 2003).

It thus appears that there has been a "double convergence" in theoretical concerns around the topic of human rights at the international and domestic levels, which centers on the idea of *constrained agency*. At the domestic level, constrained agency involves the notion of the "socially embedded unit act" (Lichbach 1997), which sees individual rational action situated in larger structural and cultural constraints. At the international level, such constrained agency centers on the idea of "embedded liberalism" (Ruggie 1982, 382–83), which sees individual rational states acting in a world system that is formed by the tension between power and "legitimate social purpose." To develop this idea of constrained agency, the chapter considers the tension between power and norms in international law and international relations; the common concerns in rationalist, structuralist, and culturalist theories in comparative politics; the crossover of concerns at the domestic and international levels; and how the international human rights regime is situated in this nexus. It then develops an empirical model based on the concepts, expectations, and propositions drawn from the various theories.

International Law and International Relations

International law and international relations have long been concerned with the ways in which states interact with one another, and both fields have traditionally built their theories on the twin assumptions of state sovereignty and nonintervention, most notably embodied in the 1648 Treaty of Westphalia. Both the modern state system and international law have developed dramatically since the end of the Thirty Years War, when international law moved from "natural" foundations to "positive" foundations (Forsyth 1992; Slaughter-Burley 1993, 207–20; Koh 1997, 2603–14) and addressed an ever-increasing variety of issues. Similarly, international relations theory evolved from a dominance of ethical and normative perspectives on the conduct of states to those that have been increasingly empirical and positivist (Boucher 1998; Schmidt 2002). For much of the post–World War II era there has been a natural tension between international law (represented by the legal positivists) on the one hand and international relations (represented by the realists) on the other.

Legal positivists focus on the "neutral" function of international law as it is meant to be applied to problem areas, devoid of any considerations of the nature of power differences between states or of the international system more generally (e.g., Austin 1975 [1954]; Kelsen 1949). This could be labeled the "law without power" perspective. In contrast, realist theories of international relations, built on the assumption of states as unitary rational actors, play down the importance of international law and relegate it to something that is merely "epiphenomenal." Realists argue that the structure of power between states as they maximize their preferences is the key determinant of political outcomes (e.g., Kennan 1951; Morgenthau 1961; Waltz 1979; Schmitz and Sikkink 2002; Donnelly 2000). This could be labeled the "power without law" perspective.[1]

These two somewhat idealized perspectives represent extreme ends of a broad continuum of scholarship on international law and international relations produced during the 1960–1989 period, which Slaughter-Burley (1993, 207) has referred to as the "polarity of law and power." Along this continuum, the Yale and Columbia schools of international law offered alternative perspectives that emphasize the importance of international community and the formality of norms on the one hand, and sovereign autonomy and informality of norms on the other (Kennedy 2000, 117–20). This legal scholarship gave way to new forms of "legal pragmatism" and "legal proceduralism" during the 1990s, both of which temper the neutral understanding of law by focusing on the "interplay between rules and social process in enunciating the law" (Koh 1997, 2618). Legal pragmatists concede not only that power and ideology influence law, but that law itself is a *continuing process* of authoritative decisions (Higgins 1968, 58–59; in Higgins 1994, 2, emphasis mine; see also Slaughter-Burley 1993, 209–14), in which any concept of law that "banishes power to the outer darkness" is pure "fantasy" and that "[t]he authority which characterizes law exists not in a vacuum, but exactly where it intersects with power" (Higgins 1994, 4).

Within international relations, there has been a similar set of moves away from extreme realism to include the consideration of how power interacts with law, norms, principles, and institutions more generally. Hegemonic stability theory concedes that certain norms become important over time, but that ultimately their enforcement depends on the existence, willingness, and capacity of powerful (or hegemonic) states. In this view, "[r]egime creation and maintenance are a function of the distribution of power and interests among states" (Krasner 1997, 140). For example, in comparing regimes on religious practices in the seventeenth century, slavery in the nineteenth century, minority rights in Central Europe in the late nineteenth and early twentieth centuries, and individual rights in the late twentieth century, Krasner (1997, 141) shows that the variance in regime success depends very much on the "capabilities and commitment of those states that supported each of these regimes." Indeed, he contends that the abolition of slavery would not have been possible without the vigorous monitoring and enforcement of the regime by the major European powers, especially Britain (Krasner 1997, 143–44, 152–55).[2] Donnelly (1986, 638) concurs, in arguing that "even weak regimes require the backing of major powers" (see also Young 1992, 185). This perspective thus moves slightly away from "power without law" to one of "law, but only with dominant power(s) willing to enforce it."

Moving beyond these strict realist perspectives, which place great emphasis on the sole importance of power, neoliberal institutionalism argues that "post-hegemonic" forms of international cooperation are possible (Forde 1992, 80). Such a perspective focuses on how institutions emerge from state interest and how they attenuate the power relations between states. In *After Hegemony*, Keohane (1984, 8) argues that rational states will cooperate out of self-interest, even though such cooperation will not always prevail. But interests are malleable, and the increased interdependence of states creates incentives for cooperation. The mutual advantage and reciprocity that emerge from international cooperation (e.g., lower transaction costs, access to information, expectations of behavior) explain why states would enter into international agreements. And unlike hegemonic stability theory, stable cooperation "equilibria" are possible without the presence of a dominant enforcer. This perspective comes very close to the legal-procedural perspective outlined above, since it too focuses on the ways in which mutual benefit and reciprocity provide the conditions under which otherwise self-interested states would cooperate with each other.

This convergence around the relationship between law and power has been further addressed by constructivist approaches in international relations, which occupy a position partly between and partly lateral to realist and legal-positivist perspectives. In contrast to accepting law or power as given, constructivists focus their attention on the ways in which law and power and the agents or "subjects" that articulate them are socially constructed within international affairs. They thus look at the origins, emergence, and maintenance of ideas, norms, principles, and laws as constitutive processes rather than some outcome of the strategic interaction of states (Wendt 1999; Fearon and Wendt 2002, 56–58). Accentuating the difference between the intentionality and holism of interstate relations and behavior, constructivist approaches embed their arguments in the logic of "appropriateness" (i.e., what the international context expects of states)[3] rather than the logic of "consequences" (i.e., the outcomes of state behavior) (March and Olsen 1998; see also Mapel and Nardin 1992; Hawkins 2002, 18). Such a constructivist perspective dovetails with the legal-procedural and neoinstitutional perspectives outlined above. On the one hand, legal-proceduralists are precisely interested in the construction of international law as an iterative political process. On the other hand, Wendt (1999) shows convincingly that the social and political construction of preferences and interests of states *precedes* any strategic interaction in which they may engage. Thus, the construction of international cooperative regimes, law, or institutions must be seen as a function of broader processes of normative transmission and internalization (see also Henkin 1979, 60–62; Falk 2000, 60–66).

Legal proceduralism, neoliberal institutionalism, and constructivism are all important for the theory of international regimes, which have increasingly become the focus of international relations scholars. For Young (1992), "[r]egimes are sets of rules, decision-making procedures, and/or programs that give rise to social practices, assign roles to the participants in these practices, and govern their interactions." A regime is a "collection of rights and rules" that "structure[s] the opportunities of the actors interested in a given activity," has a significant procedural component for the resolution of situations involving social or collective choices, and contains the expectation of compliance by its members (Young 1980, 333–42). Realist and neoliberal institutionalist theories demonstrate that regimes are created and are effective through the application of cost-benefit analysis by states, whereas constructivist theories argue that regime effectiveness is achieved through "internalized identities and norms of appropriate behaviour" (Raustiala and Slaughter 2002, 540). Like constructivism, international law differs from realism and neoliberal institutionalism in its view of regimes. It turns its attention away from cost-benefit functions of regimes and concentrates on their provision of rules. Such rules foster stable expectations for actors and establish efficient baselines and standards, criteria for the justification of action, processes of communication, opportunities for domestic and international "intermeshing" of bureaucracies, and routinized habits of compliance (Slaughter-Burley 1993, 220). There is thus a complementarity between the concerns over formal rules in international law and the reasons states become part of such systems of rules in international relations.

But not all regimes are the same, as Donnelly (1986) demonstrates. For him, regimes vary according to their level of norms and their types of decision-making activities (Donnelly 1986, 603–4). Norms can range from a fully international level to an entirely national level, and decision-making activities can include enforcement, implementation, or promotion. The combination of these two dimensions (norms and decision making) creates a typology that ranges from "strong declaratory" regimes to "weak promotional" regimes, where the strength of any one regime is determined by its normative and procedural scope, as well as by its overall acceptance and coherence (Donnelly 1986, 604–5). While the notion of acceptance is straightforward, coherence requires a match between the normative and procedural dimensions of the regime (Donnelly 1986, 605), or what Keohane (2002, 135) calls a high degree of "precision." This difference in regime type and strength is important for forming propositions about the likely impact and effectiveness of particular regimes. But before we bring together these different aspects of international law and international relations with respect to the international human rights regime, it is necessary first to consider the contribution from empirical theories of comparative politics.

Comparative Politics

The field of comparative politics has long been concerned with how and why the relationship between citizens and the state varies across different national political contexts. The substantive focus of the field has included patterns of stability and instability in advanced industrial democracies; the emergence, maintenance, and performance of liberal democracy; the origins and consequences of violent and nonviolent social mobilization; the emergence, duration, and performance of authoritarian regimes; patterns of democratic transition and consolidation; processes of regionalization and globalization; and the political economy of development (see Almond and Bingham Powell 1966; Macridis and Brown 1990; Rustow and Erickson 1991; Chilcote 1994; Apter 1996; Mair 1996; Landman 2000, 2003). Theories in comparative politics reflect concerns similar to those found in international relations: rational actors, ideas, norms, institutions, and structures. Like international relations, *rationalist, culturalist*, and *structuralist* theories in comparative politics help account for and provide an understanding of political outcomes and patterns that are observed across different political contexts (Kohli et al. 1995; Lichbach 1997). Like the tensions in the field of international relations, these theories in comparative politics have tensions that are a function of both their ontological assumptions and their analytical scope of human behavior. Rationalist perspectives concentrate on the actions of individuals who make reasoned and intentional choices based upon sets of preferences, or interests. Those who adhere to the rationalist perspective are "concerned with the collective processes and outcomes that follow from intentionality, or the social consequences of individually rational action" (Lichbach 1997, 246; see also Munck 2001).

Like realism in international relations, rationalism in comparative politics concentrates on "means-ends" calculations and how they affect political outcomes. But realism engages in "methodological nationalism" (Zürn 2002, 248), whereas rationalism, as it is deployed in comparative politics, engages in "methodological individualism" (Przeworski 1985). For realism, the ontological unit of analysis is the state as a unitary actor from which the models and explanations for events and political outcomes in international relations are derived. For rationalism, the ontological unit of analysis is the individual, whose strategic interaction forms the basis for political explanation. The difference between the two perspectives thus resides in their focus on states or individuals, whereas the common affinity of the two perspectives is their emphasis on the utility-maximizing behavior of their units of analysis.

In contrast to the rationalist perspective, culturalist perspectives in comparative politics seek an understanding of political phenomena by focusing on the broader holistic and shared aspects of collectivities. Single individual interests and actions are not understood in isolation, but are placed in the context of the shared understandings, intersubjective relationships, and mutual orientations that make human communities possible (Lichbach 1997, 246–47). These shared meanings and understandings form broader cultures and communities grouped together and analyzed as whole units. They are held together by social rules that are emblematic of the identities of both the individuals and the groups themselves (Lichbach 1997, 247).

Identifying the boundaries of these cultural units and separate identities remains problematic for systematic comparative research; however, scholars have tried to examine the world views, rituals, and symbols that provide "systems of meaning and the structure and intensity of political identity" across different geographical regions of the world (Ross 1997, 43–44). Culturalist approaches are akin to their constructivist counterparts in international relations, since both perspectives are concerned with the social construction and meaning of ideas and norms as the basis for political analysis.

Structuralists focus on the holistic aspects of politics, but unlike culturalists, they focus their attention on interdependent relationships among individuals, collectivities, institutions, and organizations. They are interested in the social, political, and economic networks that form among individuals. Structures that have become reified over time constrain or facilitate political activity such that individual actors are not completely free agents capable of determining particular political outcomes (Lichbach 1997, 247–48). Rather, individuals are embedded in relational structures that shape human identities, interests, and interaction. Relational structures have evolved through large historical processes such as capitalist development, market rationality, nation-state building, political and scientific revolutions, and technological progress (Katznelson 1997, 83), all of which provide possibilities and limits for human action.

Like the polarity of law and power in the fields of international law and international relations, rationalist and structuralist accounts of politics have created a polarity between "structureless agents" on the one hand (extreme rational choice) and "agentless structures" on the other (extreme structuralists). This polarity between agents and structures (see Hay 1995, 2002) has converged (or it has been sought to resolve this polarity) around the idea of "new-institutionalism" (March and Olsen 1984), which not only seeks to examine the constrained rationality of actors as they confront the persistence of institutional forms, but also brings in culturalist concerns over symbolic action, norms, and ideas (March and Olsen 1984, 739, 744). Like the claim that "international law matters" by public international lawyers, proponents of new institutionalism make the claim that "institutions matter" (Steinmo et al. 1992; Young 1992, 175), and it is no surprise that proponents of new institutionalism at the domestic level have turned their attention to the international level (compare March and Olsen 1984 with March and Olsen 1998).

Crossover: Two-Level Games and Liberal Republicanism

An examination of these developments in international law, international relations, and comparative politics shows that the traditional polarities in international and comparative research have been partly transcended and have produced similar convergences around the idea of constrained action. Legal-proceduralism, neoliberal institutionalism, and new-institutionalism are all concerned with the ways in which law, power, ideas, norms, and institutions intersect to both facilitate and limit choices that are available to individuals and states. For domestic politics, Lichbach (1997, 260–67) combines categories of social analysis found in Parsons and Weber to construct what he calls the "socially embedded unit act" to show how the degree of individual choice is the product of the intersection between interests, ideas, and institutions. But it seems plausible to apply this same notion to individual states, whose choices in international affairs can also be seen as a function of the intersection between interests, ideas, and institutions. Indeed, Ruggie's (1982) notion of "embedded liberalism" sees the interests and actions of states as reflective of the presence of larger liberal forces such as markets and liberal or "civic republican" states (Kant 1795, 112–15).

Combining the insights from these seemingly disparate perspectives through the notions of the "socially embedded unit act" and "embedded liberalism" contributes to our understanding of the ways in which states make agreements and how such agreements affect their behavior. Legal-proceduralism shows how norms emerge through the express consent of states, the absence of opposition to such norms, or the failure of attempts to oppose them. Obligations to abide by these norms arise through a perception that there is a reciprocal advantage in self-restraint (Higgins 1994, 16). Thus, both the emergence of norms and adherence to them can be seen as a *process* that involves the power of states to engage in activity that yields mutual benefit. Equally, for proponents of neoliberal institutionalism, individual and mutual state advantage can be achieved through the formation of agreements. At the domestic level, new-institutionalists see political outcomes as a product of the interactions between formal institutions and individual actors, where concerns over unrestrained individual rational action have led to the formation of political institutions that channel and structure the social and political interaction in ways that maintain stability and order.

Although the notion of "embeddedness" is appealing for political analysis at the international and domestic level, rarely have schools within international relations and comparative politics talked to each another. For example, international relations scholars have focused on the structure of state interaction and how that may account for outcomes such as war, peace, trade, and security, whereas comparativists have remained focused on the structure of individual interactions in larger processes of economic development, democratization, and conflict, among many other topics. The exception to this observation has been the work on "two-level" games (Putnam 1993), which brings the convergent views of international relations and comparative research together. Putnam (1993, 459) observes that "[t]he most portentous development in the fields of comparative politics and international relations in recent years is the dawning recognition among practitioners in each field of the need to take into account entanglements between the two." Any engagement of a state in international relations reflects the domestic array of social and political forces, including key actors and institutions (Putnam 1993, 435). The politics of such a two-level game is neatly summarized as follows:

> At the national level, domestic groups pursue their interests by pressuring the government to adopt favourable policies, and the politicians seek power by constructing coalitions among those groups. At the international level, national governments seek to maximize their own ability to satisfy domestic pressures, while minimising the adverse consequences of foreign developments. (Putnam 1993, 436)

Although there may be different "rational" strategies available at either level of the game, Putnam (1993, 473) argues that "there are powerful incentives for consistency between the two games." What is absent from the formulation of the two-level game is any consideration of the type of government that is in place, although it appears that Putnam implies some form of representative government, and most of his empirical examples are of advanced industrial democracies.[4] Indeed, liberal democratic states are simply more open to and reflective of competing claims from domestic groups than are authoritarian states. Nevertheless, as the elite-centered work on democratic transitions demonstrates (e.g., Przeworski 1991; Colomer 2000), authoritarian regimes are susceptible to competing demands within the authoritarian coalition as well as from groups in civil society, however repressed they may be. Indeed, Hawkins (2002) argues that during the Pinochet period in Chile (1973–90), there were "rule-oriented" elements within the authoritarian regime that became increasingly concerned over questions of political legitimacy owing to international human rights pressures. The presence of these elements within the regime helps explain some of the limited tactical concessions that were made through reform of the internal security forces and the promulgation of the 1980 Constitution. Such tactical concessions have been demonstrated within the liberalizing contexts of Kenya, Uganda, South Africa, Tunisia, Morocco, Indonesia, the Philippines, Guatemala, Poland, and Czechoslovakia (Risse et al. 1999). It is thus possible to think in broader terms about how the games played at the domestic level (whatever type of government is in place) will be important for state interaction at the international level, thereby giving the notion of the two-level game universal applicability (see Czempiel 1992, 257–58).

Drawing on the insights of the two-level game and combining them with variants of democratic peace theory, Moravcsik (1997, 2000) develops a theory of "liberal republicanism," which makes explicit reference to democratic forms of rule and how such domestic systems will have an influence on a country's propensity for making international agreements. He argues that making international agreements can "lock in" and consolidate democratic institutions, thereby enhancing their credibility and stability in the long run against possible threats from nondemocratic forces. Echoing realist language, he argues that states will make such agreements when the benefits of reducing future uncertainty outweigh the costs of membership in an international regime (Moravcsik 2000, 220). He claims that this argument really applies only to newly established democracies, since they face more immediate uncertainty, which regime membership tempers, but other scholars suggest that regime membership, particularly for human rights, is a function of democracy in general (see Zacher 1992, 94; Vincent 1986).

The International Human Rights Regime

This "double convergence" in international and comparative research, combined with concerns over the interaction of domestic and international politics, provides a rich theoretical basis that helps explain the growth and effectiveness of the international human rights regime. The growth of the international human rights regime demonstrates that human rights have now become enshrined in bodies of international law, represented most forcefully by the existence of international treaties to which states become a party and, at least in formal terms, the terms of which states agree to abide. From the International Covenant on Civil and Political Rights (1966) through the Rome Statute on the establishment of the International Criminal Court (2002), increasing types of human rights have found expression in international law, and an increasing number of states have signed and ratified the treaties. Table 2.1 summarizes these instruments and lists the dates when they became open for signature. It is clear from the table that the regime has become increasingly specialized beyond the main International Bill of Human Rights (i.e., the Universal Declaration and the two International Covenants) to include the rights of women and children, as well as prohibition of specific acts such as torture and racial discrimination. Each of the six main treaties (but not the optional protocols) has an associated treaty monitoring body comprising international human rights experts, who examine and comment on the formal reports submitted by member states on a legally mandated and periodic basis (Donnelly 1986, 609; Robertson and Merrills 1996, 97–111; Buergenthal 1997, 709–11; Alston and Crawford 2000; Bayefsky 2001, 11).

Unlike other international regimes in areas such as environmental protection and trade, which involve the regulation of the interaction between states, human rights form a special policy area, since the international regime seeks to uphold state obligations and state responsibility toward individuals and groups within its own domestic jurisdiction (Higgins 1994, 95; Moravcsik 2000, 217). States both violate and protect human rights, and they are the "principal actors governed by the regime's norms" (Donnelly 1986, 616). The international human rights regime has an extensive and coherent set of norms across the various categories of rights, which form an "interdependent and synergistically interactive system of guarantees"; however, states maintain virtual autonomy in implementing them, and the regime itself has

Table 2.1. The international human rights regime

Name	Date when open for signature
International Covenant on Civil and Political Rights (ICCPR)	1966
International Covenant on Economic, Social, and Cultural Rights (ICESCR)	1966
Optional Protocol to the International Covenant on Civil and Political Rights (OPT1)	1976
Second Optional Protocol to the International Covenant on Civil and Political Rights (OPT2)	1989
International Convention on the Elimination of All Forms of Racial Discrimination (CERD)	1966
Convention on the Elimination of All Forms of Discrimination against Women (CEDAW)	1979
Convention against Torture and Other Cruel, Inhuman, or Degrading Treatment or Punishment (CAT)	1984
Convention on the Rights of the Child (CRC)	1989

Source: OUNHCHR (Sept. 2000), *Status of Ratification of the Principal International Human Rights Treaties* (www.unhchr.ch/pdf/report.pdf), and International Service for Human Rights (Jan. 2000), *Info-Pack*, pp. 46–50. See also Bayefsky (2001, 11).

limited decision-making powers (Donnelly 1986, 607–8, 619). Thus, at best, the regime is a strong promotional one that is lacking a real capacity for international enforcement (Donnelly 1986, 614).

The growth of the regime at first appears to be counter-intuitive if one adopts a purely realist perspective, captured effectively by Moravcsik (2000, 219), who asks:

> Why would any government, democratic or dictatorial, favour establishing an effective, independent international authority, the sole purpose of which is to constrain its domestic sovereignty in such an unprecedentedly invasive and overtly non-majoritarian manner?

The inability of a purely interest-based theory of state action to explain the proliferation of human rights norms suggests that neoliberal institutionalism and legal-proceduralism offer a more satisfactory account by focusing on the historically iterative process of norm prolif-eration and the construction of state behavior. The fact that states have signed and ratified human rights treaties over the years has led to a degree of optimism among international lawyers that increased state participation in the international human rights regime ought to make a difference for human rights protection, despite Donnelly's (1986) skeptical assessment outlined above. But systematic analysis of regime effectiveness is incomplete if one merely focuses on the international law of human rights or on domestic political arrangements and insti-tutions. Legal-proceduralism, neoliberal institutionalism, and new-institutionalism help build a fuller picture of the ways in which both domestic and international factors are important to a consideration of the relationship between the international human rights regime and human rights protection.

The preceding examination of the double convergence in theories from international law, international relations, and comparative pol-itics is summarized in figure 2.1. The top of the figure charts the trans-formation in international legal and international relations scholarship,

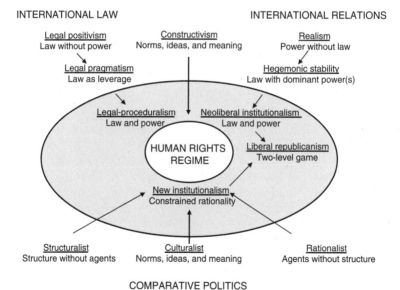

Figure 2.1. Human rights as a nexus for theories of international law, in-ternational relations, and comparative politics.

and the bottom of the figure charts the ways in which rational, structural, and cultural approaches in comparative politics have converged on the "rediscovery" of institutions. The two halves of the figure converge within the shaded elliptical area, which represents the study of regimes, including the liberal-republican perspective. Finally, the human rights regime lies at the center of the figure as the important nexus for these theories. From these theories and the figure, it is now possible to develop a preliminary empirical model from which it is possible to derive a series of hypothesized relationships and testable propositions about the growth and effectiveness of the international human rights regime.

Building an Empirical Model

If the norms contained within the international human rights regime are important, as legal-proceduralists, neoliberal institutionalists, and liberal-republicans argue, then there ought to be a positive relationship between the international law of human rights (rights in principle) and the protection of human rights (rights in practice). Such an expectation is often supported by Henkin's (1979, 47) claim that "*it is probably the case that almost all nations observe almost all principles of international law and almost all of their obligations almost all of the time*" (emphasis in the original). In response to this claim, Chayes and Chayes (1993, 176–77) argue that no such empirical attempt has been made, that "it would not be easy to devise a statistical protocol that would generate such evidence," and that "general compliance with international agreements cannot be empirically verified." In contrast, Koh (1997, 2599–2600) shows that initial empirical work on international trade, international adjudication, U.S. policy on human rights, and international environmental protection seems largely to have confirmed Henkin's "hedged but optimistic description." In addition, Simmons (2000) has systematically examined the degree to which countries comply with exchange-rate demands of the financial regime established by the International Monetary Fund.

Outside these important international issue areas, two recent studies in the field of human rights test the relationship between treaty ratification and human rights protection across a variety of human rights measures and indicators. Keith (1999) examines the relationship between ratification of the International Covenant on Civil and Political Rights (ICCPR) and the protection of personal integrity rights, and Hathaway (2002) tests the relationship between a broader range of treaties and rights protection, including torture, genocide, and women's rights. Both studies achieve mixed results, whereas simple bivariate analysis (correlation and difference in means tests) shows a positive association between treaty ratification and rights protection, which tends to drop away in their multivariate analyses. They both use data sets that are pooled over time and across space, which gives them a large number of observations, but the way in which they have carried out their analyses has masked the growth of the regime, its time-dependent effects on rights protection, its possible feedback effects, and the importance of complementary social and political developments.

These extant studies testing compliance suggest that this is a fruitful and necessary area of research that enriches our understanding of global human rights protection. Indeed, it seems paramount for political science theories and methods to provide meaningful explanations of *why* countries ratify human rights treaties in the first place and whether such ratification *makes a difference for human rights protection.* Drawing on the achievements of these extant studies and the theories outlined above, it is possible to construct an empirical model that helps explain both the growth and effectiveness of the international human rights regime. Figure 2.2 depicts the simple bivariate relationship between treaty ratification and human rights protection.

The figure captures the simple relationship as expected from legal-proceduralism, neo-institutionalism, and new-institutionalism, but fails to take into account a series of other important factors. Since norms exhibit trends and human rights protection can accumulate over time, it is necessary to add three different time-series feedback processes to the model. First, there are feedback processes between previous ratification of human rights treaties and current ratification, both of which operate within the same state as well as among states. These are known as "social" or "bandwagon" effects.[5] Second, there are feedback processes between previous and current years of human

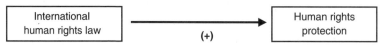

Figure 2.2. Simple bivariate relationship between international human rights law and human rights protection.

rights protection, capturing the time-dependent performance of a country with respect to human rights protection (Poe and Tate 1994; Poe et al. 1999; Keith 1999). Third, there are feedback processes between human rights protection and treaty participation itself, such that human rights protection in one year may have an effect on a country's propensity to ratify in subsequent years (Keith 1999, 100, fn 7; Hathaway 2002). This third feedback process suggests that ratification and protection are not necessarily mutually exclusive processes. Figure 2.3 depicts the simple relationship with these additional feedback processes, showing that the first two processes are expected to have positive relationships, whereas the hypothesized relationship for the third process remains opaque. If a state improves its human rights practices before ratification, the relationship should be positive, whereas if it improves its practices after ratification, the relationship should be negative. Thus, both signs are included in the model.

These relationships are complicated further by a series of important additional independent variables that reflect the issues and concerns outlined in the theories in the first part of this chapter as well as the findings from extant studies in international relations and comparative politics.[6] First, studies within the neoliberal institutional and liberal-republican traditions have repeatedly shown the benefits of democratic rule for both the ratification of treaties and the protection of human rights. In testing the liberal-republican model, Moravcsik (1997, 2000) shows that democratic states have a greater propensity to ratify the European Convention on Human Rights, a finding that may be upheld at the global level (see Landman 2002a). For the protection of human rights, empirical studies have shown that democracies are less likely to violate personal integrity rights (Poe and Tate 1994; Poe

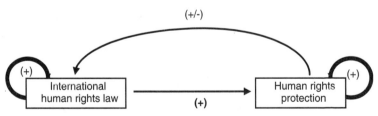

Figure 2.3. Feedback processes in human rights law and human rights protection.

et al. 1999; Keith 1999; Hathaway 2002), and even within the first year of a democratic transition, such rights violations decrease significantly (Zanger 2000a). Thus, any model of the growth and effectiveness of the international human rights regime must include democracy as an important independent variable.

Second, extant studies in comparative politics have repeatedly shown the importance of economic wealth in explaining the level and maintenance of democracy and the protection of personal integrity rights. From Lipset's (1959) seminal study on the "economic correlates of democracy" to the cross-national time-series comparative study of Przeworski et al. (2000), overall levels of wealth are positively related to the level of democracy, and rich democracies are less likely to experience breakdown (Przeworski and Limongi 1997; Przeworski et al. 2000; see also Landman 2003, 65–93). These findings are also upheld in studies on human rights, where higher levels of economic wealth are positively associated with a greater protection of personal integrity rights (Mitchell and McCormick 1988; Poe and Tate 1994; Poe et al. 1999; Keith 1999; Zanger 2000a; Hathaway 2002).

Third, international relations research on the "Kantian tripod" demonstrates the overall importance of international interdependence of countries in reducing their propensity for international conflict (e.g., Russett et al. 1998; Russett and O'Neal 2001). These findings are consistent with the work on the growth of "world culture," which maps the global evolution and proliferation of international governmental (IGOs) and nongovernmental (INGOs) organizations (Boli and Thomas 1999; see also Zacher 1992, 65). The degree of "embeddedness" of countries in global networks of IGOs and INGOs, it is argued, is positively related to their exposure to value transfers and demonstration effects that ought to have a positive impact on regime participation and compliance (see also Ruggie 1982). Indeed, in *The Power of Human Rights*, eleven comparative case studies on the protection of political and civil rights demonstrate that the existence of international human rights norms, coupled with increased activity from domestic and international NGOs, makes a positive contribution to state compliance (Risse et al., 1999). Thus, democracy, wealth, membership in IGOs, and the presence of INGOs are seen to be crucial independent variables that mediate the relationship between norms and rights.

Fourth, to these two variables of international interdependence is added a third variable on international trade. Like participation in

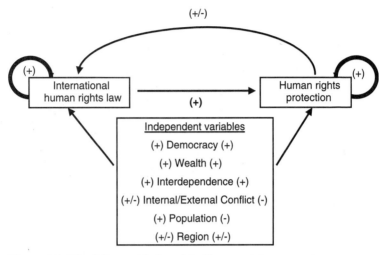

Figure 2.4. The fully specified model of human rights protection.

IGOs and the presence of INGOs, state engagement in global trade suggests that similar value transfers and demonstration effects may have an impact on regime participation and the protection of human rights. For example, Li and Reuveny (2003) review the conflicting hypotheses about the relationship between economic globalization and democracy (positive, negative, and no effect) and then test the relationship between four national aspects of economic globalization (trade openness, foreign direct investment inflows, portfolio investment inflows, and democratic diffusion) and the level of democracy. Their cross-national time-series analysis shows that trade openness and portfolio investment have a negative impact on the level of democracy, whereas foreign direct investment and democratic diffusion have a positive impact on the level of democracy. But regime participation and the protection of human rights are different from the level of democracy, and the model hypothesizes that along with IGO and INGO membership, trade openness ought to be positively associated with regime growth and effectiveness.

Finally, three further variables need to be specified for the model. Again, the extant studies argue that any explanation of personal integrity rights protection must take into account the degree of a country's involvement in international and national conflict. One of the key findings of this research, not surprisingly, is that involvement in civil war poses the largest threat to the protection of personal integrity rights (Poe and Tate 1994, 866). But involvement in international and domestic conflict may also have an impact on regime participation. On the one hand, states in conflict may need external allies and see treaty ratification as an important way in which to garner support. On the other hand, states in conflict may be so preoccupied with the immediate nature of the conflict that they simply have no interest in treaty negotiations. It is thus important to include involvement in internal and external conflict in the model. Two final variables control for the size of the population and geographical differentiation of the World Bank classified regions of Europe, North America, the Middle East and North Africa (MENA), Latin America, sub-Saharan Africa, South Asia, and East Asia and the Pacific (www.worldbank.org).

Figure 2.4 depicts the fully specified model with expected signs for all of the relationships, including those for the feedback loops and control variables. The model clearly shows that the simple bivariate relationship between treaty ratification and rights protection must take into account past state behavior with respect to treaties and rights, levels of democracy, wealth, international interdependence, involvement in conflict, size of the population, and regional differentiation. The model represents an adapted form of a more general "Grotian" model on international regimes specified by Krasner (1983b, 9), which depicts the two-way relationship between regimes and state behavior, both of which are influenced by "basic causal variables." The adapted form of the model developed here applies specifically to the case of the international human rights regime and human rights protection.

3

Data and Methods

The preceding chapter presented a synthesis of theories from international law, international relations, and comparative politics to develop the idea of constrained agency in order to address both the growth and effectiveness of the international human rights regime. This reading of theory resulted in the formulation of a stylized model that specifies a nonrecursive relationship between the international human rights regime and human rights protection that includes a series of important international, domestic explanatory, and control variables (fig. 2.4). The model is based on a series of expectations drawn from theory about the possible interrelationships between the main variables. This chapter shows how global comparative analysis can help map the evolution of the regime and test its effectiveness, along the lines specified in the previous chapter. The research design outlined here is used in the next three chapters and includes the measurement of the participation of nation-states in the international human rights regime and their variable protection of human rights and explains how such measures are assembled into a large cross-national time-series data set.

Such a global comparative research design is predicated based on several ontological, epistemological, and methodological assumptions that are broadly in line with "behavioral" and "postbehavioral" traditions in empirical political science (Sanders 1995, 67–68; Landman 2003, xvii). These traditions privilege the "evidence-inference" methodological core of mainstream comparative political science (Almond and Bingham 1966, 54) and emphasize the systematic collection and analysis of empirical data, which uncover patterns, trends, and relationships from which large-scale generalizations are made possible. To outline this perspective and mode of analysis, this chapter is divided into four parts. First, it outlines the assumptions of the research design and the strengths and weaknesses in its ability to address the main research questions. Second, it examines the different ways in which human rights can be measured, particularly their *de jure* and *de facto* protection. Third, it discusses the choice of explanatory and control variables and how they are related to the theoretical concerns and propositions outlined in chapter 2.

The Research Design: Assumptions and Trade-offs

In line with the assumptions of the behavioral and postbehavioral research traditions in the social and political sciences, the study assumes that there are observable political events, actors, interests, structures, and outcomes about which we can make reasoned, informed, and intelligent analytical statements (Landman 2003, xvii; see also Gordon 1991, 33–56; Couvalis 1997; Flyvberg 2001; Hay 2002, 1–58). The main aims of the research design are to *explain the object of inquiry* (i.e., the growth and effectiveness of the international human rights regime) and *test a number of propositions against the world of observation*, where such testing is done systematically and not through the collection of "illustrative examples" (Sanders 1995, 60–63). In contrast to the view of some sceptics (Macintyre 1971, 1981; Freeman 2001, 2002b, 76–100),[1] it accepts that valid comparisons can be made between different countries to examine empirically the kind of universal claims for human rights that are made normatively.[2]

Conducting such an inquiry in the field of human rights thus rests on a number of ontological, epistemological, and methodological assumptions. Ontologically and epistemologically, the design assumes that human rights are "more or less protected" by the states that make up the world and that this "more or less" can be measured in some fashion (Landman 2002b, 900; see also Foweraker and Landman 1997, 49–65). For decades now, monitoring human rights has been the very rationale of human rights work, with an emphasis on holding states accountable and providing redress for abuse. The United

Nations has charter (e.g., the Economic and Social Council or ECOSOC) and treaty (e.g., the Human Rights Committee or HRC) bodies charged with the responsibility of monitoring both *de jure* and *de facto* human rights developments. Moreover, one of the mainstay activities of nongovernmental human rights organizations such as Amnesty International, Human Rights Watch, the International Federation of Human Rights Leagues, and the World Organisation Against Torture is to monitor states' human rights commitments and practices in order to be able to alert the international community of patterns of abuse in the world.

There is thus a precedent in the human rights community for at least assessing the degree of human rights protection in states, and this study rests on the further assumption that such commitment and protection can be measured quantitatively for global comparative analysis. Such a design accepts the tentative nature of these measurements but does not reject their use, since to "forswear the use of available, although imperfect data, does not advance scholarship" (Strouse and Claude 1976, 52).[3] To this end, the study assembles a large cross-national time-series data set for 193 countries for the period 1976–2000, yielding a total of 4,825 observations. Methodologically, this type of global comparative quantitative analysis has a number of advantages and disadvantages, which are related to the trade-off between the scope of countries compared and the level of abstraction and depth of inquiry that are made possible by such comparisons (Sartori 1970; Mair 1996; Landman 2003, 24–26).

The main advantages of global comparative analysis include statistical control to rule out rival explanations, extensive coverage of cases, the ability to make strong inferences, and the identification of "deviant" cases or "outliers." Comparing many countries is referred to as "variable-oriented," since its primary focus is on "general dimensions of macro-social variation" and the relationship between variables at a global level of analysis (Ragin 1994, 300). The extensive coverage of cases allows for stronger inferences and theory building, since a given relationship can be demonstrated to exist with a greater degree of certainty across a wider range of cases. For all global comparative research, the emphasis is on the generalizations that can be made about the particular political phenomenon that is to be explained. Such a generalization is meant to hold for most countries, and goodness-of-fit statistics (typically the R^2 in regression analysis) allow the analyst to estimate the degree to which the explanatory variables account for the overall variation in the dependent variable. Focusing on the general patterns of macrosocial variation thus allows one to make a series of inferences drawn from a large sample.

A second advantage of global comparative analysis lies in its ability to identify so-called deviant cases, or outliers. Such cases do not conform to the general patterns that are established through global analysis. On the one hand, a deviant case may be a country in which an expected outcome, given the presence of the explanatory variables, does not occur. On the other hand, a deviant case may be a country in which an outcome is observed that is not expected, given the presence of the explanatory variables. For example, in the field of conflict studies, Muller and Seligson (1987) use a simple scatter plot to test the positive relationship between income inequality and political violence in sixty countries and to identify those countries that fit the theory. In the analysis, Brazil, Panama, and Gabon were found to have a lower level of political violence than was expected for the relatively high level of income inequality. On the other hand, the United Kingdom was found to have a particularly high level of political violence, given its relatively low level of income inequality. Other explanations may account for deviance of these cases (e.g., the Northern Ireland conflict in the case of the United Kingdom). In the field of human rights, the United States is a classic outlier, since it has ratified very few international human rights treaties (see chapter 4) and yet has a reasonable record of protecting human rights.

Despite the advantages of comparing many countries, the method has some distinct disadvantages, including those associated with the availability of data, the validity of the quantitative measures, and the quality of inferences that are drawn. First, collecting relevant data on the independent nation-states of the world can be difficult and time-consuming. Aggregate data are often published only for selected years or selected countries, making comprehensive comparison difficult. Second, measures of political science concepts are often fraught with difficulties that may undermine their validity. Valid measures closely approximate the true meaning of a concept, or what the researcher thinks he or she is measuring (King, Keohane, and Verba 1994, 25; Adcock and Collier 2001). Third, many have argued that the type of generalizations that are made may not be particularly earth shattering or illuminating and may require more attention to specify the causal mechanisms that underlie the general patterns that are observed (Dessler 1991; Waltz 1979; Rosato 2003). Empirical generalizations are limited to the parameters of the research design and normally take the form of if *x* then *y*. It is left to the analyst to use social theory to specify the ways in which he or she thinks the relationship has been obtained.

Global comparative studies have sought to overcome the worst aspects of these difficulties, and there has been a growing literature on human rights that adopts this particular mode of analysis. Extant global comparative studies on human rights protection have tended to focus on a narrow set of civil and political rights and included diachronic and synchronic analyses to estimate the effects of a series of important explanatory variables that account for their variation. Such explanatory variables have included economic development (Mitchell and McCormick 1988; Henderson 1991), population and population growth (Henderson 1991; Poe and Tate 1994; Poe, Tate, and Keith 1999), democracy and democratization (Henderson 1991; Poe and Tate 1994; Poe, Tate, and Keith 1999; Davenport 1999; Zanger 2000a), multinational corporations (Meyer 1996, 1998, 1999a), internal and external violent conflict (Poe and Tate 1994; Poe, Tate, and Keith 1999; Zanger 2000a), the end of the cold war (Cingranelli and Richards 1999), U.S. and European foreign aid (Stohl, Carleton, and Johnson 1984; Cingranelli and Pasquarello 1985; Hofrenning 1990; Poe 1990; Poe and Sirirangsi 1993, 1994; Regan 1995; Zanger 2000b), domestic constitutional provisions (Davenport 1996, 1999), and religious differences and ethnic diversity (Park 1987). Outside of a consideration of civil and political rights, other global comparative projects have focused on discrimination, minorities, and conflict (Krain 1997; Caprioli 2000; Caprioli and Trumbore 2003), U.S. refugee policy (Gibney, Dalton, and Vockell 1992), and the provision of basic human needs (Moon and Dixon 1985; Dixon and Moon 1986).

There is thus a rich tradition of using global quantitative comparative analysis to uncover key explanatory variables for the global variation in the protection of different kinds of human rights. Arguably more progress has been made in the analysis of violations of civil and political rights, since their measurement has proved more tractable than that of economic, social, and cultural rights (see below). The results of these extant global studies and the types of analytical statements that they make must be seen as empirical generalizations that hold for most of the countries in the sample, where exceptions to the overall patterns identified will necessarily appear (Meyer 1999a; Landman 2003). Such global comparisons identify the regularities that hold across the selection of countries in order to make general claims, and these general claims should be of interest to human rights scholars and practitioners (Poe and Tate 1994, 867). The empirical results help reinforce arguments about associations and relationships made in normative and legal studies, and they provide support for important prescriptions for the international community to reduce the violation of human rights.

This study thus sits squarely within this burgeoning subfield of human rights research. Almost absent from the extant studies, however, is any consideration of the impact of the international human rights regime itself. As the previous chapter made clear, there have been two global comparative studies that examine the relationship between the law and practice of human rights: Linda Camp Keith's (1999) analysis of the effects of the International Covenant on Civil and Political Rights and Oona Hathaway's (2002) more comprehensive analysis of the impact of human rights treaties on a range of different human rights. Both studies report mixed results, where simple bivariate associations between treaty obligations and human rights protection are generally positive and significant, whereas their multivariate estimations either do not achieve statistical significance or have signs in the opposite direction (i.e., treaty participation leads to an increase in human rights violations). These results tend to come from the pooled nature of their analyses and possible misspecification of the empirical relationships between treaties and rights protection.

This study seeks to overcome these two problems in five important ways. First, much more use is made of descriptive statistics to map the temporal and spatial variation in both the human rights regime and human rights protection. Second, this study specifies a nonrecursive relationship between the law and practice of human rights, something that Hathaway (2002) notes may be possible but never tests fully in her own study. Third, the model is concerned with examining the important explanatory factors that account for the growth and proliferation of the human rights regimes, something that Keith (1999) and Hathaway (2002) do not consider. Fourth, the analysis takes into account the role of reservations in treaty obligations, such that simpler coding schemes for treaty ratification are weighted by the degree to which a country has had significant reservations about the treaty (see below). Finally, the study examines the ways in which treaty ratification and rights protection may be products of larger socioeconomic processes.

Measuring Human Rights

The measurement of human rights for global comparative analysis is predicated on the incremental development of an ideal legal standard that has taken place historically, but one that has developed more rapidly in terms of norms proliferation since the 1948 UN Universal Declaration of Human Rights. As Donnelly and Howard (1988) note, attempts at human rights measurement have been hampered by the length of the list of internationally recognized rights. Indeed, the list has grown since the Universal Declaration as new and more specific treaties are promulgated and as their core content is adjudicated, most notably at the international level by the treaty bodies themselves. Beyond issues surrounding definition, conceptualization, and core content, such measurement is further hampered by a series of methodological problems, including *precision* (What exactly is to be measured?), *reliability* (Is the measure consistent across coders?), *validity* (Does it measure what it is supposed to measure?), *equivalence* (Does it have the same meaning across cultures?), and *aggregation* (Does the measure obscure important differences by combining components?) (Barsh 1993, 92–98; see also Adcock and Collier 2001).

Much progress has been made in overcoming the more obvious and striking problems of human rights measurement, with residual problems of variance truncation and reliability that affect some of the most used and dominant extant measures available (see Brysk 1994b; Foweraker and Krznaric 2000; Munck and Verkuilen 2002). Better and more reliable sources of information have been used for the raw material from which coding can take place, intercoder reliability tests show the degree to which measures have been coded accurately by different people using the same source material (see Poe and Tate 1994; Hathaway 2002), and problems of equivalence have been overcome in part by the universalizing discourse of human rights law itself. When we draw on this progress and address in part some of the methodological concerns with measurement, there appear to be three kinds of human rights measures. There are those that measure rights "in principle," or the *de jure* protection of human rights as expressed formally by states through legal commitments. There are those that measure rights "in practice," or the *de facto* enjoyment of human rights on the ground. And there are those that measure various components of public policy, such as inputs, processes, outputs, and outcomes (see Landman and Häusermann 2003). For the purposes of this study, measures of rights "in principle" and rights "in practice" are used; the implications of the results of this study for policy are discussed in chapter 7.[4]

Measuring Human Rights in Principle

At the domestic level, several studies have measured rights in principle. The precedent for such measurement was notably set by van Maarseveen and van der Tang (1978), who coded national constitutions for 157 countries across a multitude of institutional and rights dimensions for the period 1788–1975. Chapter 6 of their study compares the degree to which national constitutions contain those rights mentioned in the UN Universal Declaration of Human Rights by examining their frequency distributions across different historical epochs before and after 1948. This effort has been followed for global samples of countries by Hofrenning (1990) and Suksi (1993) and for the liberalizing authoritarian states in Brazil, Chile, Mexico, and Spain by Foweraker and Landman (1997). It is entirely possible to move such coding of "in principle" rights commitments to the international level, which has already been done for international environmental and financial regimes (see Mitchell 2004; Simmons 2000). When a state accedes to a UN or regional human rights treaty (such as the European or American Conventions on Human Rights) it is obliged to file notification with the appropriate official international bodies. These bodies provide regularly updated listings of accessions, ratifications, and reservations that have been entered by states, which provide primary source material for the assessment of state commitment to international human rights norms (see Office of the High Commissioner for Human Rights, www.unhchr.ch). Over the years, this primary information has formed the basis for coding schemes found in the United Nations Development Programme Human Development reports and in the global comparative studies carried out by Keith (1999) and Hathaway (2002) (see also www.bayefsky.com).

The Keith (1999) and Hathaway (2002) studies code the ratification of international human rights treaties by using a dummy variable that assumes a value of 1 for ratification and 0 otherwise. In contrast, the present study codes countries with a 0 for no signature, 1 for signature, and 2 for ratification. For many international lawyers such as Hathaway, ratification is the true measure of commitment to human rights norms, and therefore a simple dummy variable suffices. Using the three categories, however, allows for more nuanced comparisons. As the next chapter will show, many of the countries of the former Soviet Union signed and ratified human rights treaties simultaneously, whereas countries that preceded them often had a delay between signature and ratification. Such differences will have a slight effect on the statistical results of this study. Overall, the international human rights regime comprises six treaties and two optional protocols, which are open for signature and then come into force when enough countries have ratified them. Complementing the treaties are associated treaty bodies, five of which meet in Geneva and one in New York. The treaty bodies monitor state compliance, request reports, and make recommendations, thus forming the corpus of institutions that comprise the international human rights regime (Robertson and Merrills 1996, 97–111; Bayefsky 2001, 11; Alston and Crawford 2000). The data set thus contains ratification variables for each of the six main treaties across the entire sample of countries for the years 1976 to 2000, and the variables capture the formal commitment that states have made by ratifying these human rights treaties. In short, the variables measure what states *ought* to uphold.

To reflect accurately the intent of states in making their formal commitments, any measure of rights in principle must take into account the degree to which states lodge reservations about or exceptions to the content of the treaty to which they may have a particular objection, given their own legal culture or legal system. For example, the United States lodged a reservation about the death penalty when it signed the International Covenant on Civil and Political Rights (Malanczuk 1997, 135; see also Sherman 1994), since the jurisdiction over the death penalty is left to the individual states in the U.S. federal system. According to Article 2 (1) (d) of the Vienna Convention on the Law of Treaties, a reservation is a unilateral statement made by a state that "purports to exclude or to modify the legal effect of certain provisions of the treaty in their application to that State" (cited in Malanczuk 1997, 135; see also Brownlie 2003, 584–87).

There is an ongoing debate among international lawyers over whether such reservations invalidate the treaty, particularly since they are not meant to be incompatible with its overall "object and purpose" (Goodman 2002, 531; see also Lijnzaad 1995). The law of treaties as applied to human rights is further complicated since human rights treaties are multilateral agreements that regulate state treatment of citizens, where inter-state reciprocity has less meaning and the legal status of reservations is more in doubt. For this study, the scores that are assigned to countries for their reservations across the various treaties are not meant to solve the issues of validity and legal effect of the reservations. Rather, they are an attempt to reflect the commitment and intent of the state at the time of ratification of the treaties. They thus code the degree to which the reservations undermine such an object and purpose by creating a reservations variable for each treaty that can be combined with the ratification variables outlined above and therefore produce a "weighted" ratification variable.

The reservations variable rewards countries for making no reservations about a treaty upon ratification and punishes them in varying degrees for making reservations upon ratification.[5] The variable has four categories, which are coded as follows:

(4) *Given to countries that have no reservations with regard to said treaty, interpretive declarations that do not modify obligations, or nonsubstantial declarations.* This would include declarations such as criticism of the treaty not being open to all states, or political nonrecognition of other states.

(3) *Given to countries whose reservations could have some but not major impact on their obligations.* This would include reservations to certain aspects of a specific right that did not nullify it completely or to whole articles that are procedural (such as articles allowing one-sided referral to the International Court of Justice, ICJ).

(2) *Given to countries whose reservations have a noticeable effect on their obligations under the treaty* to a whole article, nullifying or leaving open the possibility not to abide by a whole article. This score would also be given for reservations that do not limit a whole right or article, but nevertheless contain the core obligation of the article or right.

(1) *Given to countries whose reservations can have significant and severe effects on the treaty obligations.* This would include reservations that show disregard for the object and purpose, or for rules of customary international law. Reservations that subject the whole treaty to national or religious legislation would receive this score.

These different categories are qualitative and involve subjective judgments as to the severity of the reservation and the level of commitment of a state to the treaty obligations. For example, a reservation to the freedom of movement article in the ICCPR by Belize, stating that there are statutory provisions requiring persons intending to travel abroad to furnish tax clearance certificates, is qualitatively different from Botswana's reservation to Article 7 of the ICCPR to the extent that "torture, cruel, inhuman or degrading treatment means torture, inhuman or degrading punishment or other treatment prohibited by Section 7 of the Constitution of the Republic of Botswana." In effect, Botswana's reservation could be viewed as an attempt to define for itself what it considers to be acts of torture, rather than deriving such definitions from international law. Appendix A provides further clarification of the coding of the reservation variable by treaty and discusses the sources that informed the set of judgments used in coding it. By rewarding countries for not having reservations, it is possible to multiply the two separate types of variables (ratification and reservation) to produce a third type of weighted ratification variable that takes into account a country's initial intent at the time of ratification. The following hypothetical example helps clarify the differences among these three types of treaty variables:

State A ratifies ICCPR in 1985 with no reservations:

$$[ICCPR \text{ ratification} = 2]*[ICCPR \text{ reservation} = 4]$$
$$= [\text{weighted ratification variable} = 8]$$

State B ratifies ICCPR in 1985 with serious reservations:

$$[ICCPR \text{ ratification} = 2]*[ICCPR \text{ reservation} = 1]$$
$$= [\text{weighted ratification variable} = 2]$$

The combination of the ratification variable and the reservation variable in the example above produces a weighted ratification variable, which changes fundamentally the depiction and meaning of the overall pattern of ratifications. Without the weighting variable, State A and State B would be indistinguishable in terms of their formal commitment to the ICCPR. The addition of the weighting variable "discounts" the ratification variable for State B since it had serious reservations that undermined the object and purpose of the treaty. Although both states are "rewarded" for ratifying the ICCPR, State B is "punished" for having serious reservations. In addition to the weighted ratification variables, it is possible to calculate the difference between the weighted variables and their associated ratification variables to depict patterns in ratification and reservation over time (see chapter 4), and it is possible to calculate mean ratification values for both the unweighted and weighted variables. Since there may be residual problems of reliability surrounding the reservation variables, the bivariate and multivariate analyses carried out in chapters 4 and 6 use both the raw ratification variables and their weighted versions.

Measuring Human Rights Practices

Beyond the formal commitments that states make to international human rights treaties, this study is also concerned with the conduct and practices of states with regard to their citizens, such that the data set contains measures of the *de facto* enjoyment of human rights. There are effectively three options for measuring such rights in practice, including "events-based" measures, "standards-based" measures, and "survey-based" measures. Events-based measures of human rights count specific occurrences of human rights violations, be they against individuals or groups. Standards-based measures use the legal ideal established by the international law of human rights and then code country performances on limited ordinal scales that reward and punish countries for their human rights records. Survey-based scales use survey data on individual level perceptions of human rights conditions on the ground. Each of these different types of human rights measures has its own set of strengths and weaknesses and, by extension, appropriateness for use in this study.

Over the years, NGO efforts to monitor human rights practices of states have been combined with statisticians' tools for counting and estimating human rights violations. One such effort has been pioneered by the American Association for the Advancement of Science (AAAS), which has developed a model of data capture that uses violations as the units of analysis and uses "multiple systems" of reporting to estimate the total number of violations that have occurred in a specific time and place (see Ball 1994, 2003; Ball, Spirer, and Spirer 2000). This method applies a "controlled vocabulary" of violation, victim, and perpetrator types to narrative statements received by NGOs, fact-finding missions, and truth and reconciliation commissions (TRCs) to provide macrohistorical patterns of gross human rights violations. The method has been used to estimate the number of human rights violations in the conflicts in El Salvador and Guatemala in the 1970s and 1980s (see Ball, Kobrak, and Spirer 1999; CEH 1999; Ball, Spirer, and Spirer 2000), Kosovo in the 1990s (Ball and Asher 2002), and in Peru in the 1980s and 1990s (see Ball et al. 2003). It was also used by TRCs in Haiti, South Africa, and Sierra Leone (Ball, Spirer, and Spirer 2000; see also Wilson 2001, 33–61). Although the resultant data minimize the conceptual "distance" between what is being measured and the measure itself (i.e., the measures have a great deal of validity), such estimations of violations are inappropriate for the kind of global comparative analysis used in this study. The violations data are more significantly bound by space and time constraints that limit their comparability across different political contexts. The AAAS data projects have covered discrete periods of conflict, such as those in El Salvador, Guatemala, South Africa, and Kosovo, but they have not produced such measures for a larger sample of countries. Moreover, almost by definition, the AAAS work does not cover times and places in which few or no violations have taken place, thereby providing limited variability of the kind necessary for the analysis in this study.

Survey-based data on the protection of human rights are also inappropriate for several reasons. First, perceptions of human rights practices or support for the idea of human rights as found in the *World Values Surveys* (see Inglehart 1997) tend to be bound by both time and space constraints and therefore preclude the type of analysis needed to estimate systematically the effectiveness of the international human rights regime. Second, surveys of random samples of individuals that probe the degree to which they have suffered human rights abuses elicit such a small "strike rate" that very large (and therefore expensive) mass surveys must be carried out. Extant measures of good governance tend not to use random samples, but small samples of economic and government elites to produce various measures of voice, accountability, corruption, and the rule of law. Such samples are not representative, and the errors associated with their overall point estimates preclude their use in multivariate statistical analysis (see Kaufmann, Kraay, and Zoido-Lobatón 1999a, 1999b, 2000, 2002).

Standards-based measures of human rights, on the other hand, offer the most reasonable solution for the type of analysis that is conducted in this study, which uses five extant measures and the average of the measures. The dominant and more reliable standards-based scale of human rights is the "political terror scale," which was devised initially by Raymond Gastil in 1979, was taken up by Michael Stohl in 1983, and has since been updated by a variety of academics (Davenport 1995, 1996; Dixon and Moon 1986; Fein 1995; Gibney,

Dalton, and Vockell 1992; Gibney and Stohl 1988; Henderson 1991, 1993; Moon and Dixon 1992; Poe 1991, 1992; Poe and Sirirangsi 1993, 1994; Stohl, Carleton, and Johnson 1984; Carleton and Stohl 1985; Stohl et al. 1986). The political terror scale codes country performance on a 1-to-5 scale, based on the annual reports produced by Amnesty International and the U.S. State Department. Others have labeled it a measure of the protection of "personal integrity rights," since it focuses on the state use of extrajudicial killings, torture, political imprisonment, and exile (see Poe and Tate 1994; Poe, Tate, and Keith 1999; Zanger 2000a). The five different levels of the scale code country human rights practices according to the different degrees and frequency with which political integrity rights violations are reported. These five levels include (Zanger 2000a, 218)

Level 1: "Countries . . . under a secure rule of law, people are not imprisoned for their views, and torture is rare or exceptional . . . political murders are extremely rare."

Level 2: "There is a limited amount of imprisonment for nonviolent political activity. However, few persons are affected, torture and beating are exceptional . . . political murder is rare."

Level 3: "There is extensive political imprisonment, or a recent history of such imprisonment. Execution or other political murders and brutality may be common. Unlimited detention, with or without trial, for political views is accepted."

Level 4: "The practices of [Level 3] are expanded to larger numbers. Murders, disappearances are a common part of life. . . . In spite of its generality, on this level terror affects primarily those who interest themselves in politics or ideas."

Level 5: "The terror of [Level 4] ha[s] been expanded to the whole population. . . . The leaders of these societies place no limits on the means or thoroughness with which they pursue personal or ideological goals."

The political terror scale has shown a good degree of intercoder reliability and robustness across the different studies that have deployed it for systematic comparative analysis. It still has residual problems with variance truncation, because beyond a certain level of scoring, it is not sensitive enough to distinguish between the human rights practices within the group of advanced industrial democracies and/or among those worst offenders. Across its different categories, however, it provides a reasonable measure of rights protection that makes it suitable for the kind of global analysis adopted in this study. The methodological strengths of the political terror scale have led to its adaptation by Hathaway (2002, 1970–71), who applies a similar five-point scale to measure the degree to which torture is practiced across the globe. The scale is derived directly from the legal requirements found in the 1984 Convention on Torture and codes country practices based on U.S. State Department reports.

Level 1: "There are no allegations or instances of torture in this year. There are no allegations or instances of beatings in this year; or there are only isolated reports of beatings by individual police officers or guards all of whom were disciplined when caught."

Level 2: "At least one of the following is true: There are only unsubstantiated and likely untrue allegations of torture; there are 'isolated' instances of torture for which the government has provided redress; there are allegations or indications of beatings, mistreatment or harsh/rough treatment; there are some incidents of abuse of prisoners or detainees; or abuse or rough treatment occurs 'sometimes' or 'occasionally.' Any reported beatings put a country into at least this category regardless of governmental systems in place to provide redress (except in the limited circumstances noted above)."

Level 3: "At least one of the following is true: There are 'some' or 'occasional' allegations of or incidents of torture (even 'isolated' incidents unless they have been redressed or are unsubstantiated; see above); there are 'reports,' 'allegations,' or 'cases,' of torture without reference to frequency; beatings are 'common' (or 'not uncommon'); there are 'isolated' incidents of beatings to death or summary executions (this includes unexplained deaths suspected to be attributed to brutality) or there are beatings to death or summary executions without reference to frequency; there is severe maltreatment of prisoners; there are 'numerous' reports of beatings; persons are 'often' subjected to beatings; there is 'regular' brutality; or psychological punishment is used."

Level 4: "At least one of the following is true: Torture is 'common'; there are several reports of torture; there are 'many' or 'numerous' allegations of torture; torture is 'practiced' (without reference to frequency); there is government apathy or ineffective prevention of torture; psychological punishment is 'frequently' or 'often' used; there are 'frequent' beatings or rough handling; 'occasional' incidents of beating to death; or there are 'several' reports of beatings to death."

Level 5: "At least one of the following is true: Torture is 'prevalent' or 'widespread'; there is 'repeated' and 'methodical' torture; there are 'many' incidents of torture; torture is 'routine' or standard practice; torture is 'frequent'; there are 'common,' 'frequent,' or 'many' beatings to death or summary executions; or there are 'widespread' beatings to death."

Here it is clear that each category contains a discrete set of practices, key words, and decision rules for coding the narrative reports on torture found in U.S. State Department reports. Hathaway reports 80 percent intercoder reliability for the measure using Cohen's Kappa statistic (Hathaway 2002, 1972; see also Carletta 1996). Owing to the unreliability and insufficiency of information on torture before 1985, she only codes the period 1985–99, and the United States is the only missing country for the entire period, since it never appears in the reports. For this study, the torture measure is used alongside the Amnesty International and State Department versions of the political terror scale.

Freedom House provides a less reliable but frequently used measure of rights protection. Initially developed by Raymond Gastil and then taken up in 1989 by Freedom House, the measure includes two seven-point scales that code the degree to which civil and political rights are protected. Like the political terror scale and the torture scale, a low score on the Freedom House scales denotes a better protection of rights than a high score. Freedom House uses two separate checklists for the protection of each type of rights protection, which then generate the separate scales (see table 3.1). It is clear from table 3.1 that Freedom House includes a wide range of institutional and rights concepts in its checklists, which are reflected in its overall scores (see Landman 1999). Indeed, as chapter 4 will demonstrate, time-series plots of the Freedom House scores show a more positive trend in *de facto* rights protection than other measures, which is partly explained by the institutional dimensions of the scale that rewards countries for having elections and captures the dynamics of the "third" and "fourth" waves of democratization (Huntington 1991; Doorenspleet 2000).

Over the years, the Freedom House scales have been used as a measure of state repressiveness (Muller and Seligson 1987), the level of democracy (e.g., Burkhart and Lewis-Beck 1994; Helliwell 1994; Munck and Verkuilen 2002), and the rule of law (Knack 2002) and are now one of the many components in the World Bank's measures of good governance (Kaufmann, Kraay, and Zoido-Lobatón 1999a, 1999b, 2000, 2002). Despite this variety of uses for the scales, it seems that at a base level, they are measures of civil and political rights protection and are best utilized in their separate form, since combining them into a single index can produce biases. Moreover, even though they are widely used, they are less reliable than the political terror and torture scales, since Freedom House has been less explicit about its coding frame, its source information from which it codes the scales, and its intercoder reliability. For this study, the scales are used separately and alongside the other measures of rights in practice as comparators, and for presentational and analytical consistency, they have been normalized to range from 1 to 5.

Despite the broad consensus that human rights are indivisible and should be accorded equal priority, extant measures of rights in practice of the kind used in this study have tended to focus on the protection of civil and political rights. This narrow focus on and progress with respect to this particular set of rights can be explained by several factors. First, they reflect a general tendency during early human rights monitoring to favor civil and political rights at the cost of economic, social, and cultural rights. Second, there remains a lack of clarity concerning the precise scope of state obligation and the core content of individual economic, social, and cultural rights, which in turn makes it difficult to identify events and practices that clearly amount to violations. The AAAS has sought to extend its events-based methodology to measure the violation of economic, social, and cultural rights, but to date has developed only the controlled vocabulary and has yet to code violations (see Chapman 1996, 1998). Third, there continues to be a debate over how economic, social, and cultural rights are to be realized progressively through use of the

Table 3.1. Freedom House checklists for coding civil and political liberties

Civil liberties checklist	Political liberties checklist
Freedom of expression and belief	*Electoral process*
Are there free and independent media and other forms of cultural expression?	Is the head of state and/or head of government or other chief authority elected through free and fair elections?
Are there free religious institutions, and is there free private and public religious expression?	Are the legislative representatives elected through free and fair elections?
Is there academic freedom, and is the educational system free of extensive political indoctrination?	Are there fair electoral laws, equal campaigning opportunities, fair polling, and honest tabulation of ballots?
Is there open and free private discussion?	
Associational and organizational rights	*Political pluralism and participation*
Is there freedom of assembly, demonstration, and open public discussion?	Do the people have the right to organize in different political parties or other competitive political groupings of their choice, and is the system open to the rise and fall of these competing parties or groupings?
Is there freedom of political or quasi-political organizations? (*Note:* this includes political parties, civic organizations, ad hoc issue groups, etc.)	Is there a significant opposition vote, *de facto* opposition power, and a realistic possibility for the opposition to increase its support or gain power through elections?
Are there free trade unions and peasant organizations or equivalents, and is there effective collective bargaining? Are there free professional and other private organizations?	Are the people's political choices free from domination by the military, foreign powers, totalitarian parties, religious hierarchies, economic oligarchies, or any other powerful group?
	Do cultural, ethnic, religious, and other minority groups have reasonable self-determination, self-government, autonomy, or participation through informal consensus in the decision-making process?

Table 3.1. (*continued*)

Civil liberties checklist	Political liberties checklist
Rule of law	*Functioning of government*
Is there an independent judiciary?	Do freely elected representatives determine the policies of the government?
Does the rule of law prevail in civil and criminal matters? Are police under direct civilian control?	
Is there protection from police terror, unjustified imprisonment, exile, or torture, whether by groups that support or oppose the system? Is there freedom from war and insurgencies?	Is the government free from pervasive corruption?
	Is the government accountable to the electorate between elections, and does it operate with openness and transparency?
Is the population treated equally under the law?	
Personal autonomy and individual rights	*Additional discretionary questions*
Is there personal autonomy? Does the state control travel, choice of residence, or choice of employment? Is there freedom from indoctrination and excessive dependency on the state?	For traditional monarchies that have no parties or electoral process, does the system provide for consultation with the people, encourage discussion of policy, and allow the right to petition the ruler?
Do citizens have the right to own property and establish private businesses? Is private business activity unduly influenced by government officials, the security forces, or organized crime?	Is the government or occupying power deliberately changing the ethnic composition of a country or territory so as to destroy a culture or tip the political balance in favor of another group?
Are there personal social freedoms, including gender equality, choice of marriage partners, and size of family?	
Is there equality of opportunity and the absence of economic exploitation?	

Source: http://www.freedomhouse.org/research/freeworld/2003/methodology.htm

maximum available resources (see Robertson 1994). Such a view of progressive realization implies that the protection of such rights is still relative, since it relies more heavily on the fiscal capacity of states (see Foweraker and Landman 1997). It has been impossible so far to provide meaningful and comparative measures of these rights for global comparative analysis. Moreover, for the purposes of the analysis conducted here and in line with the arguments advanced by Risse, Ropp, and Sikkink (1999, 2–3), demonstration of any effect of the international human rights regime for this more salient form of human rights, about which there is more global consensus and available data, represents an important first step in mapping and explaining the protection of human rights (see also Foweraker and Landman 1997, 14–17). Further research could certainly attempt to replicate the analysis here and try to estimate the relationship between norms and rights for economic, social, and cultural rights.

Explanatory and Control Variables

Beyond measures of rights in principle and rights in practice, the data set includes a series of additional variables that feature important explanatory and control variables in the model depicted in figure 2.4. These variables include the level of democracy, economic development, interdependence, internal and external conflict, size, and regional differentiation. Democracy is measured using the combined democracy index found in the Polity IV data set, which ranges from -10 to $+10$ and operationalizes a procedural and institutional concept of democracy that combines indicators for competitiveness of political participation, regulation of participation, competitiveness of executive recruitment, and constraints on the chief executive (see Jaggers and Gurr 1995, 472; Zanger 2000a; Foweraker and Krznaric 2000; Munck and Verkuilen 2002; Landman 1999, 2003). Democracy is further divided into three dummy variables for "old," "third wave," and "fourth wave" democracies (Huntington 1991; Lijphart 1999; Przeworski et al. 2000; Doorenspleet 2000, 2001).

The level of economic development, or overall wealth, is measured according to the logged values of per capita gross domestic product in 1995 U.S. dollars. This measure is typically adopted in most global comparative studies on democracy and human rights, and its logged form eliminates inherent problems of skewness, which can bias statistical estimates of relationships (Mitchell and McCormick

1988; Henderson 1991; Helliwell 1994; Poe and Tate 1994; Land-man 1999; Poe, Tate, and Keith 1999; Keith 1999; Przeworski et al. 2000). Other analyses have used energy consumption as a measure of economic development, which is highly correlated with per capita GDP (Burkhart and Lewis-Beck 1994; Foweraker and Landman 1997), but Przeworski et al. (2000, 5) note that per capita GDP or individual income, "[w]ith all its innumerable caveats . . . is simply the best overall indicator of the choices people enjoy in their lives."

Global interdependence is captured through the use of three variables: country membership in international governmental organizations (IGOs), the presence of international nongovernmental organizations (INGOs), and trade as a percentage of GDP. The organizational data are from Russett and O'Neal (2001) and from the Union of International Associations (www.uia.org). As the data were available only for selected years, the data set replaces the missing values with a linear interpolation and, in the case of INGOs, logs the result to control for skewness (see Appendix 2). Membership in IGOs and the presence of INGOs measures the degree to which countries are engaged with the larger world, especially in its more institutionalized dimensions. The twentieth century saw unprecedented growth and proliferation of IGOs and INGOs, the presence of which has been shown to effect patterns of democratization and to reduce the probability of international conflict (see Russett and O'Neal 2001; Li and Reuveny 2003). It is therefore important to examine the effects of such organizations on human rights treaty ratification and protection. In addition to examining this so-called embeddedness of countries, the data set includes the World Bank's estimate of total trade (exports and imports) as a percentage of GDP to measure the degree to which a country participates in the global trading system (www.worldbank.org).

Beyond these main explanatory variables, the model in figure 2.4 also specifies further controls for internal and external conflict, population size, and regional differentiation. Following Poe and Tate (1994), Keith (1999), and Zanger (2000a), the data set includes separate correlates of war (COW) variables on inter-state war and civil war for control of the central government, which are coded 1 for the years in which a country was involved in either form of conflict and 0 for all other years (Sarkees 2000; Singer and Small 1972, 1994). Population size is measured with the use of the natural log of population data from the World Bank. Finally, the data set has a number of regional dummy variables for Europe, Latin America, Africa, Asia, and the Pacific to gauge the differentiation of the empirical relationships across regions (see Landman 1999; Helliwell 1994; Foweraker and Landman 2004).

Table 3.2 summarizes all of the main variables used in the analysis, including the rights in principle measures and rights in practice measures, as well as the explanatory and control variables. The table shows the temporal ($18 \leq$ year ≤ 25) and spatial ($138 \leq n$ countries ≤ 193) coverage of the variables, the combination of which produces the total number of cross-national time-series observations ($2484 \leq n \times t$ observations ≤ 4825) used in the analysis. Table 3.3 is a bivariate correlation matrix of the main explanatory variables, which shows that the first-order relationships between them are all statistically significant ($p < .01$), with the exception of the relationships between inter-state conflict and wealth, inter-state conflict and INGOs, and intra-state conflict and IGO membership. Of note are the positive correlations between democracy, wealth, IGO membership, and INGOs, and the negative correlations between trade on the one hand and IGOs and INGOs and the two conflict variables on the other. None of the variables are correlated (all of the Pearson r values $< .70$) to the degree that multicollinearity will be a problem for the statistical analysis presented in chapters 4, 5, and 6.

The Way Forward

This chapter has established the overall method and research design of this study, which are based on the long tradition in mainstream political science concerning the relationship between economic development and democracy (see Lipset 1959) and have now been expanded to include similar systematic global analyses of human rights protection (see Landman 2002b). The discussion has shown that this particular mode of analysis rests on a number of assumptions about the observable world and how it can be measured and analyzed with systematic statistical techniques. The results of such analysis will always be empirical generalizations, which inform larger arguments about the protection of human rights and highlight the regularities and exceptions to the overall patterns in the evolution and effectiveness of the international human rights regime.

Such analysis cannot, however, "unpack" important historical, political, and sociological relationships at a lower level of analysis. It

Table 3.2. Data and variables used in the study

Concept	Measure(s)	Type of measure	Temporal coverage	Spatial coverage (N = countries)
Rights in principle (three variables for each of the six core international human rights treaties and the two optional protocols)	Ratification variable	Scale 0–2	1976–2000	193
	Reservation variable	Scale 1–4	1976–2000	193
	Weighted ratification variable	Scale 0–8	1976–2000	193
	Mean ratification	Averaged scale 0–2	1976–2000	193
	Mean weighted ratification	Averaged scale 0–1	1976	193
Rights in practice	Political terror scales/personal integrity rights (Amnesty International)	Scale 1–5	1976–2000	150
	Political terror scales/personal integrity rights (U.S. State Department)	Scale 1–5	1976–2000	150
	Torture variable (U.S. State Department)	Scale 1–5	1985–1999	148
	Freedom House political liberties	Scale 1–7 (transformed to 1–5)	1976–2000	170
	Freedom House civil liberties	Scale 1–7 (transformed to 1–5)	1976–2000	170
	Mean rights score	Average of all five rights in practice measures scaled from 0 to 1	1976–2000	170
Democracy	Polity IV	Scale −10 to +10	1976–1998	140

(*continued*)

Table 3.2. Data and variables used in the study (*continued*)

Concept	Measure(s)	Type of measure	Temporal coverage	Spatial coverage (N = countries)
Old democracy	Categorical	Dichotomous (0–1)	1976–1998	193 (30 old democracies)
Third-wave democracy	Categorical	Dichotomous (0–1)	1976–1998	193 (14 third-wave democracies)
Fourth-wave democracy	Categorical	Dichotomous (0–1)	1976–1998	193 (31 fourth-wave democracies)
Economic development	Per capita GDP (logged)	Continuous 1995 U.S. dollars	1976–2000	154
Inter-dependence	IGOs	Continuous	1976–2000	192
	INGOs	Continuous	1976–2000	184
	Trade as percentage of GDP (logged)	LN percentage	1976–2000	147
Conflict	Civil war	Dichotomous (0–1)	1976–1997	140
	External war	Dichotomous (0–1)	1976–1997	140
Size	Population (logged)	Continuous	1976–2000	193
Region	Europe Communist Europe Post-Communist Europe North America Latin America Sub-Saharan Africa Middle East and North Africa (MENA) South Asia East Asia and the Pacific	Dichotomous (0–1)	1976–2000	193

Table 3.3. Bivariate correlation matrix for the independent variables

	Ln per capita GDP	IGO membership	Ln INGOS	Ln trade	Civil war	Inter-state war	Ln population
Polity IV democracy score	0.55*	0.24*	0.34*	0.08*	−0.08*	−0.09*	0.09*
Ln per capita GDP		0.30*	0.22*	0.21*	−0.16*	0.03	−0.08*
IGO membership			0.51*	−0.20*	−.003	0.05*	0.40
LN INGOS				−0.11*	−0.13*	0.02	0.30*
Ln trade					−0.15*	−0.08*	−0.64*
Civil war						0.01	0.08*
Inter-state war							0.07*

Note: Pearson's *r* correlation coefficient, all correlations with an * are significant at $p < .01$.

cannot capture the lobbying and intimate political processes involved in treaty formation and ratification. It cannot examine the mobilizational strategies of human rights NGOs in their effort to set standards, monitor human rights developments, and raise awareness. It cannot examine domestic coalitions and pressure groups that try to bring about positive change within different political systems. It cannot carry out "process tracing" in an effort to establish the links at the domestic level made between actors and their propensity to reform political institutions (see Hawkins 2002). It cannot map intersubjective meanings and different cultural understandings of human rights, which may or may not have an effect on human rights practices. What the design can do is deliver useful, parsimonious, but ultimately limited forms of knowledge about the world. It is hoped that in this study, the incremental gains in knowledge and the ways in which they are generated are open to scrutiny, clarification, replication, and further testing, and that the lessons are helpful for continuing efforts at improving the protection of human rights.

4

The International Human
Rights Regime

The first two chapters of this study set the stage for the empirical
analysis that is conducted in this and the next two chapters. This
chapter portrays the growth of the international human rights regime
by using descriptive and analytical statistics as a first step in the overall empirical analysis of regime growth and effectiveness. The human
rights regime comprises international treaties to which countries become a party, and the six treaty bodies monitor state compliance with
their legal obligations. The first part of this chapter maps the evolution of the international human rights regime, using the unweighted
and weighted treaty ratification variables outlined in chapter 3. Time-
series charts show the historical trends in ratification, and regional
comparisons show the difference in ratification across the globe. The
second part of the chapter tests the main relationships outlined in the
left side of the model in chapter 2 (see fig. 2.4), with the use of bivariate and multivariate statistical techniques. In other words, the analysis
examines the degree to which democracy, wealth, interdependence,
conflict, size, and regional differentiation help explain the patterns
that are observed in the ratification behavior of states.

Taken together, both parts of the chapter answer a series of important questions. The first set of questions relates to the observable
patterns in the growth of the regime itself. What has been the growth
of the international human rights regime in terms of the number of
countries signing and ratifying human rights treaties? Is the propensity

to ratify some instruments greater than that for others? The second set of questions is related to the "second-order" explanations for the growth of the regime. Is the propensity to ratify human rights treaties greater for democracies? Are there discernible differences in the regime across the regions? Are there observable differences in the propensity to ratify between established, "third wave" (Huntington 1991), and "fourth wave" democracies (Diamond 1999; Doorenspleet 2000)? Is the propensity to ratify human rights treaties higher for wealthy countries? Does interdependence have an impact? Finally, does involvement in internal or external warfare have an impact on ratification? The first set of questions thus concerns the "if" and "when" of the regime, and the second set of questions concerns the "where" and "why" of the regime. They are posed in light of expectations that emerge from the theories outlined in chapter 2, and their answers paint a clearer picture of global trends in the growth of the human rights regime, how this growth is differentiated across regions and other important factors, and how the substantive inferences from the analysis inform larger theoretical debates.

The Evolution of the Human Rights Regime

By 2000 there were between 125 and 190 countries that were party to the various treaties that make up the international human rights regime. Table 2.1 provided a preview of the main instruments that make up the international human rights regime (see chapter 2); table 4.1 adds the number and proportion of states that are parties to the instruments as of 2000. It is clear from the table that the Convention on the Rights of the Child (CRC) has the largest number of state parties, and that the Second Optional Protocol to the International Covenant on Civil and Political Rights (OPT2) the least. The CRC lays out protections of rights delimited in previous instruments but applies them specifically to children, and the main objective of the Second Optional Protocol is to abolish the death penalty (Buergenthal 1995, 50–51, 76–78).

But the details in the table provide only a snapshot of the global picture of regime membership and say very little about the overall historical trends in treaty ratification. Figure 4.1 is a straight time-series plot of the ratification scores for the international instruments, where a country receives a score of 0 for no signature, 1 for signature, and 2 for ratification (see chapter 3). The figure shows a steady rate of ratification for all of the instruments and, in line with the 2000 rat-

Table 4.1. The international human rights regime: instruments, dates, and membership

Name	Date when open for signature	States parties 2000 N (%)
International Covenant on Civil and Political Rights (ICCPR)	1966	146 (75.6)
International Covenant on Economic, Social, and Cultural Rights (ICESCR)	1966	142 (73.6)
Optional Protocol to the International Covenant on Civil and Political Rights (OPT1)	1976	95 (49.2)
Second Optional Protocol to the International Covenant on Civil and Political Rights (OPT2)	1989	44 (22.8)
International Convention on the Elimination of all Forms of Racial Discrimination (CERD)	1966	156 (80.8)
Convention on the Elimination of All Forms of Discrimination against Women (CEDAW)	1979	164 (85.0)
Convention against Torture and other Cruel, Inhuman, or Degrading Treatment or Punishment (CAT)	1984	122 (63.2)
Convention on the Rights of the Child (CRC)	1989	190 (98.4)

Data source: OUNHCHR (Sept. 2000), *Status of Ratification of thePrincipal International Human Rights Treaties*, www.unhchr.ch/pdf/report.pdf and International Service for Human Rights (January 2000), Info-Pack, pp. 46–50. See also Bayefsky (2001, 11).

ification figures presented in table 4.1, shows the lowest ratification rate for the Second Optional Protocol and the highest rate for the Convention on the Rights of the Child. These trends lend support to the popular accounts of the growth of the international human rights system, which periodize the proliferation of human rights norms (e.g., Claude 1976b; Donnelly 1986, 1998; Buergenthal 1997). To add to this historical portrait of norms proliferation, figures 4.2 and 4.3 show the time series and regional trends in the unweighted and weighted ratification variables.

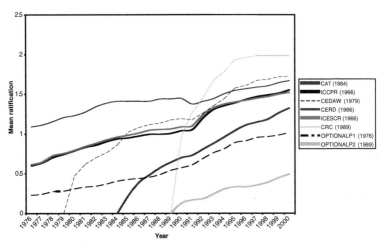

Figure 4.1. Ratification of the main treaties of the international human rights regime, 1976–2000.

Figure 4.2 shows that for all of the treaties (except CERD and CRC) there is a growing gap over time between the unweighted and weighted ratification variables. Recall from chapter 3 that the weighted ratification variable rewards countries for having fewer significant reservations. The increasing gap between the two measures thus suggests that those countries that ratified later tend to ratify treaties with fewer reservations and a greater formal intent to abide by the full obligations contained within each treaty. The gap between the unweighted and weighted ratification variables for CERD and CRC is relatively constant, suggesting that both of these treaties have been ratified on a consistent basis with few reservations. In contrast, the gap between the unweighted and weighted ratification variables is smallest for both the Convention Against Torture and the Second Optional Protocol to the ICCPR, suggesting that each of these instruments has been ratified with the largest number of significant reservations.

The regional comparisons depicted in figure 4.3 also compare the unweighted and weighted ratification variables. The between group differences for both variables are statistically significant ($18.20 \leq F \leq 151.38$; $p < .001$ for the unweighted variable and $19.04 \leq F \leq 76.18$; $p < .001$ for the weighted variable). In other words, the average values in each of the regional groupings in the figure are substantively

(*text continues on p. 71*)

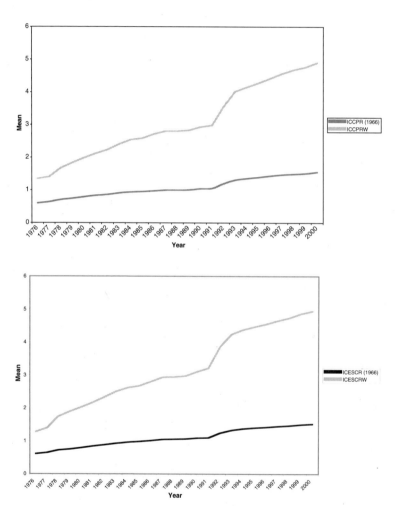

Figure 4.2. Unweighted and weighted ratification of the main human rights treaties, 1976–2000.

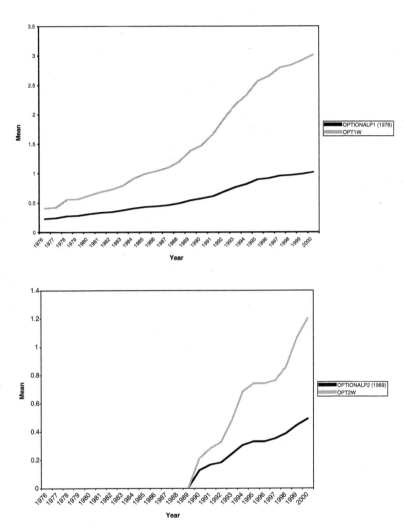

Figure 4.2. Unweighted and weighted ratification of the main human rights treaties, 1976–2000 (*continued*).

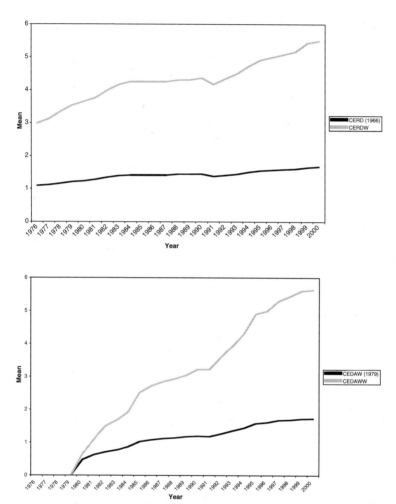

Figure 4.2. (*continued*)

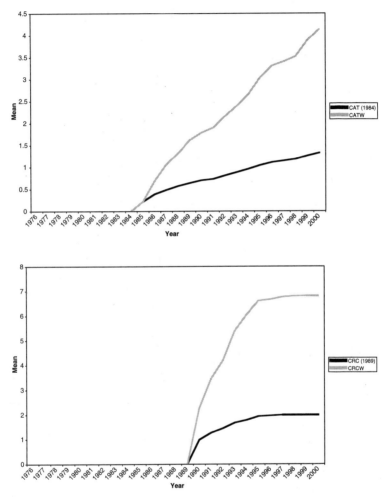

Figure 4.2. Unweighted and weighted ratification of the main human rights treaties, 1976–2000 (*continued*).

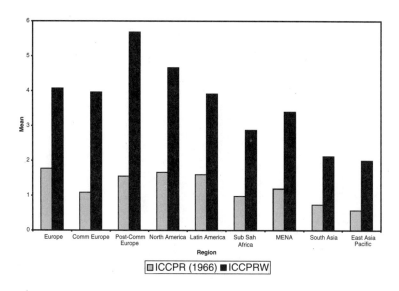

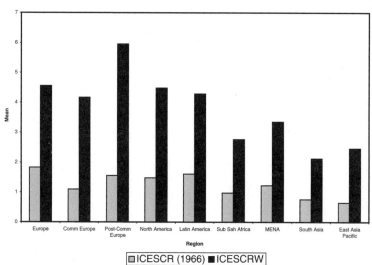

Figure 4.3. Unweighted and weighted ratification of the main human rights treaties by region, 1976–2000.

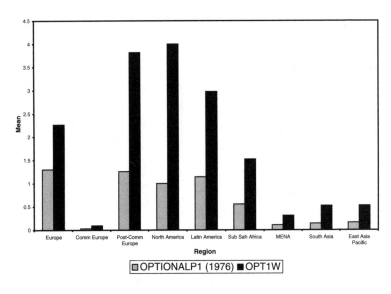

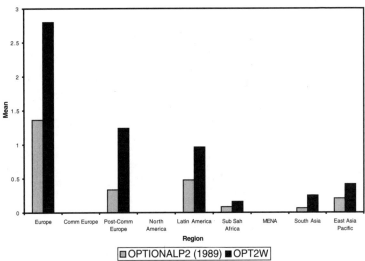

Figure 4.3. Unweighted and weighted ratification of the main human rights treaties by region, 1976–2000 (*continued*).

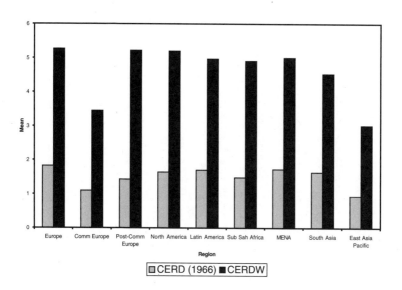

CERD (1966) ■ CERDW

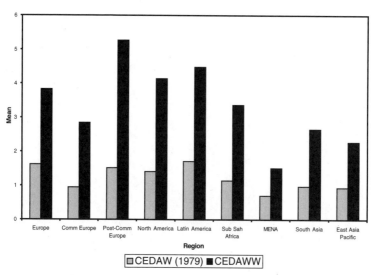

CEDAW (1979) ■ CEDAWW

Figure 4.3. (*continued*)

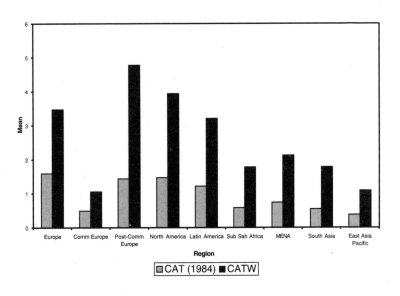

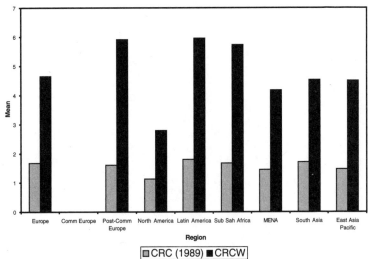

Figure 4.3. Unweighted and weighted ratification of the main human rights treaties by region, 1976–2000 (*continued*).

different. Indeed, for the ICCPR, ICESCR, CEDAW, and CAT, post-Communist Europe (Eastern Europe and the Central Asian states of the former Soviet Union) shows patterns of ratification with the least number of reservations, followed by North America and Europe. The regional differences for ratification of the other treaties are less pronounced. But the results for North America need further elaboration, since the region comprises only the United States and Canada. It is clear that Canada's behavior in terms of its formal commitment to these human rights treaties is significantly greater than that of the United States, which is notorious for not ratifying human rights instruments and lodging reservations when it does ratify. To illustrate these differences, figure 4.4 compares the weighted and unweighted ratification variables for the United States and Canada, where the between-group differences for both are statistically significant ($6.06 \leq F \leq 68.85$; $p < .02$ for the unweighted variable and $51.43 \leq F \leq 30976.00$; $p < .001$ for the weighted variable). Thus, the United States appears to be a significant outlier with respect to the ratification of human rights treaties.

The comparative table (table 4.1), time-series plots (fig. 4.1), and regional comparative charts (figs. 4.2, 4.3, and 4.4) all show that the human rights regime has grown in both depth and breadth since its inception in 1948, and especially since the International Covenant on Civil and Political Rights (ICCPR) and the International Covenant on Economic, Social, and Cultural Rights (ICESCR) came into force in 1976. Over time, a larger number of rights protections have been codified, and an increasing number of states have formally committed themselves to the protection of human rights. Although some instruments show greater membership and ratification than others, and some regions provide greater protection than others, collectively the evidence presented thus far demonstrates that the world has seen a dramatic "juridical revolution" in the area of human rights (Ignatieff 2001). More and more countries have at least formally surrendered some of their sovereignty to this emerging international legal and normative order, where such a development has formally embedded participating nation-states into larger institutional structures that seek to constrain and limit their behavior in order to protect the sanctity of the individual. Given this growing internationalization of human rights norms, it is important to start building a picture of the evolution and nature of the international system and to explore *why* independent nation-states become party to the regime.

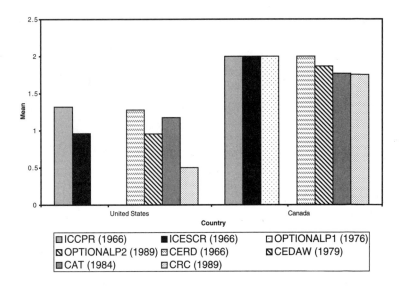

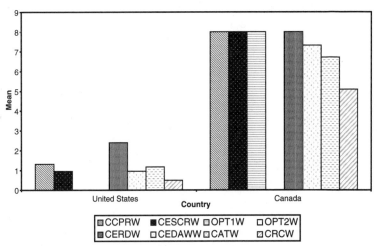

Figure 4.4. Unweighted and weighted ratification of the main human rights treaties by the United States and Canada, 1976–2000.

Explaining the Growth in the Human Rights Regime

This section of the chapter uses the model developed in chapter 2 (see fig. 2.4) to begin exploring possible explanations for the growth of the regime. In particular, the empirical analysis examines the left-hand side of the model to estimate the relationship between the regime variables and democracy, wealth, interdependence, and conflict, while controlling for size and regional differences. The analysis begins with first-order relationships between the relevant variables and then proceeds to multivariate analysis with the use of time-series cross-section regression techniques. These regression techniques also incorporate lagged values of the regime variables to capture (or control for) the time-dependent processes inherent in the evolution of the regime, and mitigate the main estimation problems associated with time-series autocorrelation (see, e.g., Stimson 1985; Gujarati 1988; Sanders and Ward 1994; Beck and Katz 1995; Fox 1997).

Tables 4.2 and 4.3 are bivariate correlation matrices of the un-weighted and weighted treaty ratification variables. Both tables show positive and significant correlations between all of the variables, suggesting a great complementarity in state behavior with regard to treaty ratification. For both the weighted and unweighted treaty ratification variables, the positive relationship is strongest for the ICCPR and ICESCR ($.90 \leq$ tau $b \leq .94$), whereas the other correlations are not as strong ($.20 \leq$ tau $b \leq .60$). These figures show that state ratification of one set of treaties is associated with state ratification of other treaties as they are promulgated and come into force. This finding holds across all of the treaties, even after recognition of reservations is taken into account. The weakest correlations for both sets of ratification variables are for the Second Optional Protocol to the ICCPR, which is not surprising, since it has the lowest ratification rate of all the treaties (see table 4.1 and fig. 4.2).

Tables 4.4 and 4.5 are bivariate correlation matrices for the un-weighted and weighted ratification variables and the main independent variables, including democracy, wealth, interdependence (IGOs, INGOs, and trade), conflict (civil war and international war), and size. The remarkable features of both tables are the strong positive correlations for the ratification of the treaties on the one hand and democracy, wealth, IGOs, and INGOs on the other. Countries with greater democracy, higher levels of per capita GDP, and a larger

(text continues on p. 78)

Table 4.2. Bivariate correlation matrix for the unweighted international human rights regime ratification variables

Independent Variables	ICCPR (1966)	ICESCR (1966)	OptionalP1 (1976)	OptionalP2 (1989)	CERD (1966)	CEDAW (1979)	CAT (1984)	CRC (1989)
ICCPR (1966)	—	.94	.59	.30	.48	.50	.48	.28
ICESCR (1966)		—	.59	.28	.48	.50	.48	.28
OptionalP1 (1976)			—	.41	.30	.38	.45	.21
OptionalP2 (1989)				—	.20	.23	.34	.16
CERD (1966)					—	.36	.36	.20
CEDAW (1979)						—	.45	.40
CAT (1984)							—	.24
CRC (1989)								—

Note: Kendall's tau *b* correlation coefficients, $p < .001$.

Table 4.3. Bivariate correlation matrix for the weighted international human rights regime ratification variables

Independent Variables	ICCPR (1966)	ICESCR (1966)	OptionalP1 (1976)	OptionalP2 (1989)	CERD (1966)	CEDAW (1979)	CAT (1984)	CRC (1989)
ICCPR (1966)	—	.90	.53	.18	.40	.45	.43	.29
ICESCR (1966)		—	.53	.20	.41	.44	.45	.27
OptionalP1 (1976)			—	.35	.29	.37	.43	.17
OptionalP2 (1989)				—	.12	.12	.30	.07
CERD (1966)					—	.32	.34	.17
CEDAW (1979)						—	.40	.40
CAT (1984)							—	.20
CRC (1989)								—

Note: Kendall's tau *b* correlation coefficients, $p < .001$.

Table 4.4. Bivariate correlation matrix for the unweighted international human rights regime ratification variables and the main independent variables

Independent Variables	ICCPR (1966)	ICESCR (1966)	OptionalP1 (1976)	OptionalP2 (1989)	CERD (1966)	CEDAW (1979)	CAT (1984)	CRC (1989)
Democracy	.38***	.38***	.46***	.42***	.16***	.33***	.40***	.16***
Wealth	.18***	.18***	.22***	.43***	.06***	.07***	.31***	−.07**
IGOs	.29***	.29***	.14***	.17***	.32***	.09***	.12***	.01
INGOs	.27***	.26***	.21***	.22***	.20***	.26***	.26***	.11***
Trade	−.01	−.002	.08***	.08***	−.09***	−.04***	−.04**	.01
Civil war	.03*	.03*	.01	−.07**	.06***	.02	.02	−.05**
International war	.02	.02	−.06***	−.03	.04**	−.07***	−.03*	−.07**
Population	.27***	.26***	.04***	.01	.24***	.23***	.28***	.06***

Note: Pearson's *r* correlation coefficients, $*p < .05$, $**p < .01$, $***p < .001$.

Table 4.5. Bivariate correlation matrix for the weighted international human rights regime ratification variables and the main independent variables

Independent Variables	ICCPR (1966)	ICESCR (1966)	OptionalP1 (1976)	OptionalP2 (1989)	CERD (1966)	CEDAW (1979)	CAT (1984)	CRC (1989)
Democracy	.23***	.27***	.35***	.33***	.08***	.27***	.28***	.09***
Wealth	.08***	.11***	.12***	.35***	−.01	.01	.18***	−.12***
IGOs	.17***	.18***	.06***	.14***	.26***	−.03	.06***	−.08***
INGOs	.31***	.33***	.26***	.29***	.32***	.29***	.34***	.05*
Trade	−.02	−.05**	.04**	.05*	−.07***	.03	−.05**	.02
Civil war	.01	.01	.01	−.07**	.05**	.01	.03	−.03
International war	.03*	.02	−.05***	−.02	.001	−.05	.07	−.07***
Population	.25***	.26***	.05***	.04*	.19***	.10***	.22***	−.03

Note: Pearson's *r* correlation coefficients, $*p < .05$, $**p < .01$, $***p < .001$.

number of IGOs and INGOs are more likely to have ratified the main human rights treaties for the 1976–2000 period. The results for the weighted ratification variables show a weaker positive relationship, and for CERD and CEDAW the overall positive relationship for wealth and IGOs drops away. Nevertheless, these first-order associations lend preliminary support to the proposition that greater democracy, wealth, and participation with and in international organizations are related to the degree to which states ratify human rights treaties. Thus it appears that treaties form part of a larger set of macrosocial processes that have included economic development, democracy, and greater international interdependence. The tables also show that international and internal conflict are not necessarily related to treaty ratification, suggesting that states experiencing such conflicts either do not seek international allies and credibility through ratification or are otherwise occupied to make such formal commitments.

To explore these relationships further, multivariate analysis is required. Such analysis harnesses the statistical properties of a large number of observations while being able to provide estimates for separate independent variables and to control for regional differentiation. The most common estimation procedure is Ordinary Least-Squares (OLS) regression, which minimizes the distance between the observed values and the predicted values of any empirical relationship between variables. But the application of standard OLS to time-series cross-sectional data of the kind used in this study is fraught with difficulties. There are both time and unit properties to the data set, which are not wholly independent or uniformly distributed. First, country observations are not independent over time, leading to the possibility of time-serial autocorrelation, which means that any error terms associated with the country will be related to one another through time. The presence of such autocorrelation is a violation of one of the basic assumptions of OLS regression (Lewis-Beck 1980; Stimson 1985) and can lead to biased estimates. Second, some countries have more time-series variation than others (e.g., the level of democracy over time for Brazil varies more than the level of democracy for Finland). Such unit differentiation in variation is known as heteroscedasticity, the presence of which also violates the assumption of OLS regression (Lewis-Beck 1980; Stimson 1985). Thus, the estimations in the following analysis include lagged values of the dependent variable (in this case, treaty ratification) to correct for the problem of autocorrelation and regional dummy variables to correct for the problem of heteroscedasticity. The general regression equation estimated for each human rights treaty is as follows:

$$\text{Treaty ratification}_t = \alpha_t + \beta_1 \text{Treaty ratification}_{t-1} + \beta_2 \text{Democracy}_t$$
$$+ \beta_3 \text{Wealth}_t + \beta_4 \text{IGOs}_t + \beta_5 \text{INGOs}_t + \beta_6 \text{Trade}_t + \beta_7 \text{Civil War}_t$$
$$+ \beta_8 \text{International War}_t + \beta_9 \text{Population}_t + \beta_{10} \text{Sub-Saharan Africa}$$
$$+ \beta_{11} \text{MENA} + \beta_{12} \text{East Asia Pacific} + \beta_{13} \text{South Asia} + \mu_t$$

where the dependent variable is ratification of the human rights treaty at time t, and the independent variables (per the model in fig. 2.4) include ratification at time $t - 1$, the level of democracy, wealth, IGO membership, INGO presence, trade, civil war, international war, population, and regional dummies for sub-Saharan Africa, MENA, East Asia and Pacific, and South Asia. The parameters to be estimated are α and $\beta_{1...14}$, and μ is the error term. The analysis first used the *xtreg* function in Stata, which takes into account the time and unit structure of the data and estimates the parameters with the use of generalized least-squares regression. It then excluded the lagged dependent variables from the equations and used *xtregar*, which estimates the parameters under the assumption of the presence of a one-year autoregressive function (AR[1]) (see Sanders and Ward 1994). The parameters for the equation above were estimated for the straight ratification and the weighted versions, with the use of both forms of regression analysis.

Tables 4.6 and 4.7 report the parameter estimates for the unweighted and weighted ratification variables, made with the use of the lagged endogenous variable model and generalized least-squares regression. For the unweighted ratification of human rights treaties, it is clear from table 4.6 that democracy is significantly related to the ratification of the ICCPR, ICESCR, the First Optional Protocol, and CEDAW. There are mixed effects for the other independent variables, where the countries of East and South Asia tend to have ratified the treaties less often than the rest of the world, especially the ICCPR, ICESCR, the First Optional Protocol, CEDAW, and CAT. For the weighted ratification of human rights treaties, which takes into account reservations, the results are similar (see table 4.7). Democracy continues to have a positive relationship; wealth is mixed, and INGOs are positive and significant for ICESCR, the Second Optional Protocol, CERD, CEDAW, and CAT. Again, the countries of East and South Asia are less likely to ratify in the first place and may lodge more reservations than other countries when they do ratify.

Tables 4.8 and 4.9 report the parameter estimates for the unweighted and weighted ratification variables, including an AR(1) in

(text continues on p. 88)

Table 4.6. Parameter estimates for human rights treaty ratification (unweighted)

Independent Variables	ICCPR (1966)	ICESCR (1966)	OptionalP1 (1976)	OptionalP2 (1989)	CERD (1966)	CEDAW (1979)	CAT (1984)	CRC (1989)
Constant	.04 (.28)	.15 (1.16)	.02 (.15)	.05 (.27)	.26** (2.23)	.10 (.59)	−.08 (−.43)	1.48*** (4.86)
Ratification$_{t-1}$	.92*** (132.71)	.92*** (135.92)	.94*** (131.29)	.94*** (68.36)	.91*** (133.92)	.86*** (95.67)	.90*** (84.76)	.47*** (31.69)
Democracy	.006*** (5.01)	.006*** (5.00)	.004*** (4.05)	.003 (1.51)	.001 (1.47)	.003** (1.95)	.003 (1.49)	.004 (1.32)
Wealth	−.01*** (−2.06)	−.01** (−2.22)	−.007 (−1.19)	.03*** (4.28)	−.005 (−.98)	−.02** (−2.14)	−.0003 (−.04)	−.04** (−3.10)
IGOs	—	—	—	—	—	.001*** (3.31)	.003*** (6.17)	—
INGOs	−.004 (−.72)	.0003 (.92)	−.005 (−.97)	−.001 (−.15)	−.001 (−.25)	−.004 (−.68)	−.002 (−.19)	.002 (.18)
Trade	.02 (1.56)	.01 (.74)	.03* (1.98)	−.005 (−.24)	−.005 (−.37)	.02 (1.43)	.008 (.42)	−.03 (−1.06)
Civil war	−.02 (−.79)	−.002 (−.06)	.004 (.13)	.03 (.86)	.01 (.47)	.002 (.06)	.02 (.50)	−.01 (−.19)

International war	−.01 (−.22)	−.01 (−.24)	−.01 (−.22)	−.07 (−.79)	−.02 (−.47)	−.12* (−1.64)	−.12 (−1.35)	−.21* (−1.79)
Population	.009* (1.76)	.004 (.82)	.002 (.34)	−.01* (−1.92)	−.001 (−.23)	.01** (1.92)	.009 (1.23)	−.003 (−.30)
Sub-Sahara	−.01 (−.65)	−.009 (−.47)	−.02 (−1.28)	−.02 (−.80)	−.03 (−1.44)	−.06** (−2.61)	−.08** (−3.10)	−.02 (−.51)
MENA	.001 (.05)	.007 (.28)	−.07** (−3.02)	−.09** (−2.60)	−.004 (−.17)	−.14** (−4.76)	−.05 (−1.58)	−.12** (−2.12)
East Asia and Pacific	−.08*** (−3.54)	−.07*** (−3.41)	−.08*** (−3.98)	−.01 (−.42)	−.03* (−1.73)	−.03 (−1.30)	−.11*** (−3.58)	−.05 (−1.17)
South Asia	−.09** (−2.81)	−.07** (−2.14)	−.08** (−2.46)	.01 (.32)	−.008 (−.28)	−.12*** (−3.21)	−.12** (−2.56)	−.04 (−.58)
N	2604	2604	2604	1194	2604	2322	1773	1200
R^2	.91	.91	.91	.86	.92	.84	.86	.53
Wald chi^2	23398.33***	24458.03***	24411.11***	7203.03***	19029.06***	12290.18***	10932.76***	1148.07***

Note: Generalized least-squares regression, unstandardized coefficients with z scores in parentheses, $*p < .05$, $**p < .01$, $***p < .001$.

Table 4.7. Parameter estimates for human rights treaty ratification (weighted for reservations)

Independent Variables	ICCPR (1966)	ICESCR (1966)	OptionalP1 (1976)	OptionalP2 (1989)	CERD (1966)	CEDAW (1979)	CAT (1984)	CRC (1989)
Constant	.17 (.34)	.66 (1.29)	.15 (.34)	−.32 (−.57)	.56 (1.21)	.29 (.51)	−.56 (−.86)	5.97*** (4.22)
Ratification$_{t-1}$	.94*** (137.05)	.93*** (131.47)	.95*** (128.29)	.96*** (68.24)	.93*** (140.25)	.91*** (102.76)	.93*** (90.15)	.65*** (41.44)
Democracy	.02*** (3.78)	.02*** (3.75)	.01*** (3.02)	.003 (.71)	—	.008* (1.66)	.004 (.76)	.01 (.83)
Wealth	−.06** (−2.61)	−.05** (−2.35)	−.04** (−1.94)	.06** (2.75)	−.02 (−1.15)	−.06** (−2.15)	−.03 (−1.05)	−.17** (−2.92)
IGOs	—	—	—	—			.004** (2.26)	−.003 (−.67)
INGOs	.03 (1.59)	.04* (1.81)	−.002 (−1.57)	.05** (2.27)	.03* (1.76)	.06* (2.59)	.11*** (3.87)	.02 (.24)
Trade	.07 (1.38)	—	.06 (1.17)	.002 (.03)	.02 (.38)	.08 (1.25)	.04 (.63)	−.17 (−1.17)
Civil war	.08 (.77)	.12 (1.06)	.11 (1.13)	.03 (.29)	−.02 (−.28)	.09 (.76)	.12 (.87)	.09 (.34)

International war	−.05	−.08	−.09	−.16	−.09	−.23	−.18	.21
	(−.23)	(−.34)	(−.41)	(−.63)	(−.53)	(−.88)	(−.59)	(.43)
Population	.01	−.002	.002	−.02	−.008	.008	.02	−.08*
	(.69)	(−.08)	(.14)	(−.87)	(−.42)	(.37)	(.63)	(−1.62)
Sub-Sahara	−.06	.09	−.09	−.07	−.12*	−.13	−.18**	−.24
	(−.89)	(−1.20)	(−1.42)	(−.88)	(−1.75)	(−1.55)	(−1.94)	(−1.19)
MENA	.05	.04	−.17**	−.18*	−.05	−.37***	−.06	−.54**
	(.58)	(.46)	(−2.10)	(−1.85)	(−.63)	(−3.55)	(−.55)	(−2.09)
East Asia and Pacific	−.16**	−.15*	−.20**	−.08	−.07	−.20**	−.26**	−.45**
	(−2.02)	(−1.86)	(−2.86)	(−.96)	(−.96)	(2.18)	(−2.56)	(−2.01)
South Asia	−.28**	−.30**	−.22**	.09	−.11	−.25*	−.19	−.69**
	(−2.35)	(−2.41)	(−2.07)	(.72)	(−.91)	(−1.84)	(−1.21)	(−1.99)
N	2604	2604	2604	1194	2604	2322	1773	1200
R^2	.91	.91	.89	.84	.94	.86	.86	.69
Wald chi^2	22846.15***	21828.47***	20902.20***	6186.23***	22459***	14336.43***	11027.98***	1930.43***

Note: Generalized least-squares regression, unstandardized coefficients with z scores in parentheses, $*p < .05$, $**p < .01$, $***p < .001$.

Table 4.8. Parameter estimates for treaty ratification (unweighted), autoregressive estimation

Independent Variables	ICCPR (1966)	ICESCR (1966)	OptionalP1 (1976)	OptionalP2 (1989)	CERD (1966)	CEDAW (1979)	CAT (1984)	CRC (1989)
AR (1)[a]	.81	.81	.82	.71	.79	.77	.74	.62
Constant	-1.50**	-1.33*	-.38	-1.28**	-.04	-1.59**	-2.69***	-.20
	(-2.07)	(-1.83)	(-.55)	(-2.13)	(-.06)	(-2.47)	(-3.84)	(-.29)
Democracy	.03***	.02***	.02***	.004	.004*	.01**	.02***	.04***
	(8.71)	(8.26)	(6.64)	(1.08)	(1.73)	(2.61)	(4.3)	(6.39)
Wealth	-.05	-.05	.05	.17***	-.005	-.03	.12**	-.08**
	(-1.27)	(-1.20)	(1.25)	(5.67)	(-.13)	(-.78)	(3.05)	(-2.48)
IGOs	—	—	-.003**	-.009***	.001*	.005***	-.01***	-.02***
			(-2.30)	(-5.15)	(1.77)	(-3.81)	(-11.12)	(-7.85)
INGOs	.19***	.20***	.15***	.12***	.14***	.23***	.19***	.12***
	(6.39)	(6.74)	(5.25)	(3.67)	(5.63)	(7.33)	(5.02)	(3.81)
Trade	.05	.03	.06	.05	-.04	.05	-.02	.20**
	(1.37)	(.91)	(1.47)	(.98)	(-1.42)	(1.01)	(-.34)	(2.97)
Civil war	-.09	-.03	-.02	-.10	.09**	.10	.04	.02
	(-1.58)	(-.52)	(-.33)	(-1.38)	(2.17)	(1.37)	(.45)	(.14)

International war	-.02 (-.30)	.01 (.19)	.01 (.19)	-.004 (-.06)	-.003 (-.07)	-.08 (-1.04)	-.04 (-.52)	.11 (.75)
Population	.12*** (3.35)	.12*** (3.07)	-.003 (-.09)	-.01 (-.51)	.06* (1.66)	.12*** (3.92)	.16*** (4.82)	.08** (2.97)
Sub-Sahara	-.20 (-1.26)	-.23 (-1.46)	-.14 (-.92)	-.006 (-.05)	.09 (.58)	-.10 (-.83)	-.24* (-1.73)	.16 (1.51)
MENA	.02 (.10)	.03 (.14)	-.77*** (-4.30)	-.32** (-2.44)	.19 (1.01)	-.58*** (-3.93)	-.13 (-.81)	.29** (2.21)
East Asia and Pacific	-.67*** (-3.51)	.67*** (-3.44)	-.72*** (-4.00)	-.10 (-.76)	-.23 (-1.22)	-.15 (-1.04)	-.76*** (-4.69)	-.22* (-1.90)
South Asia	-.92** (-3.12)	-.87** (-2.91)	-.60** (-2.16)	.07 (.37)	.05 (.17)	-.59** (-2.64)	-.71** (-2.84)	-.08 (-.43)
N	2610	2610	2610	1317	2610	2423	1892	1317
R^2	.16	.16	.24	.22	.03	.16	.26	.07
Wald chi²	191.96***	181.50***	159.97***	119.74***	58.74***	150.05***	288.29***	131.97***

Note: Generalized least-squares regression with an AR (1), unstandardized coefficients with z scores in parentheses, $*p < .05$, $**p < .01$, $***p < .001$.
[a]For the AR (1) term, rho, the estimated autocorrelation coefficient is reported.

Table 4.9. Parameter estimates for treaty ratification (*weighted for reservations*), autoregressive estimation

Independent Variables	ICCPR (1966)	ICESCR (1966)	OptionalP1 (1976)	OptionalP2 (1989)	CERD (1966)	CEDAW (1979)	CAT (1984)	CRC (1989)
AR (1)[a]	.81	.82	.83	.71	.78	.80	.78	.63
Constant	-5.76**	-5.12**	-1.10	-3.93**	-1.62	-3.89*	-8.30***	1.75
	(-2.12)	(-1.88)	(-.48)	(-2.32)	(-.60)	(-1.64)	(-3.34)	(.61)
Democracy	.08***	.08***	.06***	.004	.008	.03**	.04**	.12***
	(7.18)	(7.21)	(6.10)	(.36)	(.97)	(2.57)	(2.58)	(5.77)
Wealth	-.43**	-.37**	-.14	.34***	-.05	-.251*	.10	-.46***
	(-2.79)	(-2.39)	(-1.08)	(3.88)	(-.32)	(-1.91)	(.71)	(-3.54)
IGOs	-.004	-.002	-.01**	-.19***	.004	-.03***	-.04***	-.06***
	(-1.01)	(-.57)	(-3.00)	(-3.87)	(1.51)	(-5.84)	(-8.49)	(-7.18)
INGOs	.80***	.86***	.61***	.45***	.62***	.98***	.92***	.54***
	(7.35)	(7.71)	(6.08)	(4.87)	(6.60)	(8.50)	(7.04)	(3.84)
Trade	.23*	.09	.15	.11	-.01	.15	.08	.69**
	(1.69)	(.65)	(1.16)	(.78)	(-.13)	(.92)	(.45)	(2.55)
Civil war	-.14	-.09	-.06	-.08	.32**	.24	.16	.11
	(-.67)	(-.45)	(-.29)	(-.40)	(1.97)	(.93)	(.60)	(.24)

International war	.007 (.03)	.03 (.17)	.02 (.13)	−.01 (−.06)	−.003 (−.02)	−.09 (−.40)	−.06 (−.21)	.66 (1.30)
Population	.48*** (3.41)	.43** (3.07)	.07 (.65)	−.007 (−.10)	.20 (1.33)	.31** (2.73)	.42*** (3.51)	.18 (1.54)
Sub-Sahara	−.86 (−1.43)	−1.08* (−1.82)	−.75 (−1.52)	−.12 (−.40)	.41 (.65)	−.56 (−1.18)	−.82* (−1.66)	.23 (0.50)
MENA	.70 (.97)	.57 (.81)	−1.81** (−3.12)	−.73** (−1.95)	.36 (.46)	−2.14*** (−3.84)	−.21 (−.35)	.51 (.91)
East Asia and Pacific	−1.55** (−2.14)	−1.31* (−1.82)	−2.02*** (−3.44)	−.35 (−.96)	−.64 (−.81)	−1.38** (−2.51)	−2.03*** (−3.50)	−1.41*** (−2.71)
South Asia	−3.46** (−3.09)	−3.47** (−3.12)	−2.07** (−2.29)	.25 (.44)	−.92 (−.75)	−2.05** (−2.41)	−1.79** (−1.99)	−1.46* (−1.81)
N	2610	2610	2610	1317	2610	2423	1892	1317
R^2	.13	.16	.24	.17	.09	.20	.22	.09
Wald chi^2	169.28***	170.54***	135.74***	82.18***	63.53***	174.05***	193.81***	124.56***

Note: Generalized least-squares regression with an AR (1), unstandardized coefficients with z scores in parentheses, $^*p < .05$, $^{**}p < .01$, $^{***}p < .001$.
[a]For the AR (1) term, rho, the estimated autocorrelation coefficient is reported.

the model. It is clear from the tables that the results are different, suggesting that inclusion of the lagged dependent variable in the estimations above has masked the independent effects of the other variables in the model. Indeed, table 4.8 shows that democracy is now significant for a wider range of treaties, the only exception being the Second Optional Protocol. Wealth and IGOs show mixed effects across the different treaties, whereas INGOs are positive and significant for all of the treaties. The MENA countries and the countries of East and South Asia show generally lower levels of ratification, with the exception of the Second Optional Protocol and CERD. Across the range of weighted ratifications (table 4.9), democracy is positive and significant for all but the Second Optional Protocol and CERD, whereas wealth and IGOs continue to show mixed results. Again, INGOs have a positive and significant effect on ratification of all of the treaties, and there continues to be lower propensity to ratify in the countries of East and South Asia.

These second-order results provide empirical support for the propositions made by those adhering to both the neoliberal institutionalist and liberal-republican perspectives in international relations. On the one hand, there is empirical support for the importance of INGOs in the ratification of human rights treaties, especially in the autoregressive modeling. It is thus consistent with neoliberal institutionalism that the presence of INGOs would influence state ratification behavior. On the other hand, democracy emerges as having a significant effect on treaty ratification across both sets of results for both the weighted and unweighted ratification variables. As chapter 2 outlined, liberal republicanism argues that democracies have a greater interest in ratifying international treaties, especially human rights treaties, since they commit states to uphold a series of values that are most compatible with democracy. In the context of the ratification of the European Convention on Human Rights, Moravcsik (2000) argues that it is not necessarily democracies, but "new" democracies that would have a greater interest in ratifying the Convention, since at the time their long-term sustainability was still precarious and ratification would "lock in" future generations of politicians and state actors to international legal commitments in line with democratic values. Indeed, there is a positive and significant correlation between the level of democracy and ratification of the European Convention of Human Rights (Pearson's $r = .79$; $p < .001$).

Although Moravcsik considered only the context of Europe, his proposition is worth exploring further by dividing the global sample of countries in this study into "old" democracies (i.e., pre-1974), "third-wave" democracies (i.e., those counties that became newly democratic between 1974 and 1989), and "fourth-wave" democracies (i.e., those countries that became democratic between 1990 and 1994) to gauge whether the timing of democracy is at all related to treaty ratification (see Huntington 1991; Doorenspleet 2000, 2001). Table 4.10 lists those countries that fall into each of these categories of democracy, using lists found in Lijphart (1999), Przeworski et al. (2000), and Doorenspleet (2000, 2001). This list contains countries that have remained democratic for the duration of the period in this study (i.e., up to and including the year 2000) and excludes those countries that have made reversals. For example, Peru made a democratic transition in 1980 during the third wave, but the subsequent "autogolpe" by President Alberto Fujimoro in 1992, which has been classified as an authoritarian government, reversed democracy for a period of five years (Doorenspleet 2001; Foweraker, Landman, and Harvey 2003; Youngers 2003, 304–63). Democratic reversals during the fourth wave include Comoros in 1994, the Gambia in 1994, and Haiti in 1992 (Doorenspleet 2001, 57); however, the fact that Haiti made another democratic transition in 1994 means that it is still considered a fourth-wave democracy for the analysis presented here, since the data set stops in 2000.

The list in table 4.10 has been used to create three separate dummy variables for old, third-wave, and fourth-wave democracies with which it is possible to estimate bivariate relationships between the type of democracy and treaty ratification behavior. With the exception of the case of old democracies and the unweighted ratification of the Convention on the Rights of the Child, comparisons of means tests were all significant for both the unweighted and weighted ratification variables across the three democracy dummy variables. For the unweighted ratification variables, the F-statistic for the difference in means ranges from 99.79 to 420.01, whereas for the weighted ratification variables, it ranges from 9.25 to 220.53. In other words, these results show that ratification rates among old, third-wave, and fourth-wave countries are higher on average than for other countries in the global sample.

Figures 4.5 and 4.6 show these comparisons of means graphically; further analysis of the mean ratification scores (see fig. 4.7) across all of the treaties shows that fourth-wave democracies have the highest mean ratification scores for both the weighted and unweighted ratification variables. The difference in means for the unweighted ratification

Table 4.10. Waves of democracy

Old democracies Pre-1974[a] N = 30	Third-wave democracies 1974–1989[b] N = 14	Fourth-wave democracies 1990–1994[c] N = 31
Australia	Argentina (1982)	Albania (1992)
Austria	Bolivia (1982)	Benin (1991)
Barbados	Brazil (1985)	Bangladesh (1990)
Belgium	Ecuador (1979)	Bulgaria (1990)
Botswana	El Salvador (1984)	Cambodia (1993)
Canada	Greece (1974)	Central African Republic
Colombia	Guatemala (1985)	(1993)
Costa Rica	Honduras (1980)	Chile (1990)
Denmark	Philippines (1983)	Congo (1992)
Finland	Portugal (1974)	Czechoslovakia (1990)
France	South Korea (1988)	Guinea-Bissau (1994)
Germany	Spain (1975)	Guyana (1992)
Iceland	Thailand (1988)	Haiti (1994)
India	Uruguay (1984)	Hungary (1990)
Ireland		Lesotho (1993)
Israel		Lithuania (1991)
Italy		Madagascar (1993)
Jamaica		Malawi (1994)
Japan		Mali (1992)
Luxembourg		Mongolia (1993)
Malta		Mozambique (1994)
Netherlands		Nepal (1991)
New Zealand		Nicaragua (1990)
Norway		Niger (1993)
Sweden		Panama (1990)
Switzerland		Poland (1991)
Trinidad and		Romania (1990)
Tobago		Russia (1991)
United Kingdom		South Africa (1994)
United States		Sri Lanka (1994)
Venezuela		Taiwan (1991)[d]
		Zambia (1991)

Note: This list includes only those countries that have made a successful transition to democracy and did not suffer any reverse transition to nondemocratic forms of rule.
[a] Lijphart (1999, 50).
[b] Przeworski et al. (2000, 59–77); Doorenspleet (2001, 51–57); Foweraker, Landman, and Harvey (2003, 41).
[c] Doorenspleet (2001, 56).
[d] Taiwan is not part of the data set, since it is not a UN member state.

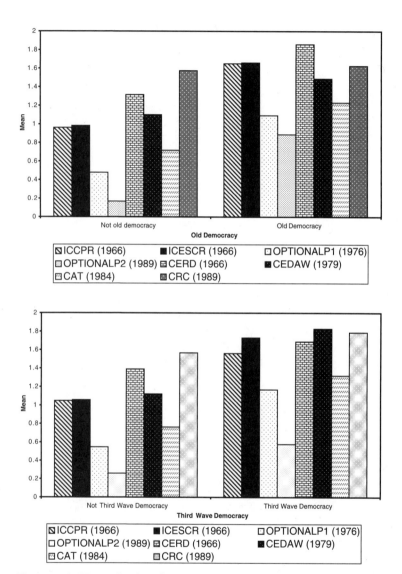

Figure 4.5. Unweighted ratification by type of democracy.

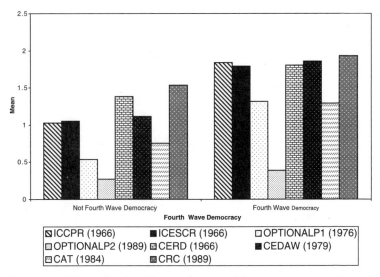

Figure 4.5. Unweighted ratification by type of democracy (*continued*).

variables is smaller than for the weighted ratification variables, suggesting that ratification by fourth-wave democracies tends to involve fewer reservations than ratification by old and third-wave democracies. These results lend strong support to the liberal republican perspective, which predicts that new democracies are most likely to ratify international human rights treaties. Indeed, the higher ratification scores for the newest democracies (i.e., fourth wave) show that old and third-wave democracies have been more reluctant to ratify the increasing number of human rights treaties, which is perhaps a reflection of the more consolidated nature of their democratic systems and less uncertainty about their democratic longevity. In contrast, new democracies of the fourth wave are less certain of their own domestic democratic institutional arrangements and may need additional international legitimacy, to be gained through ratification of international human rights treaties.

Norms Proliferation in the Age of Rights

In using time-series and regional comparisons and bivariate and multivariate analysis, this chapter has mapped and provided plausible ex-

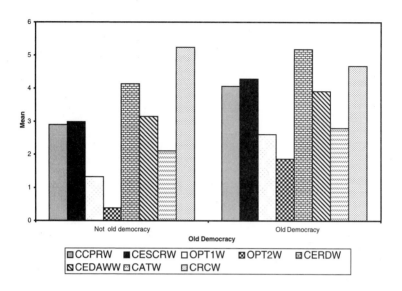

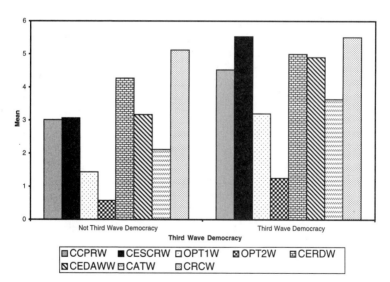

Figure 4.6. Weighted ratification by type of democracy.

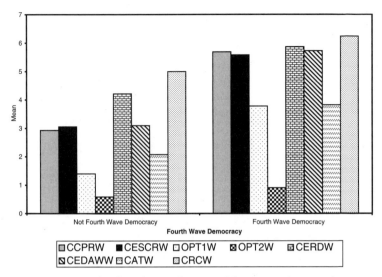

Figure 4.6. Weighted ratification by type of democracy (*continued*).

planations for the global variation in human rights treaty ratification. The time-series patterns follow the traditional narrative accounts of the proliferation of human rights norms, while highlighting the fact that those countries that ratified later during the period tended to do so with fewer reservations. The largest differences between the unweighted and weighted ratification variables were observed for CERD and CRC, and the smallest differences were observed for CAT and the Second Optional Protocol to the ICCPR. The regional comparisons showed that on balance, countries in post-Communist Europe have ratified the largest number of treaties with the smallest number of reservations, and the United States stands out as a significant outlier in comparison with Canada and European countries. The bivariate analysis showed positive correlations between treaty ratification and the level of democracy, wealth, and the greater presence of IGOs and INGOs. Multivariate analysis confirmed the importance of democracy and INGOs for the ratification of treaties, while highlighting consistently lower levels of ratification for the Middle East and North Africa, East Asia, and South Asia. Further analysis of democracy showed that all three waves of democracy have a positive relationship

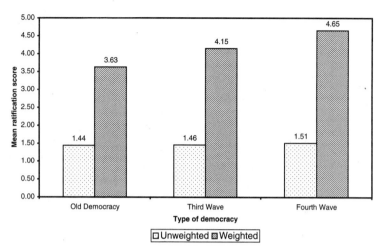

Figure 4.7. Mean ratification scores across all human rights treaties (unweighted and weighted) by type of democracy.

with treaty ratification, whereas ratification behavior is highest for fourth-wave democracies, followed by third-wave and old democracies.

The temporal and spatial mapping of the evolution of the international human rights regime helps to build a clearer picture of the proliferation of human rights norms in the so-called age of rights (Henkin 1990; Bobbio 1996), and the subsequent bivariate and multivariate analyses demonstrate the importance of domestic political arrangements and the presence of international organizations in explaining the propensity for individual states to ratify human rights treaties. On the one hand, the importance of domestic political arrangements lends empirical support to the liberal-republican view that "new" democracies are more likely to enter into international agreements in an effort to constrain future generations of politicians who have interests in eroding democracy. On the other hand, the importance of the presence of INGOs lends empirical support to the argument that more deeply embedded states will participate more widely in other forms of international commitment, which in this case involves a commitment to upholding the protection of human rights.

But this chapter has examined only the formal commitment of states to protect human rights and has said nothing about the protection of human rights in practice or the relationship between treaty membership and rights protection. Whereas chapters 1 and 2 made some preliminary claims about the persistent gap between rights in principle and rights in practice, it is necessary first to examine the global variation in human rights protection with the use of multiple measures followed by an examination of the complex relationship between rights commitments and rights protection depicted in the model in chapter 2 (see fig. 2.4). To these ends, chapter 5 examines the temporal and spatial variation in human rights protection and describes similar bivariate and multivariate analysis used to identify those factors that best account for such variation.

5

Global Variation in Human Rights Protection

The previous chapter mapped and explained the evolution of the international and regional human rights regimes with the use of descriptive and analytical statistics. Its results showed both time-series and regional variation in the ratification behavior of states, which in large part was explained by their level of democracy and exposure to a growing international network of nongovernmental organizations. Such results were obtained even after controlling for the level of wealth, trade, involvement in internal and external conflict, population size, and regional differences. In addition, the effects of the level of democracy on treaty ratification were further differentiated across old, third-wave, and fourth-wave democracies, where it was shown that fourth-wave democracies tend to ratify more human rights treaties with fewer reservations than third-wave or old democracies.

Using five measures of human rights protection, including political rights, civil rights, torture, and "personal integrity rights" (or the political terror scale), this chapter first examines the time-series trends and spatial patterns in the protection of these different categories of human rights. It then estimates the right-hand side of the model developed in chapter 2 (see fig. 2.4) by exploring the bivariate and multivariate relationships between human rights protection and the same set of independent variables used in the last chapter. The chapter concludes with a further examination of the relationship between different types of democracy and the protection of human rights and draws comparisons between the findings for ratification and rights protection in preparation for the modeling of the relationship in chapter 6.

Human Rights Protection

Although the categories of human rights include political, civil, economic, social, and cultural rights, this study is primarily concerned with the protection (or violation) of civil and political rights. As chapter 3 outlined, it uses extant measures of political and civil rights from Freedom House, a scale of torture coded based on Amnesty International country reports (Hathaway 2002), and the political terror scale, which measures the protection of personal integrity rights based on Amnesty International and U.S. State Department country reports (see, e.g., Poe and Tate 1994). Both the Freedom House and political terror scale measures of human rights cover the period 1976–2000, and the torture scale extends from 1985 to 1999. All of the measures have been transformed to range from 1 to 5, where a higher score denotes a greater violation of rights. The direction of the scaling is important since it affects the mathematical sign of the resultant coefficients in the statistical analysis and, by extension, the substantive inferences that are drawn from such analysis.

Figure 5.1 depicts the time-series trends in these five measures of rights protection, including charts for Freedom House, the political terror scale, and the torture scale, and then a combined chart with all five measures. It is apparent that the Freedom House scales show a general improvement in the protection of civil and political rights during the period, whereas the political terror and torture scales either show a mixed or declining record in the protection of rights. The differences between the two sets of measures rest mostly on the fact that Freedom House has a number of institutional and procedural indicators in its checklists for political and civil rights, which tend to result in rewarding countries for the introduction of elections (see table 3.1; Diamond 1999; Foweraker and Krznaric 2000). As the subsequent analysis in this chapter shows, it is quite possible for countries to have minimal institutional arrangements in place while the protection of other human rights remains precarious. There is also less difference between the two Freedom House scales than between the two versions of the political terror scale, which is explained by the fact the U.S. State Department reports give a take on events in

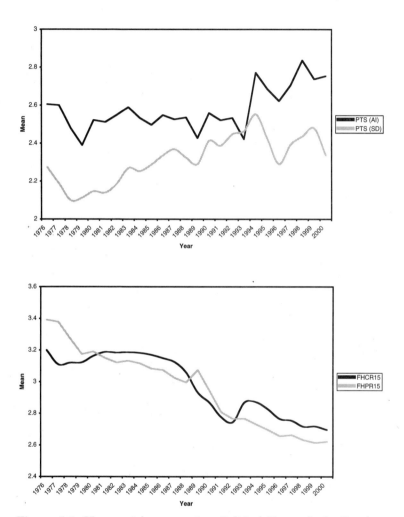

Figure 5.1. Human rights protection, Political Terror Scale, Freedom House, and Torture combined, 1976–2000.

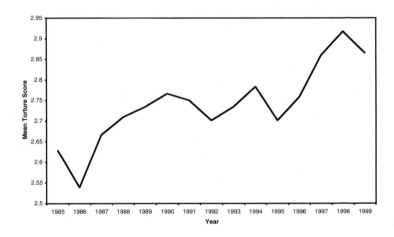

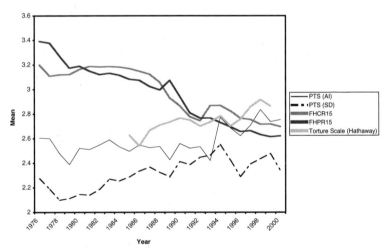

Figure 5.1. Human rights protection, Political Terror Scale, Freedom House, and Torture combined, 1976–2000 (*continued*).

countries that is slightly different from that of the Amnesty Reports (see Landman 1999), as well as by the fact that for the latter years of the period, the U.S. State Department reports cover a wider selection of countries than the Amnesty reports.

Figures 5.2 and 5.3 show human rights protection for each of the measures by region. The regional charts for the political terror scale in figure 5.2 show that South Asia and Latin America have the worst protection of rights overall, whereas the charts for the Freedom House scales show the worst protection for Communist Europe, followed by the MENA countries and sub-Saharan Africa. These differences are due partly to the different focus of each set of measures and partly to some biases of Freedom House and Amnesty International. Freedom House has been noted to be biased against the formerly Communist countries of Eastern Europe, and Amnesty International has shown some favor toward left-wing regimes (see also Foweraker and Krznaric 2000, 768). The chart for the torture scale by region shows that the worst practices have taken place in South Asia, followed by Latin America, Communist Europe, the MENA countries, and sub-Saharan Africa. The torture scale thus maps the regional variation in human rights protection more closely to the political terror scale than it does to the civil and political rights measures produced by Freedom House. The combined regional chart in figure 5.3 shows the degree to which Freedom House overestimates violations

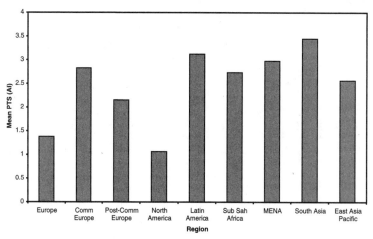

Figure 5.2. Human rights protection by region, 1976–2000.

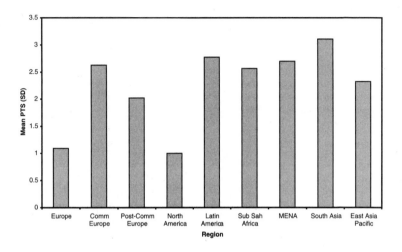

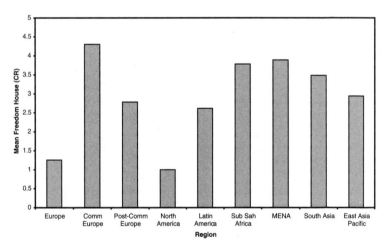

Figure 5.2. Human rights protection by region, 1976–2000 (*continued*).

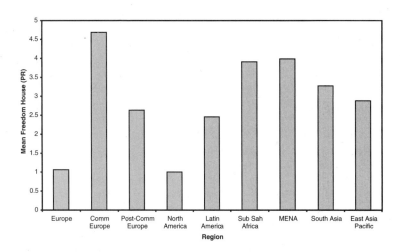

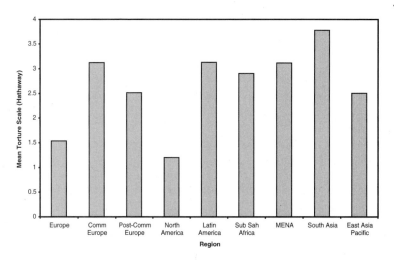

Figure 5.2. (*continued*)

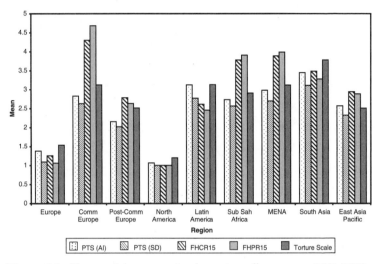

Figure 5.3. Human rights protection by region, all measures, 1976–2000.

in Communist Europe, and the other measures show, unsurprisingly, that the greatest protection of rights is in Europe and North America, followed by post-Communist Europe, Latin America, and East Asia and the Pacific.

In contrast to the ratification measures examined in the previous chapter, the human rights measures show a greater variability over time and across space, since it is possible for a country's human rights performance to improve or decline over time, whereas it is less likely for a country to "denounce" an international treaty, which would make its ratification score decline over time.[1] Thus it is important to examine each of the measures by country to show this variability in greater detail. Figures 5.4 through 5.8 depict the mean and one standard deviation above and below the mean for each of the five measures across all of the countries, which are ranked from those with the worst human rights performances to those with the best. Comparing across the figures shows that in general the same countries appear in the worst and best sets of performers with respect to the protection of human rights. The countries that rank the worst across more than one measure include Iraq, Afghanistan, Iran, Somalia, and North Korea. The top ranking countries across more than one measure include Canada, some small Caribbean countries, Europe, Australia, and New Zealand. The United States ranks very high on the Freedom

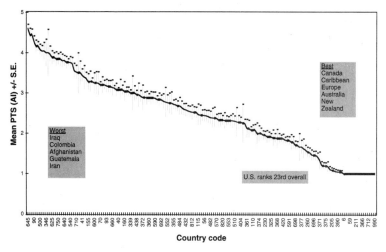

Figure 5.4. Rank order of country mean human rights protection, Political Terror Scale (Amnesty International), 1976–2000.

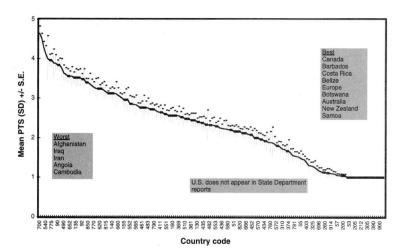

Figure 5.5. Rank order of country mean human rights protection, Political Terror Scale (U.S. State Department), 1976–2000.

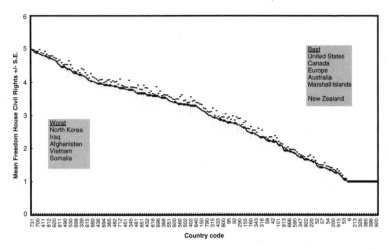

Figure 5.6. Rank order of country mean human rights protection, Freedom House civil rights, 1976–2000.

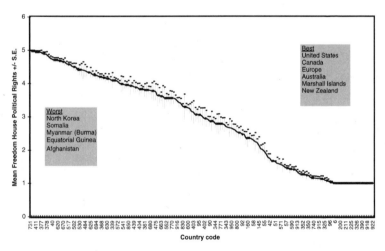

Figure 5.7. Rank order of country mean human rights protection, Freedom House political rights, 1976–2000.

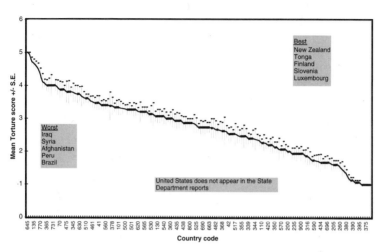

Figure 5.8. Rank order of country mean human rights protection, torture scale, 1985–1999.

House scores and does not appear in the State Department reports. Thus it does not appear in one of the political terror scales or the torture scale, since both rely on those reports as source material. Amnesty International reports do include the United States, where its mean score of 1.12 on that particular version of the political terror scale ranks it twenty-third out of the total 193 countries in the sample.

In addition to these observations, it is clear that some measures show greater variability than others. On balance, there is less overall variance in both versions of the political terror scale and the torture scale than in either of the Freedom House scales, while the variance is the greatest in the Freedom House scale of political rights (see fig. 5.7). Such variation in political rights is certainly due to the third and fourth waves of democracy, in which the number of democracies rose dramatically since the Portuguese transition to democracy in 1974. Within the two extremes of the best and worst performers, there are not statistically different means in human rights performance for the period, and within the top performers there appears to be no variation in any of the measures. This group comprises between sixteen and twenty countries across North America, Europe, parts of the Caribbean, Australia, and New Zealand. Such invariance in scores among these top performers has led some comparativists to examine alternative measures of liberal democratic performance across this set of countries, such as the protection of property rights, levels of incarceration, and minority rights protection (Foweraker and Krznaric 2003). Nevertheless, it is possible to say that the difference between the best and worst performers is statistically significant, and both sets of countries have an overall performance that is different from that of the large middle group of countries in the sample.

The general temporal and spatial distributions in the five measures of human rights protection are supported further by a simple bivariate correlation matrix, which is reported in table 5.1. The table shows that all of the rights measures are positively and significantly correlated, with the strongest correlations occurring between the two Freedom House measures ($r = .92$), followed by the two versions of the political terror scale ($r = .84$). More interestingly, however, are the correlations between the different human rights measures. The political terror scale and the torture scale are more highly correlated with one another than either set of measures is correlated with the Freedom House scales. This difference in strength in the correlations lends support to the time-series and regional differences depicted in figures 5.2 and 5.3, while suggesting further that Freedom House is providing a measure of rights protection that is different from either the political terror scale or the torture scale. Indeed, the political terror scale focuses on political imprisonment, exile, extrajudicial killings, and torture, whereas Freedom House measures a broader range of rights and institutions (Landman 1999, 614–17). The use of multiple rights measures enhances the robustness of the analysis conducted in this chapter and the one that follows, since it allows for comparative tests of empirical relationships across different measures.

Explaining Human Rights Violations

As in the previous chapter, the first step in exploring the possible explanation for the observed patterns in these different measures of human rights protection is to examine the first-order relationships between the measures and the independent variables specified in the model in chapter 2 (see fig. 2.4). Table 5.2 reports the simple bivariate correlations for the five measures and the eight main independent variables. The table shows that the signs of all of the correlations are in the expected directions and are statistically significant. Democracy,

Table 5.1. Bivariate correlation matrix for the five measures of human rights protection

Independent Variables	PTS (Amnesty)	PTS (State Department)	Freedom House (Civil Rights)	Freedom House (Political Rights)	Torture
PTS (Amnesty)	—	.84	.52	.45	.61
PTS (State Department)		—	.58	.52	.69
Freedom House (Civil rights)			—	.92	.50
Freedom House (Political rights)				—	.42
Torture					—

Note: Pearson's *r* reported, all correlations are significant at *p* < .001.

Table 5.2. Bivariate correlation matrix for the five human rights measures and the main independent variables

Independent Variables	Human rights measures				
	PTS (Amnesty)	PTS (State Department)	Freedom House (Civil Rights)	Freedom House (Political Rights)	Torture
Democracy	−.36	−.41	−.85	−.91	−.34
Wealth	−.46	−.52	−.63	−.59	−.42
IGOs	−.16	−.16	−.16	−.14	−.15
INGOs	−.08	−.08	−.22	−.23	−.11
Trade	−.35	−.38	−.21	−.17	−.28
Civil war	.34	.38	.20	.17	.20
International war	.18	.12	.10	.08	.08
Population	.31	.35	.17	.11	.36

Note: Pearson's *r* reported, all correlations are significant at $p < .001$.

wealth, IGO membership, INGO presence, and trade are significantly associated with lower levels of human rights violations, whereas civil war, international war, and population size are significantly associated with higher levels of human rights violations. But these are only first-order results and significant instances of covariation between the variables, where any number of spurious relationships may remain opaque and require further examination through multivariate analysis.

A regression equation similar to that used in the previous chapter is specified to estimate the multivariate relationship between the main independent variables and the different human rights measures:

$$\text{Human Rights Protection}_t = \alpha_t + \beta_1 \text{Human Rights Protection}_{t-1} + \beta_2 \text{Democracy}_t + \beta_3 \text{Wealth}_t + \beta_4 \text{IGOs}_t + \beta_5 \text{INGOs}_t + \beta_6 \text{Trade}_t + \beta_7 \text{Civil War}_t + \beta_8 \text{International War}_t + \beta_9 \text{Population}_t + \beta_{10} \text{MENA} + \beta_{11} \text{Sub-Saharan Africa} + \beta_{12} \text{South Asia} + \mu_t$$

Like the specification of the equations for the ratification of the human rights treaties, this equation includes variables to control for time-series autocorrelation and heteroscedasticity, whereas the parameters have been estimated with both the *xtreg* and *xtregar* procedures adopted in the last chapter. Tables 5.3 and 5.4 report the regression results for the two estimation procedures. The regression results for the multivariate effects on human rights protection build on the correlations reported in table 5.2 and largely confirm the results of previous studies on human rights protection (e.g., Mitchell and McCormick 1988; Poe and Tate 1994; Poe, Tate, and Keith 1999), even though the data set employed here has greater time-series coverage for the political terror scale than previous studies and includes Hathaway's torture scale alongside the political terror scale and Freedom House scales.

First, it is clear from tables 5.3 and 5.4 that past violations of human rights display a trend over time, whether that trend is captured by the inclusion of a lagged dependent variable or by the AR (1) term. It thus appears, unsurprisingly, that a country's human rights record from previous years has an impact on its record in the current year. Such a time-series trend is important in substantive terms. It shows that statistical methods can be used to track the variation over time in human rights protection and to correct for the methodological problems associated with such trending. Moreover, as the next chapter will make clear, it is possible to model the "anticipatory adaptation" of

(*text continues on p. 116*)

Table 5.3. Parameter estimates for human rights protection (generalized least squares)

			Human Rights Measures		
Independent Variables	PTS (Amnesty)	PTS (State Department)	Freedom House (Civil Rights)	Freedom House (Political Rights)	Torture
Constant	1.28*** (3.75)	.57** (2.09)	.68*** (4.55)	.84*** (5.04)	.58 (1.37)
$PTSAI_{t-1}$	.62*** (38.97)				
$PTSSD_{t-1}$		.67*** (46.50)			
$FHCR_{t-1}$			.80*** (71.50)		
$FHPR_{t-1}$				.66*** (57.05)	
$Torture_{t-1}$					.51** (28.06)
Democracy	-.006** (-2.41)	-.01*** (-4.40)	-.022*** (-13.34)	-.06*** (-27.94)	-.007* (-1.77)
Wealth	-.10*** (-6.40)	-.09*** (-6.74)	-.04*** (-5.44)	-.03*** (-3.80)	-.11*** (-5.82)

IGOs	-.001*	-.002***	-.001***	-.002***	-.003**
	(-1.78)	(-3.75)	(-3.52)	(-4.89)	(-2.79)
INGOs	.001	.009	-.02***	.001	-.005
	(.096)	(.91)	(-3.57)	(.23)	(-.26)
Trade	-.09**	-.02	.02	.04**	-.03
	(-2.47)	(-.72)	(1.19)	(2.53)	(-.76)
Civil war	.63***	.70***	.08**	.14***	.29*
	(9.10)	(11.56)	(2.63)	(4.07)	(3.36)
International war	.12	.12	.02	-.01	-.16
	(.88)	(.98)	(0.31)	(-.11)	(-.80)
Population	.05***	.06***	.02***	.02***	.12***
	(3.95)	(6.02)	(3.53)	(3.26)	(7.19)
South Asia	.09	.03	-.03	-.09**	.17*
	(1.20)	(0.48)	(-.83)	(-2.31)	(1.78)
MENA	.21***	.09**	.07**	-.06**	.36***
	(3.55)	(1.93)	(2.93)	(-2.18)	(4.78)
Sub-Saharan Africa	-.08*	-.08**	.003	.002	-.03
	(-1.70)	(-2.22)	(.14)	(.09)	(-.53)
N	2217	2413	2599	2597	1598
R^2	.70	.75	.94	.94	.57
Wald chi^2	4022.24***	6708.35***	38672.34***	40385.67***	2131.22***

Note: Generalized least-squares regression, unstandardized coefficients with z scores in parentheses. *p < .05, **p < .01, ***p < .001.

Table 5.4. Parameter estimates for human rights protection (generalized least squares with an AR[1] function)

Independent Variables		Human Rights Measures			
	PTS (Amnesty)	PTS (State Department)	Freedom House (Civil Rights)	Freedom House (Political Rights)	Torture
AR(1)[a]	.44	.52	.76	.76	.41
Constant	1.99**	1.11	4.83***	4.27***	.52
	(2.54)	(1.58)	(9.98)	(9.56)	(.58)
Democracy	−.02***	−.02***	−.07***	−.14***	−.02***
	(−4.31)	(−5.36)	(24.53)	(−49.85)	(−3.56)
Wealth	−.24***	−.27***	−.32***	−.20***	−.22***
	(−5.84)	(−7.59)	(−12.26)	(−8.29)	(−4.95)
IGOs	−.003**	−.007***	−.003**	−.005***	−.007***
	(−2.25)	(−5.81)	(−2.89)	(−5.10)	(−4.46)
INGOs	.03	.07*	−.04*	.01	.08*
	(.96)	(2.39)	(−1.91)	(.73)	(1.75)
Trade	−.18**	−.08	.03	—	−.05
	(−2.72)	(−1.31)	(.88)		(−.63)

Civil war	1.03*** (10.03)	1.07*** (10.89)	.15** (2.54)	.14** (2.41)	.30** (2.36)
International war	.19 (1.47)	.06 (.53)	-.02 (-.28)	-.05 (-.89)	.04 (.24)
Population	.18*** (5.08)	.22*** (7.10)	.05** (2.17)	.03 (1.41)	.24*** (6.19)
South Asia	.24 (.93)	-.09 (-.42)	-.35** (-2.20)	-.44*** (-3.09)	.30 (1.09)
MENA	.59*** (3.42)	.32** (2.18)	.59*** (5.56)	.09 (.90)	.53** (2.90)
Sub-Saharan Africa	-.10 (-.72)	-.14 (-1.15)	.06* (.66)	.03 (.40)	-.01 (-.07)
N	2296	2448	2610	2609	1728
R^2	.42	.48	.80	.86	.35
Wald chi^2	316.39***	463.79***	1572.35***	4043.62***	195.15***

Note: Generalized least-squares regression with an AR (1), unstandardized coefficients with z scores in parentheses, $*p < .05$, $**p < .01$, $***p < .001$.
[a]For the AR (1) term, rho, the estimated autocorrelation coefficient is reported.

state behavior (Haggard et al. 1993, 182; Keohane 2002, 74) for a test of the overall relationship between human rights treaty ratification and human rights protection. In other words, the model presented in the next chapter will address the relative strength of the relationship from "norms to rights" versus the strength of the relationship from "rights to norms."

Second, across both sets of results, democracy, wealth, and IGO membership are significantly related to lower levels of human rights violations regardless of the measure that is employed. This means that higher levels of democracy and wealth and a greater number of IGOs are significantly related to lower levels of human rights violations. Such a set of results is consistent with a large body of literature on the relationship between economic development and democracy, an emerging literature on the proliferation of international networks and global interdependence, and extant global studies of human rights protection. Since the late 1950s, global comparative analyses have shown a strong positive relationship between economic development and democracy (Rueschemeyer, Stephens, and Stephens 1992; Landman 2003), which has been variously interpreted as an association (e.g., Lipset 1959, 1994), a causal relationship (Helliwell 1994; Burkhart and Lewis-Beck 1994), or as supporting conditions for democratic survival (Przeworski and Limongi 1997; Landman 1999, 2003; Przeworski et al., 2000). International relations analysis has shown the positive relationship between greater global interdependence (as measured by IGO membership) and democracy, as well as the reduction of inter-state conflict (e.g., Russett and O'Neal 2001). In addition, global analyses of human rights protection have shown positive relationships between wealth and democracy and rights protection (Poe and Tate 1994; Poe, Tate, and Keith 1999; Keith 1999; Hathaway 2002).

Third, civil war and population size are significantly related to greater violations of rights, with the exception of the Freedom House political rights scale in table 5.4. As in the results for democracy and wealth, these results for civil war and population size are entirely consistent with those obtained for previous global analyses of human rights protection (Henderson 1993; Poe and Tate 1994; Poe, Tate, and Keith 1999). Building on the achievements of these earlier studies, the analysis presented here, however, uses a broader set of rights measures over a longer period of time. With regard to the substantive inferences that can be drawn at this stage, the results suggest that beyond promoting democracy and economic development, policy-makers interested in reducing the violation of human rights should also focus their efforts on the reduction of conflict and ought to encourage countries not to resort to violence to resolve disputes (see Poe and Tate 1994, 866–67).

Beyond these results obtained from the regression analysis, it is worth exploring further the relationship between democracy and human rights protection, since the analysis in the previous chapter showed that the relationship between democracy and treaty ratification varied across different types of democracy. With the list of old, third-wave, and fourth-wave democracies in table 4.10 (see chapter 4), it is possible to compare the human rights protection measures across types of democracy. Figure 5.9 is a comparative chart of the mean of the five measures for the whole period differentiated across the three types of democracy. It is clear from the figure that old democracies violate rights less than third-wave and fourth-wave democracies. Across the measures within the old democracies, the torture scale is much higher than the other four measures. This higher level for torture is due to the presence of the following three significant outliers in the group of old democracies: Colombia (mean torture score = 3.73), Venezuela (mean torture score = 3.33), and India (mean torture score = 4.07).

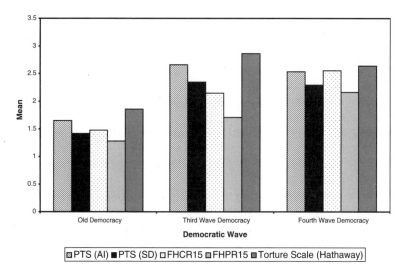

Figure 5.9. Human rights protection by type of democracy, 1976–2000.

Among the third-wave democracies, the torture score is highest, which is accounted for by the presence of three outliers: Guatemala (3.27), the Philippines (3.60), and Brazil (4.60). For the fourth-wave democracies, the torture outliers include Haiti (3.83), Mozambique (3.83), Russia (4.00), and Bangladesh (4.30). This presence of outliers across the different types of democracies lends support to the general observation that the process of democratization has seen the proliferation of "illiberal" democracies across the globe (Diamond 1999; O'Donnell 1999; Whitehead 2002; Zakaria 2003), where such countries meet minimal procedural requirements to classify them as democracies, but they are still incapable of providing protection against the abuse of human rights.

Despite the difference in human rights protection among the different groups of democracies and the presence of significant outliers with respect to torture, the average score for each group shows that old democracies have the best protection of human rights (mean protection score = 1.43), followed by third-wave democracies (mean protection score = 2.26), and fourth-wave democracies (mean protection score = 2.36). These differences in means are not surprising, since it takes time for democratic institutions to become embedded and the necessary values and practices associated with liberal democracy to develop. From a human rights perspective, the comparisons of democracies show that it takes some time indeed for the internationalization of human rights norms necessary for the reduction in human rights violations, particularly the use of torture, to take place.

But these results for democracy are all the more interesting if they are compared with the results of the previous chapter, which showed precisely the opposite relationship between the timing of democratization and the ratification of human rights treaties. Fourth-wave democracies have been more prone to ratify more treaties with fewer reservations than either third-wave or old democracies, but they have a higher average violation record than either type of democracy. Equally, third-wave democracies have a greater tendency to ratify human rights treaties but a greater propensity to violate human rights than old democracies. Thus democratic consolidation over a longer period of time has meant a lower propensity to ratify human rights treaties and a greater overall ability to protect human rights.

Such a disparity between rights in principle and rights in practice can be demonstrated empirically. Figure 5.10 plots the means for combined ratification and combined rights protection measures over

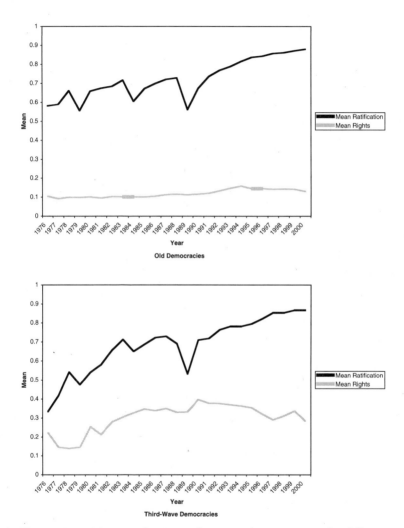

Figure 5.10. Mean ratification and mean rights protection for different types of democracy, 1976–2000.

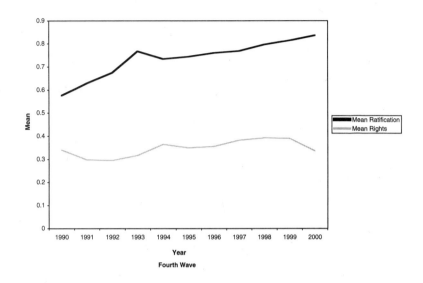

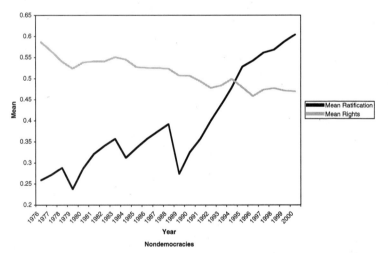

Figure 5.10. (*continued*)

time by type of democracy. The combined ratification and rights measures have been rescaled to range from 0 to 1 and then averaged. The time-series trends in figure 5.10 are unequivocal in showing that the difference between rights in principle and rights in practice is most positive for the old democracies, where rights violations remain low, whereas ratification behavior increases over the period. For third-wave democracies, ratification has also increased, whereas rights violations have risen and then declined slightly over the period. Fourth-wave democracies show a more stable trend in increasing ratification and decreasing rights violations. Most strikingly, however, is the fact that the patterns in ratification and rights protection are reversed for the nondemocracies in the sample. For the balance of the period, rights violations far exceed ratification, where the two lines cross in 1996. Figure 5.11 plots the difference in the two means by type of democracy to summarize the general relationship between the age of democracy and the narrowing of the gap between rights in principle and rights in practice.

These trends are encouraging for those promoting democracy and human rights in the world, since democracies have higher formal rights commitments and better rights protection, and it appears that there has been a closing gap over time between such commitments

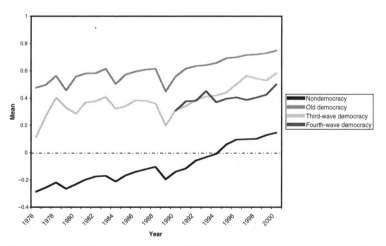

Figure 5.11. Difference in mean ratification and mean rights protection by type of democracy, 1976–2000.

and practices in the nondemocracies. What remains to be seen, however, is whether the issuing of such commitments through formal participation in the international treaties for the protection of human rights makes a difference for human rights practices, especially in the face of the other independent variables of wealth, democracy, interdependence, conflict, and regional differentiation. The differentiated results obtained across the different regions and types of democracy demonstrated in this chapter have to be taken into account in an estimation of the empirical relationship between the international law of human rights and human rights protection. This relationship and its differentiated effects across regions and type of democracy are analyzed in the next chapter.

6

Modeling Human Rights Protection

The preceding chapters have painted a descriptive and analytical comparative portrait of the growth and proliferation of the international human rights regime and the variable protection of human rights across the world. This chapter examines the direct relationship between the international human rights regime and the protection of human rights while controlling for those variables included in the model developed in chapter 2 (see fig. 2.4). The descriptive data in the previous chapters demonstrate that the international regime for human rights has indeed grown in breadth and depth, while the protection of human rights in aggregate terms has improved over the period from 1976 to 2000. Regionally, the proliferation of human rights norms and the protection of human rights are the lowest in the MENA countries, South Asia, and sub-Saharan Africa. The multivariate analysis in the previous chapters showed that democracies and countries with a greater number of INGOs tend to have higher rates of ratification, whereas democracy, wealth, and greater IGO membership had positive effects on rights protection. Consistent with extant studies on human rights protection, countries involved in civil war and countries with large populations tend to have higher levels of human rights violations.

The positive results for democracy in terms of both treaty ratification and human rights protection were explored further by comparing them across types of democracy (i.e., old, third wave, and fourth wave). The analysis showed that fourth-wave democracies have ratified more human rights treaties with fewer reservations and have higher levels of human rights violations than third-wave or old democracies. Moreover, the difference between the mean ratification of human rights treaties and mean human rights protection is greatest for nondemocracies, followed by fourth-wave democracies, third-wave democracies, and old democracies. These results suggest that although democracy is important for explaining the evolution of the international human rights regime and the protection of human rights, the timing of democratization itself further differentiates these relationships. In this way, old democracies protect human rights better and ratify fewer treaties, whereas newer democracies have a worse record at human rights protection, yet ratify more treaties.

This regional and democratic differentiation is important for the modeling of the relationship between the international human rights regime and the protection of human rights conducted in this chapter. Such modeling brings the international law of human rights to bear on the variation in state protection of human rights, using quantitative methods to test the overall levels of compliance with important dimensions of the international human rights regime while controlling for regional and democratic differentiation. The results of the analysis allow certain inferences about the relationship between international human rights law and human rights practices. The analysis is not a direct test of compliance per se, but it does allow for the covariation between regime participation and rights protection to be established in the face of other important explanatory factors. Moreover, as chapters 2 and 3 made clear, important precedents for such analysis have already been set in human rights and other fields (see Keith 1999; Krasner 1999; Simmons 2000; Hathaway 2002).

In contrast to these extant studies on compliance, the analysis conducted here moves beyond simple recursive models that specify unidirectional relationships between law and practice by estimating a series of nonrecursive models that examine their mutually constitutive and dynamic relationships over time. The traditional understanding of the relationship is that countries join a human rights regime and then improve their human rights practices, effectively demonstrating a unidirectional relationship from law to practice (Keith 1999, 100; Hathaway 2002; see also Krasner 1983b). As chapter 2 argued, however, it is entirely possible for countries to engage in "anticipatory adaptation" (Haggard et al. 1993, 182; Keohane 2002, 74) by improving their human rights practices before formally joining a human rights regime, thereby reversing the more traditional understanding of the relationship between law and practice (Hathaway 2002, 2001). Moreover, if a state is involved in a long ratification process, its human rights practices may improve during the period preceding its formal adherence to the treaty (Keith 1999, 106). Through dynamic nonrecursive modeling that takes advantage of the temporal and spatial qualities of the data set, this chapter will be able to explore this more complex relationship between human rights law and human rights practice.

To model this relationship, the chapter first examines a series of bivariate relationships between the international human rights regime and human rights protection, using the unweighted and weighted versions of the ratification variables for the International Covenant for Civil and Political Rights (ICCPR) and the Convention against Torture and other Cruel, Inhuman, or Degrading Treatment or Punishment (CAT), the five measures of human rights protection, and the mean ratification and mean rights protection. The ICCPR and CAT have been selected since they have the closest logical and substantive correspondence to the human rights measures adopted in this study. The analysis of these two treaties is complemented by the inclusion of the mean ratification of all the treaties and the mean of all the human rights measures, both of which have been transformed to range from 0 to 1. The mean ratification of all of the treaties captures countries' overall regime participation (a score of 1 for full ratification), and the mean of all the human rights measures gives a general portrait of human rights practices by combining the scores into one separate indicator (a score of 1 denotes systematic and substantial human rights violations).

The chapter then moves beyond simple bivariate relationships to estimate the fully specified model depicted in fig. 2.4. The estimations for the nonrecursive modeling are obtained by two-stage least-squares regression with instrumental variables (*xtivreg*). In this method of estimation, two stages of regression are conducted and the final results are then reported. The method allows the directional strength of the overall relationship to be tested, while controlling for other influences. The first set of two-stage least-squares regression analysis is conducted for the variables in the model (fig. 2.4), including regional dummy variables for the MENA countries, sub-Saharan Africa, and South Asia. The second set of regressions adds dummy variables for third-wave and fourth-wave democracies to gauge the variation in the overall relationship between law and practice across different types of democracy. In this way, the final models estimated in this chapter, which include the regional and democracy dummy variables, bring together the separate sets of analyses presented in chapters 4 and 5.

Bivariate Relationships

The first way to examine the bivariate relationship between international human rights law and human rights protection is to compare the human rights scores before and after ratification of the ICCPR and CAT. Figures 6.1 and 6.2 depict these differences, in which it is clear that preratification scores are higher than postratification scores. In other words, human rights practices tend to be worse before rather than after a country ratifies either treaty. These differences are statistically significant, although the two exceptions are the State Department version of the political terror scale in the case of the ICCPR and the Amnesty International version of the political terror scale for CAT. Although these simple figures lend initial support to an overall relationship, they are, at best, merely suggestive, since a simple correlation does not imply causation. Keith (1999) revealed similar significant bivariate relationships in her analysis of the relationship between ratification of the ICCPR and the protection of "personal integrity rights" (operationalized with the political terror scale), and Hathaway (2002) found similar correlations for a wider range of treaties and rights measures.

Beyond these "snapshot" views of human rights protection before and after ratification, figure 6.3 shows the time-series trends in mean ratification and mean rights score both for the whole world and differentiated by region. For the whole world, it is clear that the mean human rights score has declined across the whole period, while the mean ratification of all the international human rights treaties has increased to just over .7 on the 0 to 1 scale. This suggests that over time, as more nation-states have ratified human rights treaties, the overall protection of human rights has improved where the gap between rights in principle and rights in practice has narrowed over the period. By 1992, treaty ratification had surpassed rights protection, but the rapid increase in ratification was not met with an equivalent decrease in human rights violations. In essence, there has been a lag between increased ratification and increased protection. This general relationship appears to be quite different across the regions, where

(text continues on p. 133)

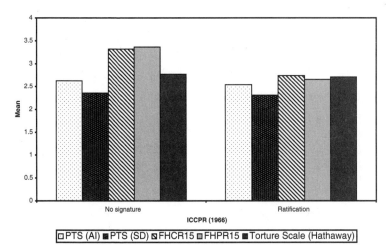

Figure 6.1. Mean human rights protection by ratification of the International Covenant on Civil and Political Rights.

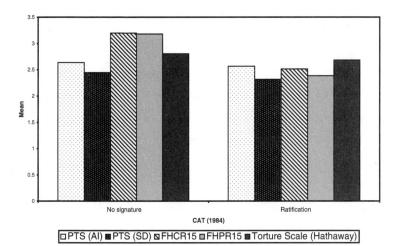

Figure 6.2. Mean human rights protection by ratification of the Convention against Torture and other Cruel, Inhuman, or Degrading Treatment or Punishment (CAT).

Note: The difference in means is significant across all the human rights measures with the exception of the Political Terror Scale (PTS) using the Amnesty International reports.

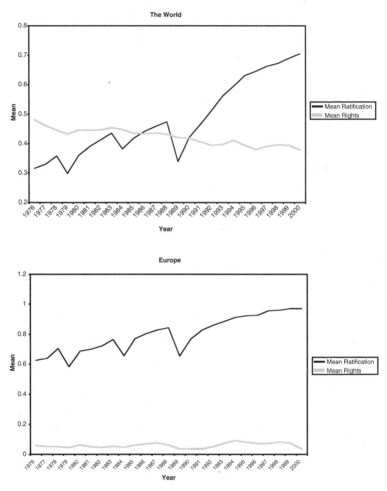

Figure 6.3. Mean ratification and mean rights protection by region and for the whole world.

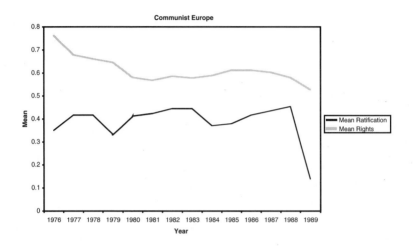

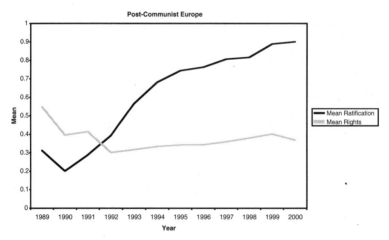

Figure 6.3. (*continued*)

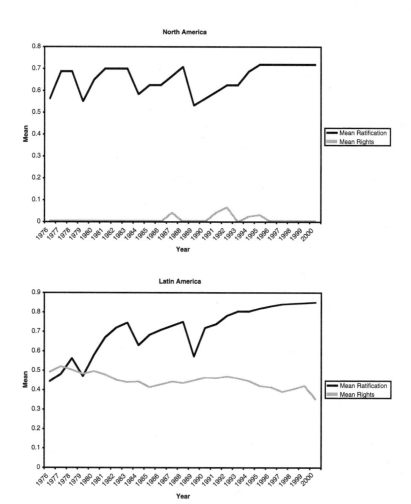

Figure 6.3. Mean ratification and mean rights protection by region and for the whole world (*continued*).

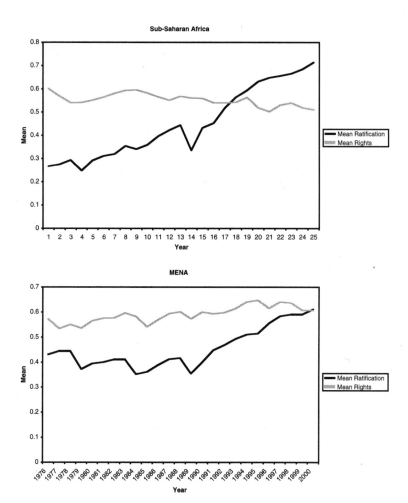

Figure 6.3. (*continued*)

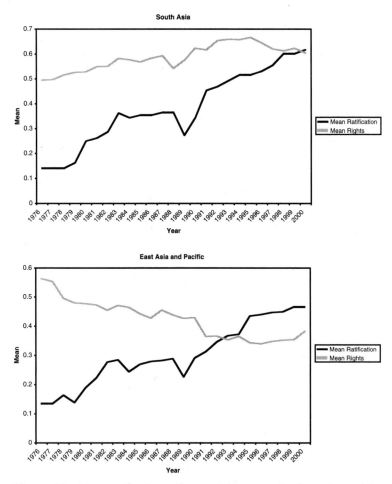

Figure 6.3. Mean ratification and mean rights protection by region and for the whole world (*continued*).

the persistence of human rights violations despite an increase in treaty ratification is evident in the MENA countries, sub-Saharan Africa, and South Asia. Indeed, for the period the mean human rights score is .66 for MENA, .63 for sub-Saharan Africa, and .66 for South Asia, where the mean human rights score has actually become worse for the MENA countries and South Asia.

The simple relationships depicted in these figures are captured further in table 6.1, which reports the bivariate correlations between the various treaty ratification and human rights protection variables, including the weighted and unweighted versions. In general, the results show that participation in the regime is associated with lower levels of human rights violations. With the exception of the Amnesty International version of the political terror scale and CAT, the unweighted ratification of the human rights treaties is consistently related to lower levels of human rights violation across the five measures, as well as the mean of the five measures. The correlations between the unweighted treaty variables and human rights measures are consistent with the analyses conducted by Keith (1999) and Hathaway (2002), but these relationships become weaker and less significant for the weighted versions of the ratification variables, suggesting that when reservations are taken into account, state participation in human rights treaties is less related to better human rights performance. Recall that those countries that ratified the treaties later did so with fewer reservations, and those countries that democratized later had poorer records of human rights protection, and thus have produced a greater dispersion in the overall relationship between treaty ratification and rights protection. Thus, over time, formal treaty ratification has included a more comprehensive acceptance of the normative content of the international human rights regime, whereas state practices themselves have lagged behind.

Nonrecursive Relationships

Such overall trends in treaty ratification and rights protection can be further examined through an estimation of the full model specified in chapter 2 (see fig. 2.4), which takes into account the possible feedback effects and the influence of other factors. Since the model has feedback loops that are between the international regime and rights protection, and both sides of the relationship are influenced by the presence of the other independent variables, there are in essence two

Table 6.1. Bivariate correlation matrix between ratification of human rights treaties and human rights protection (nonparametric correlation)

Treaty variables	Human rights measures					
	PTS (AI)	PTS (SD)	FHCR15	FHPR15	Torture scale	Mean rights score
ICCPR (unweighted)	−0.04**	−0.04*	−0.18**	−0.19**	−0.03*	−0.10***
ICCPRW (weighted)	0.01	0.02	−0.11**	−0.12**	0.01	−0.04**
CAT (unweighted)	−0.03	−0.05**	−0.21***	−0.22***	−0.05**	−0.11***
CATW (weighted)	−0.01	−0.03*	−0.18***	−0.18***	−0.02	−0.08***
Mean ratification (unweighted)	−0.09***	−0.09***	−0.23***	−0.24***	−0.12***	−0.15***
Mean ratification (weighted)	−.014	−.015	−.13***	−.14***	−.03*	−.07***

Note: Kendall's tau *b* reported, *$p < .10$, **$p < .05$, ***$p < .001$.

systems of two equations that capture the various relationships that are to be estimated. Each system, in turn, resolves its two equations into a final equation through a process analogous to solving a system of two equations in algebra. Estimating these two sets of equations and comparing their results allows us to examine (1) whether there is a systematic and sustainable relationship between norms and rights in the presence of democracy, wealth, interdependence, conflict, size, and regional differentiation, and (2) whether the relationship between norms and rights is stronger than the relationship between rights and norms.

To these ends, the first system of equations estimates the relationship between human rights norms and human rights practice while controlling for the influences of democracy, wealth, interdependence, conflict, size, and regional differentiation. It specifies treaty ratification as a function of democracy, wealth, and interdependence and then examines its relationship with rights protection in the face of international conflict, domestic conflict, and regional differentiation. In a similar fashion, the second system of equations estimates the relationship between human rights protection and human rights norms (treaty ratification) while controlling for the influences of democracy, wealth, interdependence, conflict, size, and regional differentiation. It specifies rights protection as being a larger function of democracy, wealth, and interdependence and then examines its relationship with treaty ratification in the face of international conflict, domestic conflict, and regional differentiation.

These two sets of equations (see below) are resolved into two final equations that are then estimated with the use of two-staged least squares with instrumental variables. For the norms-rights relationship, Equation 1.1 shows that human rights protection is a function of past human rights protection, ratification of the human rights treaties, international war, civil war, population size, and regional differentiation. Equation 1.2 shows that ratification of human rights treaties is a function of past values of democracy, wealth, and the three interdependence measures. Equation 1.3 resolves the system by the substitution of equation 1.2 into equation 1.1. For the rights-norms relationship, equation 2.1 shows that ratification of treaties is a function of past ratification action (no signature, signature, or ratification), human rights protection, international war civil war, population size, and regional differentiation. Equation 2.2 shows that human rights protection is a function of past values of democracy, wealth, and the three interdependence measures. As in the solution for the norms-rights system of equations, equation 2.3 resolves the rights-norms system by the substitution of equation 2.2 into equation 2.1.

The first system of equations for the relationship between human rights norms (treaty ratification) and human rights practices is

[1.1] Human rights = $\alpha_t + \beta_1$Human rights$_{t-1} + \beta_2$Treaty ratification$_t + \beta_3$International War$_t + \beta_4$Civil War$_t + \beta_5$Population$_t + \beta_6$MENA $+ \beta_7$Sub-Saharan Africa $+ \beta_8$South Asia $+ \mu_t$

[1.2] Treaty ratification$_t = \alpha_t + \beta_9$Democracy$_{t-1} + \beta_{10}$Wealth$_{t-1} + \beta_{11}$IGO membership$_{t-1} + \beta_{12}$INGOs$_{t-1} + \beta_{13}$Trade$_{t-1} + \mu_t$

which is resolved into

[1.3] Human rights = $\alpha_t + \beta_{14}$Rights at $t-1 + \beta_{15}$ (Treaty ratification$_t = \beta_9$Democracy$_{t-1} + \beta_{10}$Wealth$_{t-1} + \beta_{11}$IGO membership$_{t-1} + \beta_{12}$INGOs$_{t-1} + \beta_{13}$Trade$_{t-1}$) $+ \beta_{16}$International War$_t + \beta_{17}$Civil War$_t + \beta_{18}$Population$_t + \beta_{19}$MENA $+ \beta_{20}$Sub-Saharan Africa $+ \beta_{21}$South Asia $+ \mu_t$

The second system of equations for the relationship between human rights protection and human rights norms (treaty ratification) is

[2.1] Treaty ratification = $\alpha_t + \beta_{22}$Treaty ratification$_{t-1} + \beta_{23}$Rights$_t + \beta_{24}$International War$_t + \beta_{25}$Civil War$_t + \beta_{26}$Population$_t + \beta_{27}$MENA $+ \beta_{28}$Sub-Saharan Africa $+ \beta_{29}$South Asia $+ \mu_t$

[2.2] Human rights$_t = \alpha_t + \beta_{30}$Democracy$_{t-1} + \beta_{31}$Wealth$_{t-1} + \beta_{32}$IGO membership$_{t-1} + \beta_{34}$INGOs$_{t-1} + \beta_{35}$Trade$_{t-1} + \mu_t$

which is resolved into

[2.3] ICCPR ratification$_t = \alpha_t + \beta_{36}$ICCPR ratification at $t - 1 + \beta_{37}$ (Human rights$_t = \beta_{30}$Democracy$_{t-1} + \beta_{31}$Wealth$_{t-1} + \beta_{32}$IGO membership$_{t-1} + \beta_{34}$INGOs$_{t-1} + \beta_{35}$Trade$_{t-1}$) $+ \beta_{38}$International War$_t + \beta_{39}$Civil War$_t + \beta_{40}$Population$_t + \beta_{41}$MENA $+ \beta_{42}$Sub-Saharan Africa $+ \beta_{43}$South Asia $+ \mu_t$

To estimate parameters for the norms-rights relationship, 2SLS regresses the various treaty ratification variables (ICCPR, CAT, and Mean Ratification) on the independent variables in equation 1.2 and saves the regression "fit" values as a new variable. It then uses this new "instrumented" form of the ratification variables in a new regression of rights protection on the independent variables specified in equation 1.1 (see Kennedy 1989, 159–60; Foweraker and Landman 1997, 189–90). Since the analysis uses a pooled cross-sectional time-series data set, the 2SLS parameters were estimated with the *xtivreg* procedure in Stata 7.0. The procedure takes into account the panel and time structure of the data set (i.e., countries and years), while also carrying out the instrumental stage of the regression common to 2SLS estimation. The final parameter estimates are for equation 1.3. Exactly the same procedure was used to estimate the parameters in equation 2.3 for the rights-norms relationship; the results for both estimations across the different human rights measures are shown in tables 6.2 through 6.6.

The tables list unstandardized coefficients for the variables with *z* scores in parentheses. Parameter estimates are not reported for those variables used in the first stage of the 2SLS, since they are captured by the "instrumented" variables denoted in equations 1.2 and 2.2. Table 6.2 reports the results for the two-stage regression for the norms-rights relationship for the unweighted and weighted versions of the ICCPR and the five human rights measures and mean rights score, as well as for the two versions of CAT and the torture measure only. The coefficients for the unweighted version of the ICCPR are statistically significant across all of the human rights measures, and the coefficient for the unweighted version of CAT is also significant for the torture measure. The coefficients for past human rights practices, civil war, population, and the regional dummies, are also all significant. Substantively, these results show that there is consistent support for a limited effect of treaty ratification on human rights practices. The effect is limited, since treaty ratification has been modeled as a function of other social processes taking place in the world, including democratization, economic development, and increased interdependence. The coefficients themselves range between .18 and .53, suggesting a small effect on the overall violation of human rights, the scores for which range from 1 to 5. Taken literally, the results suggest that treaty participation may at best reduce the range of human rights violations by only 10 percent. In contrast, civil

(*text continues on p. 146*)

Table 6.2. Parameter estimates for the relationship between human rights norms (ICCPR and CAT with and without reservations) and human rights protection

Independent Variables	PTSAI		PTSSD		FHCR		FHPR		TORTURE			
Constant	−.08 (−.54)	−.22 (−1.52)	−.15 (−1.09)	−.33** (−2.56)	.21** (2.33)	.09 (1.26)	.43*** (3.66)	.15** (1.67)	−.50** (−2.16)	−.75*** (−3.51)	−.84*** (−3.43)	−.88*** (−4.21)
ICCPR (unweighted)	−.13** (−3.67)		−.19*** (−6.11)		−.12*** (−3.43)		−.25*** (−5.15)		−.29*** (−4.52)			
ICCPR (weighted)		−.02* (−1.61)		−.03*** (−3.37)		−.03*** (−3.51)		−.04*** (−4.10)		−.02** (−1.53)		
CAT (unweighted)											−.53*** (−6.81)	
CAT (weighted)												−.07*** (−4.32)
PTSAI$_{t-1}$	.73** (52.70)	.74*** (54.09)										
PTSSD$_{t-1}$			.76*** (59.66)	.77*** (61.69)								
FHCR$_{t-1}$					.90*** (73.93)	.92*** (118.99)						
FHPR$_{t-1}$							.87*** (63.21)	.91*** (110.82)				
Torture$_{t-1}$									.55*** (30.67)	.57*** (33.18)	.54*** (27.35)	.59*** (33.64)
International war	.12 (.85)	.12 (.84)	.13 (1.00)	.14 (1.06)	.03 (.43)	.04 (.60)	.03 (.38)	.04 (.44)	−.16 (−.76)	−.15 (−.71)	−.31 (−1.31)	−.26 (−1.22)

Civil war	.59**	.57***	.60***	.59***	.07**	.05*	.15***	.12**	.40***	.39***	.40***	.39***
	(8.86)	(8.66)	(9.81)	(9.58)	(2.27)	(1.68)	(3.57)	(3.04)	(4.37)	(4.44)	(3.95)	(4.25)
Population	.05***	.05***	.06***	.06***	.01**	.05*	.01**	.01*	.13***	.12***	.17***	.13***
	(5.62)	(5.63)	(6.68)	(6.83)	(2.52)	(2.41)	(1.99)	(1.81)	(9.01)	(8.86)	(9.72)	(9.36)
MENA	.16***	.21***	.09*	.16***	.15***	.14***	.19***	.18***	.32***	.37***	.18**	.31***
	(3.44)	(4.60)	(2.15)	(3.78)	(5.94)	(5.80)	(5.99)	(6.06)	(4.57)	(4.76)	(2.16)	(4.65)
Sub-Saharan Africa	.13***	.18***	.10**	.14***	.09***	.08***	.14***	.13***	.16**	.21***	-.11**	.13**
	(3.79)	(4.92)	(3.15)	(4.56)	(4.87)	(4.43)	(5.82)	(5.68)	(3.15)	(4.30)	(-1.49)	(2.53)
South Asia	.20**	.25***	.08	.14**	.02	.04	-.08	-.006	.20**	.32**	-.13	.22**
	(2.99)	(3.65)	(1.35)	(2.27)	(.65)	(1.13)	(-1.57)	(-.14)	(1.84)	(3.14)	(-.97)	(-2.20)
N	2218	2218	2433	2433	2594	2594	2609	2609	1720	1720	1720	1720
R^2	.68	.69	.72	.73	.93	.93	.91	.92	.52	.55	.43	.52
Wald chi²	4897.79	4961.98	6502.80	6760.81	32751.24	32945.34	27628.76	31346.57	1796.10	1981.40	1476.96	1988.83

Note: Estimates are from two-staged least-squares regression with instrumental variables; unstandardized coefficients reported (z scores in parentheses) $*p < .01$, $**p < .05$, $***p < .001$; chi² figures are all significant at $p < .001$.

Table 6.3. Parameter estimates for the relationship between human rights norms (mean ratification with and without reservations) and human rights protection

Independent Variables	PTSAI		PTSSD		FHCR		FHPR		Torture		Mean rights	
Constant	.06 (.38)	−.19 (−1.26)	−.03 (−.23)	−.30** (−2.33)	.46*** (3.66)	.13 (1.30)	.85*** (4.97)	.19* (2.00)	−.19 (−.77)	−.63** (−2.95)	.02 (1.09)	−.02 (−1.29)
Mean ratification (unweighted)	−.53*** (−4.59)		−.63*** (−6.70)		−.62*** (−4.32)		−1.10*** (−5.79)		−1.08*** (−6.11)		−.12*** (−6.23)	
Mean ratification (weighted)		−.23** (−1.95)		−.28** (−3.04)		−.24*** (−3.49)		−.34*** (−3.97)		−.48*** (−2.92)		−.05*** (−3.49)
$PTSAI_{t-1}$	.73*** (51.98)	.74*** (54.08)										
$PTSSD_{t-1}$			.76*** (58.65)	.77*** (62.16)								
$FHCR_{t-1}$					.87*** (52.17)	.92*** (119.77)						
$FHPR_{t-1}$							.84*** (45.73)	.91*** (114.05)				
$Torture_{t-1}$									.54*** (30.07)	.58*** (34.13)		
Mean rights$_{t-1}$											.87*** (86.02)	.90*** (116.08)

International war	.08	.10	.08	.10	−.01	.02	−.05	—	−.24	−.19	.002	.007
	(.59)	(.70)	(.65)	(.79)	(−.16)	(.25)	(−.51)		(−1.09)	(−.89)	(.12)	(.41)
Civil war	.62***	.58***	.64***	.60***	.11***	.06*	.19***	.13***	.42***	.39***	.06***	.05***
	(9.15)	(8.82)	(10.34)	(10.00)	(3.02)	(1.99)	(4.16)	(3.34)	(4.59)	(4.53)	(7.40)	(6.59)
Population	.05***	.05***	.06***	.05***	.02**	.01**	.01**	.007	.13***	.12***	.006***	.004***
	(5.65)	(5.60)	(6.92)	(6.74)	(2.89)	(2.12)	(2.02)	(1.38)	(9.13)	(9.01)	(5.05)	(4.24)
MENA	.10*	.19***	.02	.13**	.10***	.12***	.08**	.15***	.14*	.30***	.02**	.03***
	(1.81)	(3.96)	(.40)	(3.09)	(3.56)	(4.86)	(2.21)	(4.80)	(1.78)	(4.23)	(2.96)	(4.92)
Sub-Saharan Africa	.10**	.17***	.07**	.14***	.08***	.08***	.16***	.13***	.07	.18**	.02***	.02***
	(2.65)	(4.86)	(2.05)	(4.78)	(3.99)	(4.53)	(4.14)	(5.65)	(1.34)	(3.79)	(3.86)	(5.81)
South Asia	.17**	.25***	.06	.16**	−.03	.05	−.17***	.01	.11	.28**	.003	.02**
	(2.47)	(3.72)	(.93)	(2.67)	(−.59)	(1.45)	(−2.75)	(.25)	(1.05)	(2.82)	(.35)	(2.18)
N	2218	2218	2433	2433	2594	2594	2609	2609	1720	1720	2610	2610
R^2	.68	.69	.72	.74	.92	.93	.93	.90	.51	.54	.90	.91
Wald chi²	4822.00	4960.17	6511.79	6880.76	29499.63	32801.51	232293.17	29268.37	1837.18	2093.04	22599.59	24828.89

Note: Estimates are from two-staged least-squares regression with instrumental variables; unstandardized coefficients reported (z scores in parentheses) $*p < .01$, $**p < .05$, $***p < .001$; chi² figures are all significant at $p < .001$.

Table 6.4. Parameter estimates for the relationship between human rights protection and human rights norms (ICCPR and CAT with and without reservations)

Independent Variables	ICCPR (unweighted)					ICCPR (weighted)					CAT (UW)	CAT (W)
Constant	.09 (1.38)	.07 (1.04)	.13** (2.24)	.14** (2.32)	.14* (1.77)	.48** (2.09)	.37* (1.63)	.44** (2.06)	.45** (2.12)	.68** (2.31)	−.12 (−1.25)	−.21 (−.62)
PTSAI	−.01 (−.77)					.0003 (.01)						
PTSSD		−.02 (−1.35)					−.01 (−.25)					
FHCR			−.01* (−1.66)					−.02 (−.85)				
FHPR				−.01** (−2.00)					−.02 (−1.09)			
Torture					.01 (.74)					.12* (1.88)	−.11*** (−5.26)	−.19** (−2.65)
ICCPR$_{t-1}$ (unweighted)	.94*** (149.60)	.94*** (154.76)	.94*** (141.95)	.93*** (143.53)	.93*** (125.24)							
ICCPR$_{t-1}$ (weighted)						−.96*** (151.75)	.96*** (155.72)	.95*** (151.68)	.95*** (152.12)	.95*** (126.49)		
CAT$_{t-1}$ (unweighted)											.90*** (91.04)	

											.94*** (97.74)
CAT$_{t-1}$ (weighted)											
International war	−.02 (−.40)	−.02 (−.31)	−.03 (−.43)	−.03 (−.42)	−.03 (−.35)	−.06 (−.27)	−.05 (.24)	−.08 (−.35)	−.08 (−.35)	−.06 (−.23)	−.13 (−1.37) · −.24 (−.71)
Civil war	.01 (.41)	.03 (.75)	−.001 (−.03)	−.001 (−.04)	−.02 (−.46)	.11 (.86)	.12 (.97)	.09 (.93)	.09 (.95)	.05 (.40)	.07* (1.77) · .07 (.49)
Population	.004 (.77)	.005 (1.25)	.002 (.56)	.002 (.45)	−.001 (−.16)	−.009 (−.52)	.0002 (.01)	−.002 (−.12)	−.002 (−.17)	−.03 (−1.44)	.04*** (4.88) · .07** (2.73)
MENA	−.03 (−1.22)	−.02 (−1.19)	−.02 (−.89)	−.02 (−.83)	−.04* (−1.63)	−.09 (−1.20)	−.90 (−1.20)	−.06 (−.77)	−.05 (−.71)	−.19* (−1.91)	.03 (.89) · .11 (.97)
Sub-Saharan Africa	−.001 (−.11)	.006 (.39)	.006 (.37)	.009 (.55)	−.02 (−.86)	−.05 (−.90)	−.04 (−.72)	−.01 (−.25)	−.006 (−.10)	−.15** (−2.07)	−.04 (−1.49) · −.09 (−1.02)
South Asia	−.03 (−1.00)	−.03** (−1.13)	−.04** (−1.63)	−.05* (−1.72)	−.08** (−2.29)	−.12 (−1.12)	−.14 (−1.37)	−.15 (−1.48)	−.15 (−1.52)	−.34** (−2.48)	−.04 (−.79) · −.05 (−.31)
N	2297	2459	2594	2610	1848	2297	2459	2594	2610	1848	1848 · 1848
R^2	.91	.91	.91	.91	.91	.91	.91	.91	.91	.91	.85 · .85
Wald chi^2	24295.97	25761.90	25760.48	26048.26	17023.96	23947.56	25413.48	25325.33	25698.07	17023.96	10181.51 · 10547.98

Note: Estimates are from two-staged least-squares regression with instrumental variables; unstandardized coefficients reported (z scores in parentheses)

$^*p < .01$, $^{**}p < .05$, $^{***}p < .001$; chi^2 figures are all significant at $p < .001$.

143

Table 6.5. Parameter estimates for the relationship between human rights protection and human rights norms (mean ratification with and without reservations)

Independent Variables	Mean ratification (unweighted)						Mean ratification (weighted)					
Constant	.06** (2.81)	.05** (2.33)	.09*** (4.17)	.10*** (4.17)	.07** (2.91)	.07*** (3.28)	.06** (2.97)	.05*** (2.68)	.06** (3.13)	.06*** (3.22)	.08*** (3.31)	.05*** (2.86)
PTSAI	-.008* (-1.83)						.0004 (.11)					
PTSSD		-.01** (-2.41)						-.0006 (-.15)				
FHCR			-.008** (-3.05)						-.002 (-1.15)			
FHPR				-.007*** (-3.42)						-.003 (-1.58)		
Torture					-.01** (-1.99)						.004 (.85)	
Mean rights						-.04** (-2.91)						-.01 (-.75)
Mean ratification$_{t-1}$ (unweighted)	.92*** (133.19)	.92*** (138.03)	.91*** (120.04)	.91*** (122.51)	.91*** (116.01)	.91*** (128.55)						
Mean ratification$_{t-1}$ (weighted)							.95*** (146.21)	.95*** (150.57)	.95*** (140.83)	.95*** (142.37)	.95*** (130.32)	.95*** (145.66)

International war	−.006	−.004	−.010	−.010	−.006	−.008	.003	.0008	−.0008	−.0008	.01	−.0004
	(−.28)	(−.19)	(−.47)	(−.46)	(−.24)	(−.38)	(.02)	(.04)	(−.05)	(−.05)	(.42)	(−.02)
Civil war	.02	.02*	.004	.003	.007	.01	.008	.006	.006	.006	.003	.006
	(1.55)	(1.82)	(.44)	(.37)	(.68)	(.96)	(.69)	(.57)	(.68)	(.71)	(.32)	(.67)
Population	.002	.002	.0004	.0001	.002	.001	−.001	−.0008	−.0006	−.0006	−.002	−.0004
	(.93)	(1.57)	(.32)	(.10)	(1.17)	(.82)	(−.84)	(−.49)	(−.49)	(−.55)	(−1.22)	(−.39)
MENA	−.02**	−.02***	−.02**	−.02**	−.02***	−.02***	−.02**	−.02**	−.02**	−.02**	−.02**	−.02**
	(−2.98)	(−3.38)	(−2.70)	(−2.75)	(−2.66)	(−2.84)	(−2.67)	(−3.00)	(−2.34)	(−2.26)	(−3.16)	(−2.57)
Sub-Saharan Africa	−.01**	−.01**	−.007	−.007	−.01**	−.009	−.01**	−.01**	−.007	−.006	−.01**	−.008*
	(−2.11)	(−1.91)	(−1.23)	(−1.10)	(−2.15)	(−1.47)	(−2.17)	(−2.27)	(−1.38)	(−1.13)	(−2.66)	(−1.66)
South Asia	−.008	−.01***	−.02**	−.02**	−.02**	−.02*	−.008	−.01	−.01	−.01**	−.02**	−.01
	(−.79)	(−1.43)	(−1.93)	(−2.12)	(−1.78)	(−1.66)	(−.85)	(−1.48)	(−1.32)	(−1.35)	(−2.11)	(−1.30)
N	2262	2422	2556	2572	1821	2572	2262	2422	2556	2572	1821	2572
R^2	.90	.91	.90	.90	.90	.90	.91	.91	.91	.91	.92	.91
Wald chi²	20728.43	22370.20	20696.47	21015.44	16488.56	21139.07	22521.79	24233.49	22776.35	23260.51	18448.56	23214.06

Note: Estimates are from two-staged least-squares regression with instrumental variables; unstandardized coefficients reported (z scores in parentheses)
*$p < .01$, **$p < .05$, ***$p < .001$; chi² figures are all significant at $p < .001$.

145

war alone accounts for up to a 10 percent increase in the total level of human rights violations, and on balance the overall relationship is mediated by higher violations across the MENA countries, sub-Saharan Africa, and South Asia.

The results for weighted versions of treaty ratification (i.e., those that take into account the presence of reservations), though still statistically significant, show a dramatic decrease in the substantive effect of norms on rights. The coefficients range from .02 to .07, suggesting that taking reservations into account means that treaty ratification at best reduces up to 1 percent of the total range measuring human rights violations. But the results for past human rights violations, international war, civil war, and regions are broadly the same as those that were obtained with the unweighted version of treaty ratification. Table 6.3 reports the results for the regression analysis, which uses mean ratification, the five human rights measures, and the mean rights measure. Like those reported in table 6.2, the coefficients for the unweighted and weighted versions of mean ratification of all of the main human rights treaties are statistically significant, and the effects for the remaining variables are roughly similar to those in the previous table. Substantively and not surprisingly, it appears that mean ratification of all of the treaties (i.e., a measure of total participation in the international human rights regime) appears to have a slightly higher effect on human rights protection than single treaty ratification, which is reduced when reservations are taken into account. Again, civil war increases the violation of human rights, whereas the overall relationship between treaty participation and rights protection is mediated by higher violations across the three regions.

Tables 6.4 and 6.5 list the results for the relationship between human rights protection and treaty ratification. Here the two-stage regression was carried out with treaty ratification as the dependent variable to examine the degree to which variation in human rights protection is related to state participation in the international human rights regime. Overall, the relationship in this direction for the ICCPR and CAT is less strong, where there are statistically significant coefficients for the Freedom House Civil Rights score and the unweighted ICCPR variable, and for torture and the weighted ICCPR, as well as for the two versions of CAT. The regional effects are not as strong, although for the unweighted ICCPR, South Asia consistently shows a generally level of treaty ratification. For the unweighted version of mean ratification, however, the results are slightly stronger, where there are statistically significant coefficients for all of the rights measures and the regions appear to have a generally lower level of treaty ratification. The significant effects between rights and norms drop away when the weighted version of mean ratification is used.

Comparing the results from tables 6.2 and 6.3 on the one hand against those reported in tables 6.4 and 6.5, on the other, shows that on balance, there is a weakly reciprocal relationship between norms and rights, which the global empirical evidence suggests is generally stronger for the effect of norms on rights than for the effect of rights on norms. In other words, it appears that treaty participation as a function of other underlying social processes has a significant but limited effect on reducing human rights violations, and that this effect is further mediated by regional differences. On the one hand, such a result suggests that norms matter, albeit to a very limited degree. On the other hand, the importance of the normative proliferation in human rights should be seen as a larger function of democratization, economic development, and interdependence. In addition, civil war remains a significant explanatory factor for the violation of human rights. What remains to be analyzed is whether considering the impact of democratization on the overall relationship between norms and rights is further differentiated across types of democracy.

Tables 6.6 through 6.9 repeat the two-stage least-squares estimations carried out above but include a dummy variable for third-wave and fourth-wave democracies alongside international war, civil war, population, and the regions. The results across the four tables show that the main relationship between norms and rights remains intact, but that it is further mediated by the presence of controls for third- and fourth-wave democracies. Recall that fourth-wave democracies had higher ratification rates and lower protection scores than third-wave and old democracies. The regression results have captured these differences. The regression coefficients are larger for fourth-wave democracies than for third-wave democracies, which, like the regional differences, suggest that although the same overall relationship between norms and rights is obtained for these different types of democracy, they both have worse levels of human rights protection.

Taken together, the results of the final sets of regressions show that the proliferation of human rights norms has had a limited impact on the protection of human rights, which is differentiated across

(*text continues on p. 157*)

Table 6.6. Parameter estimates for the relationship between human rights norms (ICCPR and CAT with and without reservations) and human rights protection, adding type of democracy

Independent Variables	PTSAI	PTSAI	PTSSD	PTSSD	FHCR	FHCR	FHPR	FHPR	Torture	Torture	Torture	Torture
Constant	-.05 (-.30)	-.20 (-1.39)	-.10 (-.74)	-.31** (-2.34)	.28** (2.84)	.11 (1.51)	.52*** (4.11)	.17 (1.88)	-.35 (-1.44)	-.63** (-2.94)	-.82*** (-3.40)	-.89*** (-4.18)
ICCPR (unweighted)	-.18*** (-4.57)		-.24*** (-7.08)		-.19*** (-3.94)		-.31*** (-5.55)		-.43*** (-5.81)			
ICCPR (weighted)		-.03** (-2.47)		-.05*** (-4.49)		-.03*** (-3.85)		-.04*** (-3.97)		-.06** (-3.03)		
CAT (unweighted)											-.59*** (-7.60)	
CAT (weighted)												-.08*** (-4.92)
PTSAI$_{t-1}$	.73** (51.00)	.74*** (52.91)										
PTSSD$_{t-1}$			.76*** (57.37)	.77*** (59.79)								
FHCR$_{t-1}$					.88*** (63.27)	.92*** (113.29)						
FHPR$_{t-1}$							.85*** (57.29)	.91*** (109.08)				
Torture$_{t-1}$									.54*** (28.52)	.57*** (32.63)	.55*** (27.22)	.58*** (32.89)

International war	.13 (.95)	.14 (1.00)	.15 (1.13)	.17 (1.28)	.04 (.47)	.05 (.68)	.03 (.28)	.04 (.41)	-.14 (-.62)	-.11 (-.53)	-.33 (-1.35)	-.26 (-1.18)
Civil war	.61** (9.01)	.58*** (8.71)	.63*** (9.92)	.59*** (9.53)	.08** (2.44)	.06* (1.65)	.15*** (3.50)	.11** (2.94)	.43*** (4.47)	.40*** (4.58)	.43*** (4.23)	.39*** (4.34)
Population	.05*** (5.68)	.05*** (5.70)	.06*** (6.63)	.06*** (6.88)	.01** (2.94)	.01** (2.70)	.01** (2.47)	.01* (2.16)	.13*** (8.68)	.12*** (8.76)	.16*** (9.70)	.13*** (9.25)
Third wave	.09* (1.80)	.10* (1.98)	.08* (1.68)	.10** (2.14)	-.04 (-1.37)	.01 (.52)	-.11*** (-3.21)	-.07** (-2.27)	.18** (2.41)	.19** (2.74)	.18** (2.35)	.16** (2.37)
Fourth wave	.14** (2.35)	.09 (1.51)	.17*** (3.52)	.13** (2.70)	.03 (.82)	.01 (.34)	-.02 (-.47)	-.08** (-2.24)	.24*** (3.30)	.14** (2.03)	.22** (3.06)	.11* (1.81)
MENA	.18*** (3.59)	.23*** (4.92)	.10* (2.30)	.18*** (4.15)	.15*** (5.70)	.15*** (5.63)	.18*** (5.45)	.17*** (5.64)	.36*** (4.74)	.40*** (6.03)	.21** (2.57)	.35*** (5.00)
Sub-Saharan Africa	.13*** (3.63)	.17*** (4.93)	.09** (2.77)	.13*** (4.27)	.09*** (4.42)	.08*** (4.07)	.13*** (5.17)	.12*** (5.50)	.15** (2.64)	.20*** (3.88)	-.13* (-1.77)	.14** (2.58)
South Asia	.18** (2.49)	.23*** (3.24)	.05 (.73)	.10 (1.60)	-.01 (-.30)	.02 (.52)	-.13** (-2.26)	-.02 (-.37)	.10* (.87)	.25** (2.28)	-.20 (-1.43)	.21** (2.03)
N	2218	2218	2433	2433	2594	2594	2609	2609	1720	1720	1720	1720
R^2	.68	.69	.72	.71	.92	.92	.90	.92	.48	.52	.42	.51
Wald Chi²	4804.14	4894.19	6251.13	6497.96	30435.76	31755.00	24890.49	30146.96	1650.78	2027.34	1550.15	1949.81

Note: Estimates are from two-staged least-squares regression with instrumental variables; unstandardized coefficients reported (z scores in parentheses)

$*p < .01$, $**p < .05$, $***p < .001$; chi² figures are all significant at $p < .001$.

Table 6.7. Parameter estimates for the relationship between human rights norms (mean ratification with and without reservations) and human rights protection, adding the type of democracy

Independent Variables	PTSAI	PTSSD	FHCR	FHPR	Torture	Mean rights
Constant	.15 (.89) / −.16 (−1.06)	.05 (.33) / −.27** (−2.08)	.81*** (4.62) / .14 (1.84)	1.06*** (5.52) / .20* (2.18)	.008 (.03) / −.53** (−2.46)	.04*** (1.90) / −.02 (−1.05)
Mean ratification (unweighted)	−.73*** (−5.68)	−.80*** (−7.76)	−1.13*** (−5.19)	−1.41*** (−6.33)	−1.42*** (−7.25)	−.16*** (−7.00)
Mean ratification (weighted)	−.35** (−2.73)	−.40** (−3.87)	−.28*** (−3.67)	−.34*** (−3.82)	−.72*** (−3.92)	−.06*** (−3.79)
PTSAI$_{t-1}$	.72*** (49.31) / .74*** (52.94)					
PTSSD$_{t-1}$		.75*** (55.80) / .76*** (60.95)				
FHCR$_{t-1}$			.82*** (34.94) / .92*** (118.75)			
FHPR$_{t-1}$				.81*** (40.58) / .91*** (118.67)		
Torture$_{t-1}$					.53*** (28.10) / .57*** (33.10)	
Mean rights$_{t-1}$						.85*** (77.74) / .90*** (114.21)

	(1)	(2)	(3)	(4)	(5)	(6)	(7)	(8)	(9)	(10)	(11)	(12)
International war	.09 (.63)	.10 (.76)	.10 (.72)	.11 (.86)	-.03 (-.38)	.02 (.24)	-.07 (-.60)	—	-.23 (-1.01)	-.17 (-.79)	.003 (.21)	.007 (.41)
Civil war	.65*** (9.45)	.60*** (8.97)	.68*** (10.62)	.62*** (10.14)	.16*** (3.47)	.06* (1.94)	.21*** (4.14)	.13*** (3.26)	.46*** (4.81)	.41*** (4.69)	.07*** (7.51)	.05*** (6.59)
Population	.05*** (5.71)	.05*** (5.64)	.06*** (6.88)	.06*** (6.73)	.02* (3.26)	.01** (2.28)	.02** (2.24)	.009* (1.67)	.13*** (8.81)	.12*** (8.81)	.006*** (5.15)	.002*** (.28)
Third wave	.14** (2.76)	.11** (2.12)	.12** (2.67)	.09** (2.08)	.04 (1.00)	-.02 (-.56)	-.04 (-.88)	-.08** (-2.32)	.24*** (3.19)	.20** (3.97)	.009* (1.68)	.003 (.57)
Fourth wave	.19** (3.09)	.09 (1.55)	.19*** (3.91)	.09** (2.04)	.14** (2.76)	-.01 (-.52)	.06 (1.13)	-.11*** (-3.48)	.24*** (3.57)	.13** (2.02)	.02** (2.58)	.0006 (.09)
MENA	.09* (1.75)	.20*** (4.18)	.02 (.35)	.14*** (3.27)	.08*** (2.40)	.11*** (4.62)	.06** (1.40)	.13*** (4.45)	.14* (1.73)	.31*** (4.40)	.02** (2.54)	.03*** (4.74)
Sub-Saharan Africa	.09** (2.42)	.17*** (4.98)	.06* (1.71)	.14*** (4.76)	.07** (2.85)	.08*** (4.33)	.10*** (3.18)	.13*** (5.66)	.06 (.99)	.19*** (3.81)	.02** (3.11)	.02*** (5.55)
South Asia	.13* (1.87)	.24*** (3.47)	.02 (.35)	.14** (2.38)	-.13*** (-2.18)	.04 (1.20)	-.24*** (-3.44)	.01 (.26)	.04 (.35)	.25** (2.45)	-.005 (.51)	.02** (1.90)
N	2218	2218	2433	2433	2594	2594	2609	2609	1720	1720	2572	2572
R^2	.67	.69	.71	.73	.89	.93	.88	.93	.48	.53	.89	.91
Wald chi²	4672.76	4915.88	6263.20	6796.07	19964.08	33143.14	19058.59	3282.01	1732.24	2051.01	20596.12	24498.49

Note: Estimates are from two-staged least-squares regression with instrumental variables; unstandardized coefficients reported (z scores in parentheses)
$*p < .01$, $**p < .05$, $***p < .001$; chi² figures are all significant at $p < .001$.

Table 6.8. Parameter estimates for the relationship between human rights protection and human rights norms (ICCPR and CAT with and without reservations), adding type of democracy

Independent Variables	ICCPR (unweighted)					ICCPR (weighted)					CAT (UW)	CAT (W)
Constant	.09 (1.33)	.07 (1.05)	.13** (2.27)	.14** (2.34)	.14* (1.75)	.48** (2.10)	.37* (1.63)	.45** (2.08)	.45** (2.12)	.67** (2.23)	−.13 (−1.30)	−.24 (−.69)
PTSAI	−.01 (−1.04)					−.004 (−.09)						
PTSSD		−.18 (−1.57)					−.02 (−.42)					
FHCR			−.01 (−1.56)					−.02 (−.72)				
FHPR				−.01* (−1.78)					−.02 (−.73)			
Torture					.009 (.52)					.11* (1.65)	−.11*** (−5.53)	−.20** (−2.83)
ICCPR$_{t-1}$ (unweighted)	.94*** (146.32)	.94*** (151.09)	.93*** (139.70)	.93*** (142.00)	.93*** (119.77)							
ICCPR$_{t-1}$ (weighted)						.96*** (148.61)	.95*** (151.73)	.95*** (147.90)	.95*** (149.45)	.95*** (120.83)		
CAT$_{t-1}$ (unweighted)											.90*** (89.67)	
CAT$_{t-1}$ (weighted)												.94*** (96.62)

International war	−.02 (−.34)	−.01 (−.24)	−.02 (−.39)	−.02 (−.39)	−.02 (−.29)	−.05 (−.24)	−.04 (.18)	−.07 (−.30)	−.07 (−.30)	−.05 (−.19)	−.13 (−1.30)	−.22 (−.66)
Civil war	.02 (.65)	.03 (.97)	.0003 (.01)	−.0007 (−.02)	−.01 (−.32)	.12 (.93)	.15 (1.12)	.09 (.96)	.09 (.96)	.07 (.54)	.09* (1.97)	.10 (.64)
Population	.004 (.82)	.005 (1.22)	.001 (.40)	.001 (.31)	−.0007 (−.11)	−.009 (−.56)	—	−.004 (−1.25)	−.004 (−.30)	−.03 (−1.33)	.04*** (4.96)	.07** (2.80)
Third wave	.05** (2.11)	.04** (2.11)	.03 (1.54)	.03 (1.35)	.03 (1.26)	.12 (1.57)	.12 (1.59)	.11 (1.47)	.10 (1.37)	.07 (.75)	.06** (1.93)	.13 (1.21)
Fourth wave	.02 (.71)	.02 (1.08)	.02 (.95)	.02 (.75)	.03 (1.30)	.003 (.04)	.07 (.93)	.09 (1.18)	.08 (1.06)	.11 (1.40)	.04* (1.68)	.14 (1.57)
MENA	−.02 (−.69)	−.01 (−.70)	−.14 (−.66)	−.01 (−.67)	−.03 (−1.17)	−.07 (−.87)	−.06 (−.80)	−.04 (−.54)	−.04 (−.54)	−.16 (−1.49)	.05 (1.40)	.16 (1.33)
Sub-Saharan Africa	.007 (.43)	.01 (.84)	.009 (.52)	.01 (.64)	−.01 (−.55)	−.03 (−.50)	−.02 (−.35)	−.008 (−.13)	−.003 (−.05)	−.14* (−1.79)	−.03 (−1.02)	−.06 (−.72)
South Asia	−.02 (−.67)	−.02 (−.86)	−.04 (−1.53)	−.04 (−1.62)	−.08** (−2.11)	−.10 (−.86)	−.12 (−1.18)	−.14 (−1.43)	−.14 (−1.47)	−.14** (−1.79)	−.03 (−.60)	−.04 (−.23)
N	2297	2459	2594	2610	1848	2297	2459	2594	2610	1848	1848	1848
R^2	.91	.91	.91	.91	.91	.91	.91	.91	.91	.91	.85	.85
Wald chi^2	24322.16	25779.36	25769.20	26049.56	16339.38	23959.36	25425.76	25210.65	25701.28	16170.41	10139.87	10533.29

Note: Estimates are from two-staged least-squares regression with instrumental variables; unstandardized coefficients reported (z scores in parentheses)

*$p < .01$, **$p < .05$, ***$p < .001$; chi^2 figures are all significant at $p < .001$.

Table 6.9. Parameter estimates for the relationship between human rights protection and human rights norms (mean ratification with and without reservations), adding type of democracy

Independent Variables	Mean ratification (unweighted)						Mean ratification (weighted)					
Constant	.06** (2.62)	.05** (2.19)	.10*** (4.27)	.10*** (4.29)	.07** (2.75)	.08*** (3.39)	.05** (2.76)	.05*** (2.47)	.06** (3.15)	.06*** (3.18)	.07** (3.07)	.06** (2.93)
PTSAI	−.01** (−2.56)						−.001 (−.36)					
PTSSD		−.01** (−3.22)						−.001 (−.37)				
FHCR			−.008** (−2.95)						−.002 (−.88)			
FHPR				−.007*** (−3.04)						−.002 (−1.01)		
Torture					−.01** (−2.57)						.002 (.44)	
Mean rights						−.04** (−2.99)						−.007 (−.63)
Mean ratification$_{t-1}$ (unweighted)	.92*** (128.79)	.92*** (133.35)	.90*** (117.26)	.90*** (120.55)	.91*** (109.58)	.90*** (124.11)						
Mean ratification$_{t-1}$ (weighted)							.95*** (142.44)	.94*** (141.55)	.94*** (136.69)	.94*** (138.76)	.95*** (121.75)	.94*** (140.13)

154

	(1)	(2)	(3)	(4)	(5)	(6)	(7)	(8)	(9)	(10)	(11)	(12)
International war	−.003 (−.14)	−.0006 (−.03)	−.009 (−.41)	−.008 (−.40)	−.003 (−.14)	−.006 (−.30)	.002 (.12)	.003 (.19)	.0005 (−.03)	.0005 (.03)	.01 (.51)	−.0009 (−.05)
Civil war	.03** (2.25)	.03* (2.57)	.006 (.59)	.004 (.46)	.01 (1.07)	.01 (1.14)	.01 (1.15)	.01 (1.06)	.007 (.80)	.006 (.79)	.006 (.64)	.007 (.83)
Population	.002 (1.36)	.003 (1.92)	.0002 (.17)	−.0004 (−.03)	.003 (1.52)	.001 (.78)	−.0007 (−.54)	−.0003 (−.20)	−.0008 (−.63)	−.0008 (−.68)	−.002 (−.90)	−.0006 (−.53)
Third wave	.02** (2.40)	.02** (2.15)	.01 (1.37)	.008 (1.06)	.009 (1.04)	.01 (1.63)	.009 (1.42)	.009 (1.41)	.009 (1.38)	.008 (1.23)	.003 (39)	.01 (1.41)
Fourth wave	.03*** (4.12)	.03*** (4.40)	.03*** (3.96)	.03*** (3.53)	.02*** (3.20)	.03*** (4.00)	.02*** (3.55)	.02*** (3.96)	.03*** (4.12)	.02*** (3.89)	.02*** (3.24)	.03*** (4.13)
MENA	−.02** (−2.04)	−.02** (−2.56)	−.02** (−2.39)	−.02** (−2.59)	−.02** (−1.97)	−.02** (−2.40)	−.01** (−1.96)	−.02** (−2.31)	−.01** (−2.07)	−.01** (−2.12)	−.02** (−2.59)	−.02** (−2.20)
Sub-Saharan Africa	−.008** (−1.37)	−.007 (−1.4)	−.008 (−1.30)	−.008 (−1.32)	−.01* (−1.78)	−.008 (−1.40)	−.008* (−1.66)	−.01* (−1.89)	−.008 (−1.49)	−.008 (−1.42)	−.01** (−2.44)	−.009* (−1.66)
South Asia	−.007 (−.69)	−.01 (−1.36)	−.02** (−2.20)	−.02** (−2.39)	−.02* (−1.78)	−.02* (−1.87)	−.008 (−.90)	−.01 (−1.57)	−.01 (−1.62)	−.01* (−1.67)	−.03** (−2.23)	−.01 (−1.58)
N	2262	2422	2556	2572	1821	2572	2262	2422	2556	2572	1821	2572
R^2	.90	.90	.90	.90	.90	.90	.91	.91	.91	.91	.92	.91
Wald chi²	20802.06	22336.91	20510.24	20795.09	15550.73	20720.19	22655.84	22859.46	22650.94	23051.03	17007.49	22920.14

Note: Estimates are from two-staged least-squares regression with instrumental variables; unstandardized coefficients reported (z scores in parentheses) $*p < .01$, $**p < .05$, $***p < .001$; chi² figures are all significant at $p < .001$.

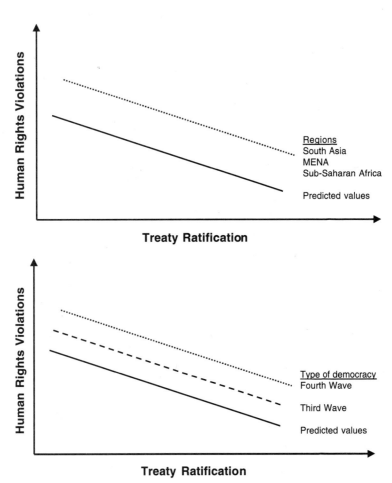

Figure 6.4. Stylized relationship between international human rights treaty ratification and human rights violations, controlling for regions and type of democracy.

regions and types of democracy. Figure 6.4 depicts this generalization graphically. On the left side of the figure, the solid line represents the overall relationship between norms and rights and the dotted line represents the relationship for the regions. On the right side of the figure, the solid line again represents the overall relationship between norms and rights, and the different dotted lines represent the relationship for third- and fourth-wave democracies. The figure shows that there is a significant "intercept shift" in the overall relationship between law and practice that has been captured by the inclusion of the regional and democracy dummy variables. Both within the regions and across third- and fourth-wave democracies, human rights practices have generally been worse, but both sets of countries still demonstrate a significant but limited effect of norms on rights.

The bivariate findings presented in this chapter differ little from the extant quantitative political science research on the effectiveness of the international human rights regime (Keith 1999; Hathaway 2002), although they have been obtained with the use of a broader set of rights measures and a longer time period. The multivariate results, however, do differ from these two studies, since they show consistent evidence for a limited but significant impact of human rights treaty participation on an improvement in human rights practice. Such an impact should not be overstated, however, since treaty participation itself has been modeled as a larger function of underlying processes of democratization, economic development, and global interdependence, the full theoretical and practical implications of which are the subject of the final chapter.

7

Protecting Human Rights

This study has been concerned with the mutual relationship between the norms of human rights specified by the international human rights regime, country participation in that regime, and the degree to which such participation makes a difference for human rights protection. It approached these areas of concern using empirical theories drawn from international law, international relations, and comparative politics. It showed that against certain sceptical corners within each of these three traditions, there has been a convergence of ideas around the notion of constrained agency at the domestic and international levels. Such constrained agency suggests that norms, ideas, and institutions limit the degree to which individuals and states can act. In this study these norms and institutions relate to human rights protection. Unlike the norms and institutions that constrain agency for inter-state relations around issues such as trade, environmental protection, and finance, human rights norms seek to constrain the agency of states, in order to prevent the violation of the human rights of their own citizens. Thus, the international human rights regime is a special type of regime that uses the mechanism of inter-state relations to govern the capacity of states to protect individual human dignity, formally codified as a set of rights. Human rights activists and scholars have long argued that the growth and proliferation of the human rights regime ought to make a difference for the *de facto* protection of human rights.

The analysis presented here was conducted against the backdrop of competing claims about the degree to which the international human rights regime can be effective in promoting and protecting human rights. On the one hand, popular commentary on the growth and proliferation of the regime since the Universal Declaration in 1948 suggests that great achievements have been made in terms of the expansion in the number of rights that have received express legal protection and the dramatic increase in the number of countries willing to make a formal commitment to the burgeoning body of human rights norms. On the other hand, sceptics have cautioned against any premature exhilaration over the growth and proliferation of the human rights regime. At a theoretical level, critics simply do not see how the mere articulation and codification of human rights norms at the international level will make any difference to states that are largely motivated by the pursuit of their own self-interest, especially since the enforcement mechanisms are still relatively weak. Empirically, such a claim is supported by the continued violation of human rights evident throughout the twentieth century (Watson 1999) and the selective support for human rights in the foreign policies of dominant powers, which are seen as a larger function of their geostrategic interests (Krasner 1997, 1999; Forsythe 2000; Ignatieff 2001).

An answer to the main question posed by this study can only really be provided by systematic comparative analysis. A number of single-case studies and small-*N* comparative studies have set important precedents for the ways in which human rights norms and discourse may have an impact on state practices. For example, as a "most likely" case for human rights research (Landman 2003, 215–18), Argentina has been the focus of many studies on the degree to which human rights norms affected the behavior of the military regime (1976–82). The separate studies of Guest (1990) and Weissbrodt and Bartolomei (1991) show that international efforts to challenge the military regime for its human rights abuses were limited because of the cold war machinations of the Reagan administration, the lack of consensus among key human rights actors, and strong allies within and outside Latin America. For Brysk (1994a, 2–3), domestic mobilization against the regime achieved substantive changes, including international delegitimation of the regime, the establishment of a government commission on disappearances, trials of the former military rulers and officers, new legislation to safeguard civil liberties, and the introduction of new social norms and institutions within civil society. In similar fashion, Hawkins (2002) uses the case of Chile to show the degree to which international and domestic pressure on Pinochet's regime led to concessions that ultimately opened the way for the 1988 plebiscite and subsequent democratic transition. Small-N studies have also achieved mixed results. For example, A. Brown's (2002) study of East Timor, Tiananmen Square, and the plight of Australia's indigenous people shows that dominant strategies adopted by the international human rights movement have resulted in selective and exclusionary activism that has left some groups receiving "too much" international attention (e.g., the protesters at Tiananmen Square), while leaving other groups marginalized on the "borders of suffering" (e.g., Australia's aborigines, and the East Timorese under the occupation of Indonesia). Foweraker and Landman (1997) compare social mobilization and the protection of citizenship rights within the liberalizing authoritarian cases of Franco's Spain, Pinochet's Chile, the one-party-dominant state of Mexico, and military Brazil. Their analysis shows that social movements have increasingly adopted the language of civil and political rights in their challenges against authoritarianism, which in the end produced differing degrees of democratic transformation across the four cases. Finally, Risse, Ropp, and Sikkink (1999, 17–35) use their eleven case studies to illustrate the ways in which linkages between domestic and international advocacy can achieve differing degrees of institutionalization of human rights norms through changes in domestic policy and state behavior.

The common theme running through all of these studies is the gap between rights in principle and rights in practice and how such a gap can be closed through international activism, domestic mobilization, or a combination of the two. Common also are the ways in which the international law of human rights provides the moral compass and normative language to challenge authoritarianism and oppression across different political contexts. In moving beyond single-case and small-N comparative studies, global comparative analysis also examines the gap between rights in principle and rights in practice by operationalizing the international human rights regime and human rights protection, and then testing the relationship between them with statistical techniques (Keith 1999; Hathaway 2002). As chapter 3 made clear, such analysis does not capture advocacy or domestic mobilization, nor is it capable of representing the type of elite negotiations at the domestic level that may or may not lead to concessions and a change in state behavior. Rather, the analysis focuses on global patterns of macrosocial variation by estimating the general relationship between international law and state practice, while controlling for other domestic and international factors.

This study adds to the findings of these earlier studies and contributes to our knowledge of the protection of human rights in several important ways. First, the study carried out a separate analysis by mapping and explaining both the international law of human rights and the protection of human rights *before* estimating the relationship between the two. Second, it included ratification variables that took into account the degree to which countries filed reservations upon making a formal commitment to human rights norms. Third, it extended the time-series and substantive coverage of human rights violations by using the latest versions of the Political Terror Scale and Hathaway's (2002) torture scale alongside the Freedom House scales on the protection of political and civil rights. Fourth, it specified a nonrecursive model of rights protection that takes into account time-series feedback loops between the international regime and rights protection, as well as for each of them separately. Fifth, it included consideration of global interdependence through the inclusion of IGOs and INGOs, as well as a measure of trade openness. Finally, it further differentiated the analysis through inclusion of regional dummy variables and dummy variables for old, third-wave, and fourth-wave democracies. These different dimensions of the study and their associated achievements are discussed in turn. This is then followed by a discussion of why the inferences that have been drawn in this study matter for the theory and practice of human rights.

The Findings

Separate consideration of the growth of the international human rights regime on the one hand and the global variation in human rights protection on the other revealed a number of important findings. The descriptive analysis in chapter 4 showed that the international regime for human rights has grown in breadth and depth, and the correlations showed that states ratifying one set of treaties have a greater tendency to ratify subsequent treaties. These general patterns were further differentiated across treaties, regions, and democracies. Participation of states is highest for the CRC, followed by CEDAW, CERD, ICESCR, ICCPR, CAT, and the two optional protocols. Regionally, the MENA countries, sub-Saharan Africa, and Southeast and South Asia have the lowest ratification scores, and the relatively low participation of the United States affected the comparative results for North America. Politically, the regression analysis showed that democracies are more likely to ratify human rights treaties, but further analysis showed that fourth-wave democracies ratify the most treaties with the least number of significant reservations, followed by third-wave and old democracies. In addition to the importance of democracy for treaty ratification, the regression analysis also showed no effects for conflict, mixed effects for IGOs and wealth, but consistent positive effects for INGOs, whether the unweighted or weighted versions of the ratification variables were used.

The descriptive analysis of the different measures of rights protection in chapter 5 showed that, depending on the collection of rights, time-series trends show general improvement in political rights and mixed results for civil rights protection and the use of torture. The country analysis showed similar sets of countries at the extreme ends of the global rank ordering. Iraq, Afghanistan, Iran, Somalia, and North Korea rank as the worst overall performers, and Canada and the United States, some small Caribbean countries, Europe, Australia, and New Zealand rank as the best performers (however, the United States features in only three of the five measures). Regionally, some of the worst performers are in the MENA region, sub-Saharan Africa, and South Asia. The correlations showed a reasonable consistency between all of the measures (especially between the Political Terror Scale and the torture scale), although the strongest interrelationships are, not surprisingly, within the two versions of the Freedom House and Political Terror scales. The regression analysis again confirmed that the level of democracy is an important explanatory variable for human rights protection, but that such protection among democracies is highest for old democracies, followed by third-wave and fourth-wave democracies. Among the old democracies, Colombia, Venezuela, and India stand out as outliers with respect to high levels of torture; among the third-wave democracies, Guatemala, the Philippines, and Brazil are outliers; and among the fourth-wave democracies the outliers include Haiti, Mozambique, Russia, and Bangladesh. The regression analysis showed further that wealth and IGO membership have consistent relationships with lower human rights violations, and civil war is consistently related to higher levels of violation.

Chapter 6 brought the two separate sets of analyses together by testing the relationship between the international human rights regime and the protection of human rights. The analysis used ratification of the ICCPR, CAT, and mean ratification across all of the treaties to represent the international human rights regime. The bivariate analysis confirmed a positive relationship between state participation in the international regime (ICCPR, CAT, and mean ratification) and greater protection of human rights (the five measures and the mean protection score). This overall relationship was shown to be different across the regions, especially in the MENA countries, sub-Saharan Africa, and South Asia. The multivariate analysis demonstrated a significant but limited effect between norms and rights, which was further differentiated as an "intercept shift" for the different regions and democracies. This limited effect was modeled as a function of the larger social processes of democratization, economic development, and global interdependence.

The inclusion of weighted versions of the ratification variables enriched the analysis, since it showed that later ratifiers and newer democracies tended to ratify more human rights treaties with fewer reservations than earlier ratifiers or older democracies. When coupled with worse human rights protection in later ratifiers and new democracies, this result meant that the overall relationship between norms and rights is weaker when reservations are taken into account. Statistically, the coefficients on balance were smaller and less significant between the weighted versions of the ratification variable and rights protection. Substantively, these results mean that despite the good intentions of the later ratifiers and newer democracies, much work at protecting human rights among these sets of countries needs to be done.

The greater time-series coverage and wider use of rights measures have helped make the analysis presented here more robust, since rights protection has been differentiated across those measures that include political rights and institutions for upholding those rights, personal integrity rights, and the specific use of torture. The demonstration of a consistent effect of international law on the protection of these rights strengthens to some degree the types of inferences that can be drawn. In this way, the analysis has built on the earlier achievements of the studies carried out by Keith (1999) and Hathaway (2002). Clearly, further differentiation of rights measures particularly for the protection of economic, social, and cultural rights can only strengthen our understanding of rights protection and its relation to the international regime.

Inclusion of time-series feedback loops has also advanced our understanding of the complex relationship between norms and rights. On the one hand, the lagged variables used in the separate analyses of the international regime (chapter 4) and rights protection (chapter 5) showed that there are important time-dependent effects of past ratification behavior on current ratification behavior and past rights protection on current rights protection. On the other hand, the nonrecursive modeling in chapter 6 showed that states do not necessarily engage in "anticipatory adaptation" by improving their rights practices before joining the regime, but that the balance of evidence suggests that treaty participation *precedes* an improvement in rights protection. Both sets of findings show that time itself is an important factor in the protection of human rights and that the proliferation of human rights norms may have a long-term impact on state practice.

Finally, the analysis presented here included consideration of interdependence in a way that has not been operationalized before in global comparative human rights research. The inspiration for the inclusion of IGOs, INGOs, and trade came primarily from the literature on globalization (e.g., Held et al., 1999; Boli and Thomas 1999), its effects on democracy (e.g., Li and Reuveny 2003), and the research testing the main propositions outlined in Kant's (1795) *Perpetual Peace* (e.g., Russett and O'Neal 2001). These fields in international relations and comparative politics have shown a growth in the number of IGOs and INGOs over the course of the twentieth century and the positive influences of IGOs and trade openness on democracy and inter-state peace. The results of this study add a further dimension to the consideration of global interdependence. Trade openness had mixed results for treaty ratification and rights protection. Larger numbers of INGOs are significantly related to greater degrees of treaty ratification, and higher levels of IGO membership are significantly related to greater protection of human rights. In either case, greater internationalization through growth in the number of IGOs and INGOs has mediated the relationships between norms and rights.

Theoretical and Practical Implications

Beyond the statistical results and the various findings of each of the chapters, the substantive inferences that can be drawn from the study have important implications for the theory and practice of human rights and inform larger debates within the fields of international law, international relations, and comparative politics. The results of the analysis here suggest that we ought to be cautiously optimistic about the tangible benefits of human rights norms proliferation. On the one hand, the statistical results show that the norms-rights relationship appears to be stronger than the rights-norms relationship, across different measures of treaty ratification and a variety of civil and political rights measures. A crude reading of these results would suggest that the international law of human rights "matters." On the other hand, the positive statistical results for ratification of the ICCPR and CAT and the mean ratification of all treaties are obtained in the presence of patterns of democratization, international interdependence, and wealth, while conflict, regional differentiation, and population size are controlled for. Moreover, the overall norms-rights relationship weakens significantly when reservations are taken into account.

Thus, the growth of the international human rights regime and the protection of human rights themselves complement larger social and political processes occurring in the world. Wealthy countries that are democratic and increasingly interdependent are more likely to ratify human rights treaties and more likely to protect civil and political rights. Such a reading suggests that larger social and political processes mediate the direct relationship between norms and rights. Increased levels of democratization, wealth, and global interdependence in terms of IGOs and INGOs have produced in some sense a "club" of nations that also participates in the international human rights regime. The regime thus complements these other processes, which have a significant bearing on rights protection. Keith (1999) and Hathaway (2002) have both shown that the existence of the regime alongside democracy, wealth, and other independent variables does not appear to have a significant impact on rights practices. However, the analysis presented here, which considers the regimes as a function of these factors as well as interdependence, shows that it does.

For the international law of human rights, it appears that norm proliferation as seen as a larger function of other sociopolitical processes in the postwar period is important for consolidating a set of norms and values first articulated formally in the 1948 Universal Declaration of Human Rights. It seems equally important, however, that the articulation of these norms and values through law must be complemented by political developments at the domestic and international levels. Democracy, wealth, interdependence, and conflict resolution are important factors in the consideration of the overall impact of the international law of human rights. It may be that such developments in international law simply mirror what is happening anyway, lending some credibility to the realist claim that international organizations, institutions, and law are merely epiphenomenal.

But the evidence presented here shows that states *do join* this particular regime, and those states that have ratified earlier treaties tend to continue to ratify subsequent human rights treaties. As of May 2003, a total of 89 states had ratified the 1998 Rome Statute, which universalizes criminal liability for genocide, crimes against humanity, war crimes, and crimes of aggression and gives authority to the International Criminal Court to prosecute offenders. Using the ratification data in this study as at the year 2000, the ratification of the Rome Statute by these 89 states is positively and significantly correlated with the ratification of all of the other human rights treaties, where the mean ratification score is .89 out of 1 for those who have ratified the Rome Statute and .60 for those who have not ($F = 46.55$, $p < .001$). Thus, the willingness of states to ratify treaties based on past behavior includes ratification of the Rome Statute, which arguably extends greater enforcement mechanisms over member states and limits their capacity to commit the most serious forms of human rights abuse with impunity.

Such willingness for states to ratify human rights treaties was shown to be higher for those countries with higher levels of democracy, and it is among the fourth-wave democracies where such willingness is the highest. For international relations theory, such evidence confirms the propositions found in liberal republicanism, which makes a direct link between the domestic regime type and international behavior with respect to the ratification of human rights treaties. New democracies uncertain of their future seek a greater degree of commitment to those international treaties that at least formally seek to limit the ways in which governments may behave toward their citizens. Moravcsik's (1997, 2000) findings for the European Convention for Human Rights can be generalized to include the international human rights treaties across the third- and fourth-wave democracies. Thus, this "liberal effect" on the international behavior of states ought to continue if more and more states become democratic, while with this democratic advance comes a greater protection of human rights.

Wealth, trade openness, and conflict do not have a significant impact on treaty ratification, but a larger number of INGOs does, suggesting some form of internationalization and interdependence through the proliferation of such organizations. For rights protection, however, greater wealth and IGO membership have a positive impact on rights protection, whereas civil war was shown to have a consistent negative impact. The positive and significant relationship between economic development and democracy (Rueschemeyer, Stephens, and Stephens 1992; Burkhart and Lewis-Beck 1994; Helliwell 1994; Przeworki et al. 2000; Landman 2003, 66–75) appears to be upheld for the protection of human rights (Mitchell and McCormick 1988; Poe and Tate 1994; Poe, Tate, and Keith 1999), where rights performance is indeed better for those countries that form part of the advanced industrial world (see also Foweraker and Landman 2004). IGO membership has been shown to reduce the probability of interstate conflict (Russett and O'Neal 2001, 157–96), and this study shows that such membership is associated with better rights protection. Although IGO membership does not appear to be related to the absence of civil war (see table 3.3), it does appear to help reduce the propensity for states to commit "state terror" against their citizens. Civil war itself, however, continues to have the most negative impact on rights protection.

The results of the study challenge in some degree the extreme versions of legal positivism and realism, while taking on board the main insights offered by empirical theories in comparative politics. The proliferation of human rights norms suggests a greater attention to a particular set of values that is receiving validation through the participation of an increasing number of states, but its overall effectiveness is mediated through international and domestic political considerations. In this way, "the legalization of politics has led primarily to the politicization of law" (Loughlin 2000, 233), where the mere presence of norms, rules, and codes at the international level is not enough without the development of democratic political institutions, interstate connections, and the capacity for states to realize in practice what they commit to in principle.

It is ultimately down to the individual states, which have the primary responsibility of protecting the rights of their citizens, and it is the presence of domestic political institutions that has the best chance of limiting state action that leads to the violation of human rights. The establishment of liberal democratic institutions provides the formal constraints on state action through vertical and horizontal mechanisms of accountability (O'Donnell 1999; Whitehead 2002) and informal constraints on state action, since the establishment of liberal democratic institutions shares a commitment to upholding the norms and values found in international human rights discourse. But it is liberal democracy and not hollow democracy that is essential for rights protection, where horizontal and vertical accountability are enshrined in constitutionalism and the rule of law, where rights abuses cannot take place with impunity. In addition, it appears that higher levels of wealth are associated with a lower level of human rights violations, evidence perhaps of the indirect connections between the greater overall fiscal capacity of states to provide for the protection of human rights and to distribute the benefits of development in order to satisfy rising expectations and demands within any society seeking to construct liberal democracy (Landman 2001c, 239).

But what do the results of this study mean for the human rights practitioner and what sorts of foreign and public policy recommendations flow from the general set of inferences about the growth and effectiveness of the international human rights regime? At a base level, the study shows that in contrast to opinions of some of its harshest critics, the development of the international human rights regime has not been in vain. International standard setting, advocacy, monitoring, and negotiation have produced a body of international law that seeks to uphold an important set of values to which an increasing number of states have formally committed themselves. Alongside economic development, increased organizational interdependence, democratization, and conflict resolution, the development of this body of law has provided an important discourse for improving the promotion and protection of human rights across a larger number of countries. The significant but limited effect of international human rights law suggests that much work has yet to be done, since the focused international advocacy on human rights must be accompanied by continued international work on the promotion of democracy, economic development, and greater internationalization of states.

To the extreme realists, who argue that the "real world is a realist world" and that it has been dominated by realist discourse for the "past seven centuries or more" (Mearsheimer 2001), human rights activists and advocates should find perhaps not a new discourse that *challenges* realism (see, e.g., Ruggie 1998; Wendt 1999), but one that argues that the promotion of democracy, the rule of law, and the protection of human rights at home and abroad are in the interests of the dominant powers both as an end in themselves as well as a means to achieving greater overall security and peace. Indeed, if we combine the results of this study with that on the democratic peace, it appears that greater democracy and interdependence are associated empirically with a reduction of human rights violations and a reduction in inter-state conflict. In analyzing 40,000 dyadic observations between 1885 and 1992, Russett and O'Neal (2001) show convincingly that democracy, inter-state commerce, and joint IGO membership significantly reduce the probability of inter-state conflict, *even after traditional realist explanatory factors, such as distance, power, and the formation of alliances, are controlled for.*

If realist discourse is indeed a self-fulfilling prophesy and a dominant discourse that has described and explained inter-state relations over the last seven or eight hundred years, then recasting realist arguments to include the promotion of democracy, the rule of law, and the protection of human rights may change the way states behave at the international level (i.e., less inter-state conflict), which in turn can inform arguments for the self-restraint of states at the domestic level (i.e., greater protection of human rights). The lessons are clear: the protection of human rights is not guaranteed by the single-minded pursuit of more international law; nor is it a hopeless prospect in the face of powerful states pursuing realist objectives. Rather, it is the result of concerted efforts across the arenas of democracy promotion, economic development, and multilateral governmental and nongovernmental associationalism that provide the best hope for improving overall levels of human dignity.

Appendix A

Coding Reservations

Analysis of the reservations to human rights treaties presented a complex task. Some of the existing measurements of human rights commitments (UNDP 1999; Keith 1999; Hathaway 2002) do not give proper weight to reservations, which can have a serious impact on the obligations of the ratifying country. However, merely painting a black-and-white picture by coding for the presence or absence of reservations could lead to possible biases due to overestimation of the impact of some reservations and underestimation of the impact of others. Certain reservations can have very little, if any, effect on the commitments of the reserving country, whereas others raise serious doubts about the intention of the reserving country to comply with the treaty at all. To permit a slightly more accurate assessment of the reservations, chapter 3 showed that a scoring system of 1–4 has been adopted. The highest score of 4 was given to countries that entered no reservation, and those that did have a reservation received a score of 1–3, depending on the content of the reservation. This method can at times appear insufficient, as it groups together reservations not always alike in their severity, but can nevertheless provide a certain necessary level of analysis that takes reservations into account when the commitments made by states are assessed. A number of sources have been used to form the basis for many of the decisions made in this assessment. These include the treaties themselves; the reservations and objections by other states (though these cannot be relied upon alone, since they are often inconsistent); the general comments, summary records, and concluding observations of the various treaty bodies; and certain publications (Cook 1990; Clarke 1991; Lijnzaad 1995; Schabas 1995a, 1995b, 1995c, 1997; Hodgkin and Newell 1998; Fottrell 2000; International Law Commission 2002).

The reservations were assessed according to the level of commitment to the treaty obligations the state displays. This is not necessarily equal to the questions often raised about the legal effect of a reservation, which center around issues of the validity of the reservations, whether the state might remain bound or not, and how this might affect inter-state relationships. The law of treaties and particularly all that relates to reservations become more complicated when applied to human rights treaties. In other fields of international law, treaties often appear to be a web of inter-state exchanges of mutual obligations (as described by the Human Rights Committee). Thus, a reservation by one country leading to an objection to this reservation by a second country can have an effect on the application of the treaty between these two states. The rules concerning reservations are closely linked to issues of reciprocity of obligations between states. When it comes to human rights treaties, the obligations are largely those of the state to individuals, and the inter-state reciprocity has less meaning. This may be one of the reasons why countries have lodged such a large number of reservations. The legal validity of reservations and their effect are therefore problematic in the case of human rights treaties, leading some commentators to speak of a need for revision or new developments to clarify the difficulties. The scores given in this study are not meant to solve the issues of validity and legal effect of the reservations, but rather are an attempt to reflect the commitment and intent of the state at the time of ratification of the treaty.

States may choose different titles for their comments when they ratify a treaty, such as "reservation," "declaration," "interpretive declaration," "interpretive statement," and "understanding." However, the title chosen does not necessarily reflect the content. Certain "declarations" can have significantly more adverse effects than certain other "reservations." All such terms have been reviewed for the assessments made in this study, and scores were given according to content, not title, based on whether the countries appear to attempt to exclude or modify their treaty obligations.

The assessment of reservations used three helpful concepts drawn from legal theory and the law of treaties, which include "object and purpose," "core obligation," and "nonderogatable" rights. Often the legal validity of a reservation is determined by the degree to which it is compatible with the object and purpose of the treaty itself, where extreme forms of incompatibility led to an assignment of a lowest score of 1. But it is not entirely clear how the object and purpose of a human rights treaty can be objectively determined across the treaties considered in this study. Whereas some treaties have a clear focus, such as the prohibition of torture, other treaties include a multitude of rights with little direct connection between them. Moreover, there is the view that the object and purpose of a human rights treaty can change over time. Thus, the notions of "core obligation" (i.e., identifying the fundamental content of the treaty) and "nonderogatable rights" add to the assessment of the object and purpose of the treaty and how a reservation would affect it. In addition to these three concepts, the principle of nondiscrimination was also used, such that reservations with discriminatory effects are likely to have received a low score.

Although the coding scheme has the same four basic categories, the assessment of reservations is relative to the particular treaty under consideration. The comparisons and evaluation are between states and their stated commitments to the content of each treaty, and are not comparisons of one treaty to another. Thus, even if the scoring may be slightly different for two separate treaties, the crucial fact is that within each treaty all countries party to it have undergone the same assessment procedure and are treated equally. The score is given to each country per year according to each treaty, but scores can change over the years as a result of a country withdrawing a reservation. It is based on the combined effect of reservations the country has with regard to the specific treaty, and not on the number of reservations (i.e., quality versus quantity). Its assignment is based on the most serious reservation of the country. Although a multitude of "light" reservations by one country does not equal one "heavy" reservation by another country, a combination of a few "heavy" reservations may push the country into the lowest score.

In addition, the potential adverse effect of the reservation is measured in terms of its depth (i.e., the level of modification or exclusion from the treaty obligation) and breadth (i.e., the proportion of people who stand to be affected). Certain reservations are formulated in vague language concerning a particular provision or how the country intends to implement its obligations overall. Although detailed and precise reservations may at first glance seem more serious, vague reservations may have the potential for the widest and most sweeping adverse effects. A state that formulates a reservation of this kind raises serious doubts and concerns about its commitment to the relevant obligations. These types of reservations are often the ones that mention the overriding authority of domestic or religious laws and that the treaty or provision will be subjected to these laws. Without entering the debate on cultural relativism, any sweeping and undefined subjugation of a treaty or provision to domestic laws undermines the concept and purpose of creating international human rights obligations. This type of reservation receives a low score in the assessment of commitment to the treaty. It should be noted that religious laws, such as Sharia, are considered for the purpose of this assessment in the same way as any domestic legislation. Finally, it is not considered a reservation if a state does not opt into further commitments, such as accepting competence of the treaty bodies associated with CAT and CERD to receive complaints; however, it is considered a reservation if a state opts out of a particular procedure within a treaty (such as the CAT committee's competence to conduct investigations). Further detailed clarifications of the coding per treaty are listed below.

CERD

1. There is tension between CERD hate speech and freedom of expression. There are different types of reservations: those that give predominance to freedom of expression based on their domestic law, or leave themselves the option to legislate according to need, have a score of 3; those that interpret it in accordance with other international human rights instruments can be considered a legitimate interpretive declaration, with a score of 4.
2. Reservations containing the sentence "Acceptance of the Convention by the Government of (. . .) does not imply the acceptance of obligations going beyond the constitutional limits nor the acceptance of any obligations to introduce judicial processes beyond those provided in the Constitution" or sentences of similar content attempt to remove outside scrutiny of compatibility and imply that obligations and commitments can change together with domestic law. These are the type of vague, sweeping reservations with a potential for undermining the whole treaty and are scored as 1.

ICCPR

1. As above, any reservation that may affect a whole right or the core of it receives a score of 2.
2. Reservations that could allow for violation of nonderogatable rights, particularly those accepted as customary international law (e.g., torture) or fundamental principles such as nondiscrimination, receive a score of 1.

CEDAW

1. A number of commentators have defined articles 2, 7, 9, 11, 15, and 16 as core articles, such that any reservation to them would be against the object and purpose of the treaty. Article 2 seems to carry extra weight, as it is a general article on discrimination. Any significant reservation to this article would therefore gain a score of 1. As for the others, as these have also been identified as possible object and purpose articles, a reservation completely nullifying the core of one of these would receive a score of 1, and a partial but significant reservation to these articles would receive a score of 2. A partial and very restricted reservation would receive a score of 3. Reservations to the whole of other articles receive a 2, and partial reservations to others receive a 3.
2. Statements giving predominance to religious (e.g., Sharia) laws or national legislation, depending on whether they refer to one full article or the whole treaty, receive a score of 2 or 1.

CAT

1. The object and purpose should be understood as more than the mere prohibition of torture, since that is already a rule of general international law. The object of CAT can also be understood as creating the grounds for the prosecution and extradition of offenders.
2. Opting out of procedures (committee investigation) is counted as a reservation (albeit an allowed one, but still a reservation that signifies less commitment to the content of the treaty) and receives a score 3. Not opting in (state and individual complaints) does not count as a reservation, since it involves no statement or action.

3. Subjecting the whole treaty or limiting fundamental elements, such as the definition of torture or cruel, inhuman, or degrading treatment or punishment, to religious or national legislation results in a score of 1. This is also the score for reservations that seek to limit the scope of responsibility (e.g., acquiescence in article 1 and superior orders in article 2).

CESCR

1. Although the treaty speaks of progressive implementation, it has been acknowledged by the Committee on Economic, Social, and Cultural Rights that such implementation takes time. But full implementation should be the ultimate goal, and states should take deliberate and concrete steps toward achieving it as swiftly as possible. Therefore, statements on the lack of resources can still be considered a reservation to obligations, if they could allow for stagnation and no clear progress toward the goal.
2. Reservations to a whole right or article receive a score of 2. Furthermore, within the rights there can be a core, as identified by the Committee, such as minimal health essentials. Reservations to core elements of the right receive a score of 2.
3. The principle of nondiscrimination is fundamental to the whole treaty and cannot be violated. Reservations subjecting the whole treaty or a number of articles, including article 2 and nondiscrimination, to national or religious laws receive a score of 1.

CRC

1. Key articles that have been mentioned as essential to the treaty are 2, 3, 6, and 12, which contain principles such as the best interests of the child and recognition of the child as a bearer of rights. Attempts to nullify or subject the whole treaty or these key principles to national or religious laws receive a score of 1.
2. Reservations to a whole other article or right, or to the core of a right, receive a score of 2.
3. Statements that seek to highlight the inadequacy of the treaty and offer a higher level of protection, such as those that take it upon themselves to raise the minimum age for military recruitment, are not treated as reservations.

Appendix **B**

IGOs and INGOs

The data analysis employed two measures of "organizational" inter-dependence. The first is the number of international governmental organizations (IGOs) of which each country is a member. The second is the number of international nongovernmental organizations (INGOs) with a registered office in each country. Both sets of numbers come from the Union of International Associations (UIA), which publishes statistical yearbooks with membership figures. In both cases, the analysis uses the total number of organizations across the different categories. Although the IGO data come from the UIA, Bruce Russet at Yale University kindly provided the tabulated figures by country. The INGO numbers were obtained from the UIA yearbooks and input into the data set by Gemma Mackman, a researcher at the University of Essex who worked on this study in 2003.

The data are provided at five-year intervals, so the missing observations were replaced with figures from a linear interpolation. For the INGO numbers, the data analysis used the logged transformation of the membership figures to reduce the amount of skewness in the distribution, which was not a problem for the IGO numbers. Figure B.1 shows histograms for the original distribution IGOs and INGOs. The distribution for the IGOs is quite normal (skewness = .49 and kurtosis = .35), whereas the distribution for INGOs is skewed with a long tail of a very few observations in which there are a large number of INGOs (skewness = 2.06 and kurtosis = 4.16). Figure B.2 shows histograms for IGOs and INGOs after the linear interpolation. The mean for each variable changes a little, but the

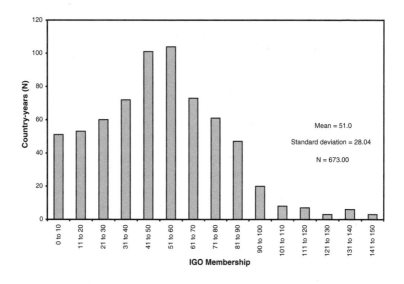

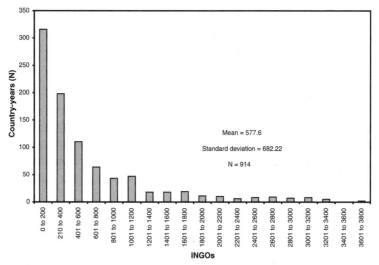

Figure B.1. Histogram for the raw figures on IGOs and INGOs by country and year.

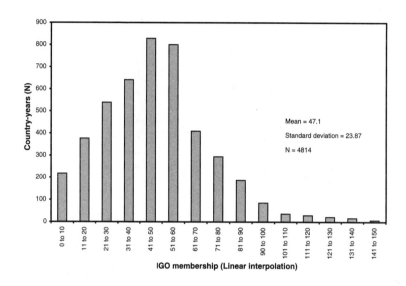

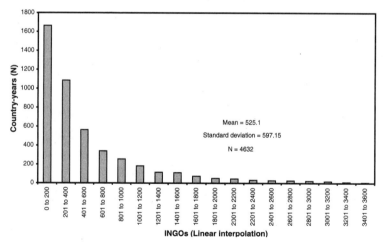

Figure B.2. Histogram for IGOs and INGOs by country and year, linear interpolation.

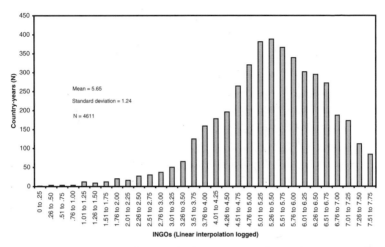

Figure B.3. Histogram for INGOs by country and year, linear interpolation and log transformation.

number of observations increases dramatically, and the standard deviation is reduced slightly. Again, it is clear that the distribution for INGOs is skewed (skewness = 2.09 and kurtosis = 4.71). Figure B.3 shows the histogram for the logged transformation of the INGO numbers after linear interpolation, where it is clear that the distribution is much more normal (skewness = −.60 and kurtosis = .68). Using these transformed versions of IGO and INGO figures does not change their basic properties but does make them more tractable for the analysis conducted in the study. Russett and O'Neal (2001) have used similar transformations for their IGO figures.

Notes

Chapter 1

1. By "certain collectivities," I refer to the various ways in which minority rights have become increasingly protected, for example, by the 1957 International Labour Organisation Convention No. 107 on the Protection of Indigenous and Other Tribal and Semi-Tribal Populations in Independent Countries, the 1989 ILO Convention No. 169 on Indigenous and Tribal peoples, and the 1992 UN Declaration on the Rights of Minorities (Philips 1997, viii–xiii). Such protection means that certain groups in society (typically nondominant and numerically small) have special protections against majority incursions in areas such as education, health, employment, language, and religion.

2. The classification of old democracy follows Lijphart (1999); third-wave democracy, Huntington (1991) and Przeworski et al. (2000); and fourth-wave democracy, Doorenspleet (2000, 2001). See table 4.10.

Chapter 2

1. Kennan (1951, 95–99) argues that international law rests on "the belief that it should be possible to suppress the chaotic and dangerous aspirations of governments in the international field by the acceptance of some system of legal rules and restraints . . . [and that such a] legalistic approach to international relations is faulty in its assumptions concerning the possibility of sanctions against offenses and violations." In similar fashion, Morgenthau (1958, 73) has an equal disdain for legalistic approaches to international relations whose "common denominator . . . is the substitution for the national interest of an assumed supranational standard of action" (see Henkin 1979, 322–23, 330).

2. In another example, Donnelly (1986, 625) argues that the hegemonic authority of the United States supported the creation of the inter-American regional system for the protection of human rights, with its relatively strong monitoring powers.

3. Henkin (1979, 93) goes so far as to say that "[m]uch of law, and the most successful part, is a codification of existing mores, of how people behave and they feel they ought to behave. To that extent law reflects rather than imposes, existing order. To say that nations act pursuant to law only as they would act anyhow may indicate not that law is irrelevant, but rather that it is sound and viable, reflecting the true interests and attitudes of nations, and that it is likely to be maintained."

4. In drawing on the two-level game, Ripsman (2002) shows that different degrees of executive autonomy in Britain, France, and the United States affect the ways in which they conducted foreign policy in the immediate postwar period.

5. In her study of IMF compliance, Simmons (2000, 833) adds a regional norm variable, which captures contiguous participation in IMF article VIII by countries from the same region.

6. Young (1992, 163) notes that in any analysis of regime effectiveness and compliance, "multivariate relationships will constitute the norm rather than the exception."

Chapter 3

1. Macintyre (1971, 1981) has argued that the contextual specificities of different nation-states and cultures preclude a "science of comparative politics" that can discover Hempelian "covering laws" and that human rights do not exist either as principles or objects of inquiry. Although Freeman (2001, 2002b, 76–100) is not sceptical of human rights themselves, he does see an unresolved tension between the positivist foundation of behavioral social science and the natural law origins of human rights.

2. The term "normative" is understood in two ways: (1) as legal norms that maintain a certain objectivity of law that is free from political and social construction or influence and (2) as moral and ethical norms in political theory, which inform larger statements about how political systems *ought* to be organized (see Glaser 1995; Steiner and Alston 1996, 50–52; Hutchings 1999).

3. In the field of political science, King, Keohane, and Verba (1994) have reiterated this sentiment more generally in providing strategies for reducing the presence of systematic error in any research project, while reporting and accepting the uncertainty of findings. This is also the case in the field of human rights violations–based analysis, where the most advanced techniques for analyzing large-scale gross violations of human rights include multiple

sources of data, which are then matched and used to estimate total numbers of violations and an associated margin of error (see ABA/AAAS 2000; Ball et al. 2003).

4. Measures that use scales to rank-order human rights performance of countries have a tendency to collapse information and lose important differences across cases, such that either those cases at the high end of a scale (i.e., heavy violators) or those cases at the low end of the scale (i.e., reasonable protectors) are all grouped together. In addition, some producers of human rights measures have not been altogether clear about either the source of information that is used or the ways in which scores are assigned to the information. For example, despite its wide use, Munck and Verkuilen (2002, 21) bemoan the lack of available information on how Freedom House uses its checklist to convert its base of information into its two seven-point scales of civil and political liberties. The solution for this study is to use multiple measures separately for all of the analyses, while comparing and cross-checking the results that are obtained.

5. I am grateful for the assistance of Noam Lubell, an international human rights lawyer and Ph.D. student in the Department of Law at the University of Essex. The legal research, judgments, and residual doubts were discussed further with Professor Sir Nigel Rodley, former UN Special Rapporteur on Torture and Member of the UN Human Rights Committee; Professor Françoise Hampson, member of the UN Sub-Commission on the Promotion and Protection of Human Rights; and Dr. Basak Cali.

Chapter 5

1. The official legal term for pulling out of an international treaty is "denunciation," and those treaties from which it is possible to withdraw have a specific clause to be invoked to do so. For example, Article 31 of the Convention against Torture and other Cruel, Inhuman, or Degrading Treatment or Punishment (CAT) states:

(a) A State Party may denounce this Convention by written notification to the Secretary-General of the United Nations. Denunciation becomes effective one year after the date of receipt of the notification by the Secretary-General.

(b) Such a denunciation shall not have the effect of releasing the State Party from its obligations under this Convention in regard to any act or omission which occurs prior to the date at which the denunciation becomes effective, nor shall denunciation prejudice in any way the continued consideration of any matter which is already under consideration by the Committee prior to the date at which the denunciation becomes effective.

(c) Following the date at which the denunciation of a State Party becomes effective, the Committee shall not commence consideration of any new matter regarding that State.

It is not common practice for states to denounce international human rights treaties, although Trinidad and Tobago denounced the First Optional Protocol to the International Covenant on Civil and Political Rights.

Bibliography

Abbott, K. W., R. O. Keohane, A. Moravscik, A. Slaughter, and D. Snidal. 2000. The concept of legalization, *International Organization* 54, no. 3:401–19.

Abbott, K. W., and D. Snidal. 2000. Hard and soft law in international governance, *International Organization* 54, no. 3:421–56.

Adcock, R., and D. Collier. 2001. Measurement validity: a shared standard for qualitative and quantitative research, *American Political Science Review* 95, no. 3:529–46.

Adler, E. 2002. Constructivism and international relations, in *Handbook of International Relations*, ed. W. Carlsnaes, T. Risse, and B. Simmons, pp. 95–118. London: Sage.

Almond, G., and G. Bingham Powell. 1966. *Comparative Politics: A Developmental Approach*. Boston: Little, Brown.

Alston, P. 2002. Resisting the merger and acquisition of human rights by trade law: a reply to Petersmann, *European Journal of International Law* 13, no. 4:815–44.

Alston, P., and Crawford, J., eds. 2000. *The Future of the UN Human Rights Treaty Monitoring*. Cambridge: Cambridge University Press.

American Bar Association (ABA). and the American Association for the Advancement of Science (AAAS). 2000. *Political Killings in Kosova/Kosovo, March-June 1999*. Washington, DC: American Bar Association.

Amnesty International. 1990. *Annual Report 1990*. London: Amnesty International, www.amnesty.org.

———. 2002. *Annual Report 2002*. London: Amnesty International, www.amnesty.org.

Apodaca, C., and M. Stohl. 1999. United States human rights policy and foreign assistance, *International Studies Quarterly* 43:185–98.

Apter, D. E. 1996. Comparative politics, old and new, in *The New Handbook of Political Science*, ed. R. E. Goodin and H. Klingemann, pp. 372–97. Oxford: Oxford University Press.

Arat, Z. F. 1991. *Democracy and Human Rights in Developing Countries*. Boulder, CO, and London: Lynne Rienner Publishers.

Austin, J. [1875] 1954. *Lectures on Jurisprudence or the Philosophy of Positive Law*, 5th ed. Robert Campbell, ed. London: John Murray.

Ball, P. 1994. *Who Did What to Whom? Planning and Implementing a Large Scale Human Rights Data Project*. Washington, DC: American Association for the Advancement of Science.

———. 2003. On the quantification of horror: field notes on statistical analysis of human rights violations. Unpublished book chapter. On file with University of Essex, Department of Government.

Ball, P. B., and J. Asher. 2002. Statistics and Slobodan: using data analysis and statistics in the war crimes tribunal of former president Milosevic, *Chance* 15, no. 4:15–24.

Ball, P. B., J. Asher, D. Sulmont, and D. Manrique. 2003. How many Peruvians have died? An estimate of the total number of victims killed or disappeared in the armed internal conflict between 1980 and 2000. Washington, DC: American Association for the Advancement of Science.

Ball, P., R. Cifuentes, J. Dueck, R. Gregory, D. Salcedo, and C. Saldarriaga. 1994. *A Definition of Database Design Standards for Human Rights Agencies*. Washington, DC: American Association for the Advancement of Science and Human Rights Information and Documentation Systems International.

Ball, P. B., P. Kobrak, and H. Spirer. 1999. *State Violence in Guatemala, 1960–1996: A Quantitative Reflection*. Washington, DC: American Association for the Advancement for Science.

Ball, P., H. Spirer, and L. Spirer. 2000. *Making the Case: Investigating Large Scale Human Rights Violations Using Information Systems and Data Analysis*. Washington, DC: American Association for the Advancement of Science.

Banks, A. S. 1994. *Cross-Polity Time-Series Data Archive*. Binghamton, NY: State University of New York at Binghamton.

Barbalet, J. M. 1988. *Citizenship: Rights, Struggle and Class Inequality*. Milton Keynes: Open University Press.

Barnett, M. N., and M. Finnemore. 1999. The politics, power, and pathologies of international organizations, *International Organization* 53, no. 4: 699–732.

Barsh, R. L. 1993. Measuring human rights: problems of methodology and purpose, *Human Rights Quarterly* 15, no. 1:87–121.

Bayefsky, A. F. 2001. *The UN Human Rights Treaty System: Universality at the Crossroads*. North York, Canada: York University Human Rights Project (www.yorku.ca/hrights).

Beck, N., and J. N. Katz. 1995. What to do and not to do. with time-series cross-section data, *American Political Science Review* 89, no. 3:634–47.

Beetham, D., S. Bracking, I. Kearton, and S. Weir. 2002. *International IDEA Handbook on Democracy Assessment.* The Hague: Kluwer Law International.

Beitz, C. R. 2001. Human rights as a common concern, *American Political Science Review* 95, no. 2:269–82.

Bell, D. 1960. *The End of Ideology: On the Exhaustion of Political Ideas in the 1950s.* New York: Free Press.

Berejekian, J. 1997. The gains debate: framing state choice, *American Political Science Review* 91, no. 4:789–805.

Berger, V. 1995. *Case Law of the European Court of Human Rights.* Dublin: Round Hall Press.

Bobbio, N. 1996. *The Age of Rights.* Cambridge, England: Polity Press.

Boli, J., T. A. Loya, and T. Loftin. 1999. National participation in world-polity organization, in *Constructing World Culture*, ed. J. Boli and G. Thomas, pp. 50–80. Stanford: Stanford University Press.

Boli, J., and G. Thomas, eds. 1999. *Constructing World Culture.* Stanford: Stanford University Press.

Bollen, K. A. 1992. Political rights and political liberties in nations: an evaluation of rights measures, 1950 to 1984, in *Human Rights and Statistics: Getting the Record Straight*, ed. T. B. Jabine and R. P. Claude, pp. 188–215. Philadelphia: University of Pennsylvania Press.

Boucher, D. 1998. *Political Theories of International Relations.* Oxford: Oxford University Press.

Boyle, K. 1995. Stock-taking on human rights: the World Conference on Human Rights, Vienna 1993, *Political Studies* 43:79–95.

Bratton, M., and N. van de Walle. 1997. *Democratic Experiments in Africa: Regime Transitions in Comparative Perspective.* Cambridge: Cambridge University Press.

Brito, A. B. de. 1997. *Human Rights and Democratization in Latin America: Uruguay and Chile.* Oxford: Oxford University Press.

Brohman, J. 1996. *Popular Development.* Oxford: Blackwell.

Bronkhorst, Daan 1995. *Truth and Reconciliation: Obstacles and Opportunities for Human Rights.* Amsterdam: Amnesty International Dutch Section.

Brown, A. 2002. *Human Rights and the Borders of Suffering: The Promotion of Human Rights in International Politics.* Manchester, England: Manchester University Press.

Brown, C. 2002. *Sovereignty, Rights and Justice: International Political Theory Today.* Cambridge, England: Polity Press.

Brownlie, I. 2003. *Principles of Public International Law*, 6th ed. Oxford: Oxford University Press.

Brysk, A. 1994a. *The Politics of Human Rights in Argentina: Protest, Change, and Democratization.* Stanford: Stanford University Press.

————. 1994b. The politics of measurement: the contested count of the disappeared in Argentina, *Human Rights Quarterly* 16:676–92.

Buergenthal, T. 1995. *International Human Rights in a Nutshell*. St. Paul, MN: West Publishing Co.

————. 1997. The normative and institutional evolution of international human rights, *Human Rights Quarterly* 19, no. 4:703–23.

Burkhart, R. E., and M. Lewis-Beck. 1994. Comparative democracy, the economic development thesis, *American Political Science Review* 88, no. 4: 903–10.

Buur, L. 2001. The South African Truth and Reconciliation Commission: the technique of nation-state formation, in *States of Imagination: Ethnographic Explorations of the Postcolonial State*, ed. Thomas Blom Hansen and Finn Stepputat, pp. 149–81. Durham, NC, and London: Duke University Press.

Calhoun, C., P. Price, and A. Timmer, eds. 2002. *Understanding September 11*. New York: The Free Press.

Cammack, P. 1997. *Capitalism and Democracy in the Third World: The Doctrine for Political Development*. London and Washington: Leicester University Press.

Campbell, D. T., and J. C. Stanley. 1963. *Experimental and Quasi-Experimental Designs for Research*. Chicago: Rand McNally.

Caprioli, M. 2000. Gendered conflict, *Journal of Peace Research* 37, no. 1:51–68.

Caprioli, M., and P. Trumbore. 2003. Ethnic discrimination and interstate violence: testing the international impact of domestic behavior, *Journal of Peace Research* 40, no. 1:5–23.

Carey, H. 2002. The Grotian eclectic and human rights: four recent books by Richard A. Falk, *Human Rights Quarterly* 24, no. 3:799–829.

Carleton, D., and M. Stohl. 1985. The foreign policy of human rights: rhetoric and reality from Jimmy Carter to Ronald Reagan, *Human Rights Quarterly* 7:205–29.

Carletta, J. 1996. Assessing agreement on classification tests: the Kappa statistic, *Computational Linguistics* 22:249–53.

Carlsnaes, W., T. Risse, and B. Simmons, eds. 2002. *Handbook of International Relations*. London: Sage.

Chapman, A. 1996. A "violations approach" for monitoring the International Covenant on Economic, Social, and Cultural Rights, *Human Rights Quarterly* 18, no. 1:23–66.

————. 1998. *Conceptualizing the Right to Health: A Violations Approach*. Washington, DC: AAAS, Science and Human Rights Program.

Chayes, A., and A. H. Chayes. 1993. On compliance. *International Organization* 47, no. 2:175–205.

Chilcote, R. H. 1994. *Theories of Comparative Politics: The Search for a Paradigm Reconsidered*, 2nd ed. Boulder, CO: Westview Press.

Churchill, R. R., and J. R. Young. 1992. Compliance with judgements of the European Court of Human Rights and the decisions of the Committee of

Ministers: the experience of the United Kingdom, 1975–1987, *British Yearbook of International Law* 63:283–345.

Cingranelli, D., and T. Pasquarello. 1985. Human rights practices and the distribution of U.S. foreign aid to Latin American countries, *American Journal of Political Science* 29:539–63.

Cingranelli, D. L., and D. L. Richards. 1999. Measuring the level, pattern, and sequence of government respect for physical integrity rights, *International Studies Quarterly*, 43: 407–417.

Cingranelli, D., and C. Tsai. 2002. Democracy, workers' rights and income inequality: a comparative cross-national analysis. Paper prepared for the 98th Annual Meeting of the American Political Science Association, Boston.

Cioffi-Revilla, C. 1998. *Politics and Uncertainty: Theory, Models, and Applications.* Cambridge: Cambridge University Press.

Clarke, B. 1991. The Vienna Convention Reservations Regime and the Convention on Discrimination Against Women, *American Journal of International Law* 85, no. 2:281–321.

Claude, R. P., ed. 1976a. *Comparative Human Rights.* Baltimore and London: Johns Hopkins University Press.

———. 1976b. The classical model of human rights development, in *Comparative Human Rights*, ed. R. P. Claude. Baltimore and London: Johns Hopkins University Press.

Claude, R. P., and T. B. Jabine. 1992. Exploring human rights issues with statistics, in *Human Rights and Statistics: Getting the Record Straight*, ed. T. B. Jabine and R. P. Claude, pp. 5–34. Philadelphia: University of Pennsylvania Press.

Claude, R. P., and B. H. Weston. 1989. International human rights: overviews, in *Human Rights in the World Community: Issues and Action*, ed. R. P. Claude and B. H. Weston, pp. 2–12. Philadelphia: University of Pennsylvania Press.

Cochran, M. 1999. *Normative Theory in International Relations.* Cambridge: Cambridge University Press.

Cohen, Y. 1987. Democracy from above: the origins of military dictatorship in Brazil, *World Politics* 30–54.

———. 1994. *Radicals, Reformers, and Reactionaries: The Prisoner's Dilemma and the Collapse of Democracy in Latin America.* Chicago: University of Chicago Press.

Collier, D., ed. 1979. *The New Authoritarianism in Latin America.* Princeton: Princeton University Press.

———. 1991. New perspectives on the comparative method, in *Comparative Political Dynamics: Global Research Perspectives*, ed. D. A. Rustow and K. P. Erickson, pp. 7–31. New York: HarperCollins.

———. 1993. The comparative method, in *Political Science: The State of the Discipline*, ed. A. Finifter. Washington, DC: American Political Science Association.

————. 1995. Translating quantitative methods for qualitative researchers: the case of selection bias, *American Political Science Review* 89 (June):461–66.

Collier, D., and R. B. Collier. 1991. *Shaping the Political Arena: Critical Junctures, the Labor Movement, and Regimes Dynamics.* Princeton: Princeton University Press.

Colomer, J. M. 2000. *Strategic Transitions: Game Theory and Democratization.* Baltimore: Johns Hopkins University Press.

Colomer, J. M., and M. Pascual. 1994. The Polish games of transition, *Communist and Post-Communist Studies* 27, no. 3:275–94.

Comisión para el Easclarecimiento Histórico (CEH). 1999. *Guatamala Memoria del Silencio: Informe de la Comisión para el Easclarecimiento Histórico, Tomo I.* New York: UNOPS.

CONADEP. 1984. *Nunca Más Argentina: Informe Sobre la Desaparición Forzada de Personas.* Buenos Aires: CONADEP.

Cook, R. 1990. Reservations to the Convention on the Elimination of all Forms of Discrimination Against Women, *Virginia Journal of International Law* 30:643.

Council of Europe. http://conventions.coe.int.

Couvalis, G. 1997. *The Philosophy of Science: Science and Objectivity.* London: Sage.

Cox, D. R., and D. Oakes. 1984. *Analysis of Survival Data.* London: Chapman and Hall.

Crabb, Cecil V., Jr. 1982. *Doctrines of American Foreign Policy: Their Meaning, Role, and Future.* Baton Rouge: Louisiana State University Press.

Czempiel, E. O. 1992. Governance and democratization, in *Governance without Government: Order and Change in World Politics*, ed. J. Rosenau. Cambridge: Cambridge University Press.

Dassin, J. 1986. *Torture in Brazil.* New York: Vintage Books.

Davenport, C. 1995. Multi-dimensional threat perception and state repression, *American Journal of Political Science* 39, no. 3:683–713.

————. 1996. Constitutional promises and repressive reality, *Journal of Politics* 58, no. 3:627–54.

————. 1999. Human rights and the democratic proposition, *Journal of Conflict Resolution* 43, no. 1:92–116.

Davenport, C., and D. Armstrong. 2002. *Democracies Love Me, They Love Me Not: Exploring the Relationship between Human Rights and Democracy in the Third Wave.* College Park, MD: Center for International Development and Conflict Management, University of Maryland.

Davidson, S. 1993. *Human Rights.* Buckingham, England: Open University Press.

De Brito, Alexandra Barahona. 1997. *Human Rights and Democratization in Latin America: Uruguay and Chile.* Oxford: Oxford University Press.

de Meur, G., and D. Berg-Schlosser. 1994. Comparing political systems: establishing similarities and dissimilarities, *European Journal of Political Research* 26:193–219.

Dessler, D. 1991. Beyond correlations: towards a causal theory of war, *International Studies Quarterly* 3, no. 35:337–55.

Diamond, L. 1999. *Developing Democracy: Toward Consolidation.* Baltimore: Johns Hopkins University Press.

Di Maggio, P., and W. W. Powell. 1983. The iron cage revisited: institutional isomorphism and collective rationality in organizational fields, *American Sociological Review* 48 (April):147–60.

Dinges, J. 2004. *The Condor Years: How Pinochet and His Allies Brought Terrorism to Three Continents.* New York: The New Press.

Dixon, W., and B. Moon. 1986. Military burden and basic human rights needs, *Journal of Conflict Resolution* 30, no. 4:660–83.

Dogan, M., and D. Pelassy. 1990. *How to Compare Nations: Strategies in Comparative Politics,* 2nd ed. Chatham, NJ: Chatham House.

Donnelly, J. 1986. International human rights: a regime analysis, *International Organisation* 40:599–642.

———. 1989. *Universal Human Rights in Theory and Practice.* Ithaca and London: Cornell University Press.

———. 1998. *International Human Rights.* Boulder, CO: Westview.

———. 1999. Democracy, development, and human rights, *Human Rights Quarterly* 21, no. 3:608–32.

———. 2000. *Realism and International Relations.* Cambridge: Cambridge University Press.

Donnelly, J., and R. Howard. 1988. Assessing national human rights performance: a theoretical framework, *Human Rights Quarterly* 10:214–48.

Doorenspleet, R. 2000. Reassessing the three waves of democratization, *World Politics* 52, no. 3:384–406.

———. 2001. The fourth wave of democratization: identification and explanation. Ph.D. thesis, University of Leiden.

Dorussen, H. 1999. Balance of power revisited: a multi-country model of trade and conflict, *Journal of Peace Research* 36, no. 4:443–62.

Douzinas, C. 2000. *The End of Human Rights: Critical Legal Thought at the Turn of the Century.* Oxford: Hart Publishing.

Dowding, K., and M. Van Hees. 2003. The construction of rights, *American Political Science Review* 97, no. 2:281–93.

Downs, G. W., D. M. Rocke, and P. N. Barsoom. 1998. Managing the evolution of cooperation, *International Organization* 52, no. 2:397–419.

Doyle, M. W., and N. Sambanis. 2000. International peacebuilding: a theoretical and quantitative analysis, *American Political Science Review* 94, no. 4:779–801.

Dueck, J. 1992. HURIDOCS standard formats as a tool in the documentation of human rights violations, in *Human Rights and Statistics: Getting the Record Straight,* ed. T. B. Jabine and R. P. Claude, pp. 127–58. Philadelphia: University of Pennsylvania Press.

Dunne, T., and N. J. Wheeler. 1999. *Human Rights in Global Politics.* Cambridge: Cambridge University Press.

Duvall, R., and M. Shamir. 1980. Indicators from errors: cross-national, time serial measures of the repressive disposition of government, in *Indicator Systems for Political, Economic, and Social Analysis*, ed. Charles Lewis Taylor. Cambridge, MA: Oelgeschlager, Gunn, and Hain, Publishers, Inc.

Dworkin, R. 2002. The threat to patriotism, in *Understanding September 11*, ed. C. Calhoun, P. Price, and A. Timmer, pp. 273–84. New York: The Free Press.

Eckstein, H. 1975. Case-study and theory in political science, in *Handbook of Political Science, Vol. 7: Strategies of Inquiry*, ed. F. I. Greenstein and N. S. Polsby, pp. 79–137. Reading, MA: Addison-Wesley.

Ersson, J., and E. Lane. 1996. Democracy and development: a statistical exploration, in *Democracy and Development: Theory and Practice*, ed. A. Leftwich. Cambridge, England: Polity Press.

Esty, D. C., J. Goldstone, T. R. Gurr, B. Harff, P. T. Surko, A. N. Unger, and R. Chen. 1998. The state failure project: early warning research for US foreign policy planning, in *Preventive Measures: Building Risk Assessment and Crisis Early Warning Systems*, ed. J. L. Davies and T. R. Gurr. Boulder, CO, and Totowa, NJ: Rowman and Littlefield.

Etzioni, A. 2001. *Political Unification Revisited: On Building Supranational Communities*. Lanham, MD: Lexington Books.

Evans, P. B., H. K. Jacobson, and R. D. Putnam, eds. 1993. *Double-Edged Diplomacy: International Bargaining and Domestic Politics*, pp. 330–62. Los Angeles: University of California Press.

Falk, R. 1989. Theoretical foundations of human rights, in *Human Rights in the World Community: Issues and Action*, ed. R. P. Claude and B. H. Weston, pp. 29–41. Philadelphia: University of Pennsylvania Press.

———. 2000. *Human Rights Horizons*. London: Routledge.

Faure, A. M. 1994. Some methodological problems in comparative politics, *Journal of Theoretical Politics* 6, no. 3:307–22.

Fearon, J., and A. Wendt. 2002. Rationalism v. constructivism: a skeptical view, in *Handbook of International Relations*, ed. W. Carlsnaes, T. Risse, and B. Simmons, pp. 52–72. London: Sage.

Fein, H. 1995. More murder in the middle: life-integrity violations and democracy in the world, *Human Rights Quarterly* 17, no. 1:170–91.

Finer, S. 1997. *The History of Government*. Oxford: Oxford University Press.

Finkel, S. E. 1995. *Causal Analysis with Panel Data*. London: Sage.

Finnemore, M., and Sikkink, K. 1998. International norm dynamics and political change, *International Organization* 52, no. 4:887–917.

Flyvberg, B. 2001. *Making Social Science Matter*. Cambridge: Cambridge University Press.

Forde, S. 1992. Classical realism, in *Traditions of International Ethics*, ed. T. Nardin and D. Mapel, pp. 62–84. Cambridge: Cambridge University Press.

Forsyth, M. 1992. The tradition of international law, in *Traditions of International Ethics*, ed. T. Nardin and D. Mapel, pp. 23–41. Cambridge: Cambridge University Press.

Forsythe, D. 1998. Human rights fifty years after the Universal Declaration, *PS: Political Science and Politics* 31, no. 3:507–11.

———. 2000. *Human Rights in International Relations*. Cambridge: Cambridge University Press.

Fottrell, D. 2000. *Revisiting Children's Rights: 10 Years of the Convention on the Rights of the Child*. The Hague: Kluwer.

Foweraker, J. 1995. *Theorizing Social Movements*. London: Pluto.

———. 1998. Institutional design, party systems and governability: differentiating the presidential regimes of Latin America, *British Journal of Political Science* 28:651–76.

Foweraker, J., and R. Krznaric. 2000. Measuring liberal democratic performance: a conceptual and empirical critique, *Political Studies* 45, no. 3: 759–87.

———. 2003. Differentiating the democratic performance of the west, *European Journal of Political Research* 42, no. 3:313–40.

Foweraker, J., and T. Landman. 1997. *Citizenship Rights and Social Movements: A Comparative and Statistical Analysis*. Oxford: Oxford University Press.

———. 1999. Individual rights and social movements: a comparative and statistical inquiry, *British Journal of Political Science* 29 (April):291–322.

———. 2002. Constitutional design and democratic performance, *Democratization* 9, no. 2:43–66.

———. 2004. Economic development and democracy revisited: why dependency theory is not yet dead, *Democratization* 11, no. 1:1–21.

Foweraker, J., T. Landman, and N. Harvey. 2003. *Governing Latin America*. Cambridge, England: Polity Press.

Fox, G. H., and B. R. Roth. 2000a. Introduction: the spread of liberal democracy and its implications for international law, in *Democratic Governance and International Law*, ed. G. H. Fox and B. R. Roth, pp. 1–24. Cambridge: Cambridge University Press.

———, eds. 2000b. *Democratic Governance and International Law*. Cambridge: Cambridge University Press.

Fox, J. 1997. *Applied Regression Analysis, Linear Models, and Related Methods*. Thousand Oaks, CA, and London: Sage Publications.

Freeman, M. 2001. Is a political science of human rights possible? *The Netherlands Quarterly of Human Rights* 19, no. 2:121–37.

———. 2002a. Anthropology and the democratisation of human rights, *The International Journal of Human Rights* 6, no. 3:37–54.

———. 2002b. *Human Rights: An Interdisciplinary Approach*. Cambridge, England: Polity.

Frost, Mervyn. 1996. *Ethics in International Relations: A Constitutive Theory*. Cambridge: Cambridge University Press.

Fukuyama, F. 1992. *The End of History and the Last Man.* Harmondsworth, England: Penguin.

Gartner, S., and P. Regan. 1996. Threat and repression, *Journal of Peace Research* 33, no. 3:273.

Gastil, R. D. 1980. *Freedom in the World: Political Rights and Civil Liberties.* Westport, CT: Greenwood Press.

———. 1987. *Freedom in the World: Political and Civil Liberties, 1986–1987.* New York: Freedom House.

———. 1989. *Freedom in the World: Political and Civil Liberties, 1988–1989.* New York: Freedom House.

———. 1990. The comparative survey of freedom: experiences and suggestions, *Studies in Comparative International Development* 25:25–50.

Gautier, D. 1986. *Morals by Agreement.* Oxford: Oxford University Press.

Geddes, B. 1990. How the cases you choose affect the answers you get: selection bias in comparative politics, *Political Analysis* 2:131–50.

Gelpi, C. F., and M. Griesdorf. 2001. Winners or losers? Democracies in international crisis, 1918–94, *American Political Science Review* 95, no. 3: 633–48.

Gibney, M., and M. Dalton. 1996. The political terror scale, in *Human Rights and Developing Countries*, ed. D. L. Cingranelli, pp. 73–84. Greenwich, CT: JAI Press.

Gibney, M., M. Dalton, and M. Vockell. 1992. U.S.A. refugee policy: a human rights analysis update, *Journal of Refugee Studies* 5, no. 1:37–46.

Gibney, M., and M. Stohl. 1988. Human rights and U.S. refugee policy, in *Open Borders? Closed Societies? The Ethical and Political Issues*, ed. M. Gibney. New York: Greenwood Press.

Giffard, C. 2002. *Torture Reporting Handbook.* Colchester, England: Human Rights Centre, University of Essex.

Glaser, C. L. 1994–1995. Realists as optimists: cooperation as self-help, *International Security* 19, no. 3:50–90.

Glaser, D. 1995. Normative theory, in *Theories and Methods in Political Science*, ed. D. Marsh and G. Stoker, pp. 21–41. London: Macmillan.

Goldstein, J., M. Kahler, R. O. Keohane, and A. Slaughter. 2000. Introduction: legalization and world politics, *International Organization* 54, no. 3: 385–99.

Goodman, R. 2002. Human rights treaties, invalid reservations, and state consent, *American Journal of International Law* 96, no. 3:531–60.

Gordon, S. 1991. *The History and Philosophy of Social Science.* London: Routledge.

Green, M. 2001. What we talk about when we talk about indicators: current approaches to human rights measurement, *Human Rights Quarterly* 23: 1062–97.

Guest, Iain. 1990. *Behind the Disappearances: Argentina's Dirty War Against Human Rights and the United Nations.* Philadelphia: University of Pennsylvania Press.

Gujarati, D. N. 1988. *Basic Econometrics*, 2nd ed. London: McGraw-Hill.

Gurr, T. R. 1968. A causal model of civil strife, *American Political Science Review* 62:1104–24.

————. 1993. Why minorities rebel: a cross national analysis of communal mobilization and conflict since 1945, *International Political Science Review* 14, no. 2:161–201.

Haggard, S., M. A. Levy, A. Moravscik, and K. Niolaides. 1993. Integrating the two halves of Europe: theories of interests, bargaining and institutions, in *After the Cold War: International Institutions and State Strategies in Europe, 1989–1991*, ed. R. O. Keohane, J. Nye, and S. Hoffman, p. 182. Cambridge: Harvard University Press.

Hague, R., M. Harrop, and S. Breslin. 1992. *Political Science: A Comparative Introduction*. New York: St. Martin's Press.

Hall, J. A. 1996. *International Orders*. Cambridge, England: Polity Press.

Hansclever, A., P. Mayer, and V. Rottberger. 1997. *Theories of International Regimes*. Cambridge: Cambridge University Press.

Harris, D. 1998. Regional protection of human rights: the inter-American achievement, in *The Inter-American System of Human Rights*, ed. D. Harris and S. Livingstone, pp. 1–29. Oxford: Oxford University Press.

Harris, D., and S. Livingstone, eds. 1998. *The Inter-American System of Human Rights*. Oxford: Oxford University Press.

Hart, H. L. A. 1961. *The Concept of Law*. Oxford: Clarendon Press.

Hathaway, O. 2002. Do treaties make a difference? Human rights treaties and the problem of compliance, *Yale Law Journal* 111:1932–2042.

Hawkins, D. 2002. *International Human Rights and Authoritarian Rule in Chile*. Lincoln: University of Nebraska Press.

Hay, C. 1995. Structure and agency, in *Theories and Methods in Political Science*, ed. D. Marsh and G. Stoker, pp. 189–206. London: Macmillan.

————. 2002. *Political Analysis*. London: Palgrave.

Hayner, P. B. 1994. Fifteen Truth Commissions—1974–1994: A comparative study, *Human Rights Quarterly* 16:597–655.

————. 2002. *Unspeakable Truths: Facing the Challenge of Truth Commissions*. London: Routledge.

Held, D., A. McGrew, D. Goldblatt, and J. Perraton. 1999. *Global Transformations: Politics, Economics and Culture*. Cambridge, England: Polity Press.

————. 1990. *The Age of Rights*. New York: Columbia University Press.

Helliwell, J. F. 1994. Empirical linkages between democracy and economic growth, *British Journal of Political Science* 24:225–48.

Henderson, C. 1991. Conditions affecting the use of political repression, *Journal of Conflict Resolution* 35, no. 1:120–42.

————. 1993. Population pressures and political repression, *Social Science Quarterly* 74:322–33.

Henkin, L. 1979. *How Nations Behave: Law and Foreign Policy*. New York: Columbia University Press.

Hershberg, E., and K. W. Moore, eds. 2002. *Critical Views of September 11: Analyses from Around the World.* New York: The Free Press.

Higgins, R. 1968. Policy considerations and the international judicial process, *International and Comparative Law Quarterly* 17.

———. 1994. *Problems and Process: International Law and How We Use It.* Oxford: Oxford University Press.

Hobbes, T. 1651/1985. *Leviathan.* London: Penguin.

Hofrenning, D. J. B. 1990. Human rights and foreign aid: a comparison of the Reagan and Carter administrations, *American Political Quarterly* 18.

Hodgkin, R., and P. Newell. 1998. *Implementation Handbook for the Convention on the Rights of the Child.* New York: UNICEF.

Hollis, M. and S. Smith. 1990. *Understanding and Explaining International Relations.* Oxford: Clarendon Press.

Hoothe, L., and G. Marks. 2003. Unraveling the central state, but how? Types of multilevel governance, *American Political Science Review* 97, no. 2: 233–43.

Hosmer, D. W., Jr., and S. Lemeshow. 1999. *Applied Survival Analysis: Regression Modelling of Time to Event Data.* New York: John Wiley and Sons.

Hougaard, P. 2000. *Analysis of Multivariate Survival Data.* New York: Springer.

Humana, C. 1987. *World Human Rights Guide.* London: Pan Books.

———. 1992. *World Human Rights Guide.* Oxford: Oxford University Press.

Hunt, P. 1996. *Reclaiming Social Rights: International and Comparative Perspectives.* Aldershot, England: Dartmouth.

Huntington, S. P. 1991. *The Third Wave: Democratization in the Late Twentieth Century.* Norman: University of Oklahoma Press.

Huntington, S. P. 1996. *The Clash of Civilizations and the Remaking of the World Order.* New York: Simon and Schuster.

Hurrell, A. 2002. Norms and ethics in international relations, in *Handbook of International Relations*, ed. W. Carlsnaes, T. Risse, and B. Simmons. London: Sage.

Hutchings, K. 1999. *International Political Theory.* London: Sage, 137–54.

Ignatieff, M. 2001. *Human Rights as Politics and Idolatry.* Princeton, NJ: Princeton University Press.

Inglehart, R. 1997. *Modernization and Postmodernization.* Princeton, NJ: Princeton University Press.

Innes, J. E. 1992. Human rights reporting as a policy tool: an examination of the State Department country reports, in *Human Rights and Statistics: Getting the Record Straight*, ed. T. B. Jabine and R. P. Claude, pp. 235–57. Philadelphia: University of Pennsylvania Press.

International Law Commission. 2002. Reservations to treaties, in *Report of the International Law Commission*, 54th Session, 2002, A/57/10. New York.

Jackson, R. 2000. *The Global Covenant: Human Conduct in a World of States.* Oxford: Oxford University Press.

Jaggers, K., and T. R. Gurr. 1995. Tracking democracy's third wave with the Polity III data, *Journal of Peace Research* 32, no. 4:469–82.

Jones, M. P. 1995. *Electoral Laws and the Survival of Presidential Democracies*. Notre Dame, IN: University of Notre Dame Press.

Kant, I. 1795. *The Perpetual Peace and Other Essays on Politics, History, and Morals*, trans. T. Humphrey. Indianapolis and Cambridge: Hackett Publishing.

Katznelson, I. 1997. Structure and configuration in comparative politics, in *Comparative Politics: Rationality, Culture, and Structure*, ed. M. Lichbach and A. Zuckerman, pp. 81–112. Cambridge: Cambridge University Press.

Kaufmann, C. D., and R. A. Pape. 1999. Explaining costly international moral action: Britain's sixty-year campaign against the Atlantic slave trade, *International Organization* 53, no. 4:631–68.

Kaufmann, D., A. Kraay, and P. Zoido-Lobaton. 1999a. Aggregating governance indicators. Policy Research Working Paper No. 2195. Washington, DC: World Bank.

———. 1999b. Governance matters. Policy Research Working Paper No. 2196. Washington, DC: World Bank

———. 2000. Governance matters: from measurement to action. *Finance and Development* 37, no. 2. Washington, DC: International Monetary Fund.

———. 2002. Governance matters II: updated indicators for 2000–01. Policy Research Working Paper No. 2772. Washington, DC: World Bank.

Keck, M., and K. Sikkink. 1998. *Activists Beyond Borders: Advocacy Networks in International Politics*. Ithaca: Cornell University Press.

Keith, L. C. 1999. The United Nations International Covenant on Civil and Political Rights: does it make a difference in human rights behavior? *Journal of Peace Research* 36, no. 1:95–118.

Kelsen, H. 1949. *General Theory of Law and the State*. New York: Russell and Russell.

———. 1961. *General Theory of Law and State*, trans. A. Wedberg. New York: Russell and Russell.

Kennan, G. F. 1951. *American Diplomacy*. Chicago: University of Chicago Press.

Kennedy, D. 2000. My talk at the ASIL: what is new thinking in international law? *American Society of International Law* 94:104–25.

———. 2001. The forgotten politics of international governance, *European Human Rights Law Review* 2:117–25.

Kennedy, P. 1989. *A Guide to Econometrics*. Cambridge, MA: MIT Press.

Keohane, R. 1984. *After Hegemony: Cooperation and Discord in World Political Economy*. Princeton, NJ: Princeton University Press.

Keohane, R. O. 2001. Governance in a partially globalized world, *American Political Science Review* 951, no. 1:1–13.

———. 2002. *Governance in a Partially Globalized World*. London: Routledge.

King, G., R. O. Keohane, and S. Verba. 1994. *Designing Social Inquiry: Scientific Inference in Qualitative Research*. Princeton, NJ: Princeton University Press.

Klug, F., K. Starmer, and S. Weir. 1996. *The Three Pillars of Liberty: Political Rights and Freedom in the United Kingdom.* London: Routledge.

Knack, S. 2002. Governance and growth: measurement and evidence. Paper prepared for the Forum Series on the Role of Institutions in Promoting Growth, IRIS Center and USAID, Washington, DC, February 2002.

Koh, H. H. 1997. Review essay: why do nations obey international law? *Yale Law Journal* 106:2598–2659.

Kohli, A., P. Evans, P. J. Katzenstein, A. Przeworski, S. H. Rudolph, J. C. Scott, and T. Skocpol. 1995. The role of theory in comparative politics: a symposium, *World Politics* 48:1–49.

Kornbluh, P. 2003. *The Pinochet File: A Declassified Dossier of Atrocity and Accountability.* New York and London: The New Press.

Krain, M. 1997. State-sponsored mass murder: the onset and severity of genocides and politicides, *Journal of Conflict Resolution* 41, no. 3:331–60.

Krasner, S., ed. 1983a. *International Regimes.* Ithaca and London: Cornell University Press.

———. 1983b. Structural causes and regime consequences: regimes as intervening variables, in *International Regimes*, ed. S. Krasner, pp. 1–22. Ithaca and London: Cornell University Press.

———. 1983c. Regimes and the limits of realism: regimes as autonomous variables, in *International Regimes*, ed. S. Krasner, pp. 355–68. Ithaca and London: Cornell University Press.

Krasner, S. D. 1997. Sovereignty, regimes, and human rights, in *Regime Theory and International Relations*, ed. V. Rittberger, pp. 139–67. Oxford: Clarendon Press.

———. 1999. *Sovereignty: Organized Hypocrisy.* Princeton, NJ: Princeton University Press.

Landman, T. 1999. Economic development and democracy: the view from Latin America, *Political Studies* 47, no. 4:607–26.

———. 2000. *Issues and Methods in Comparative Politics: An Introduction.* London: Routledge.

———. 2001a. Measuring the international human rights regime. Paper presented at the 97th Annual Meeting of the American Political Science Association, San Francisco.

———. 2001b. Measuring human rights and the impact of human rights policy. Paper presented at the EU Conference on Human Rights Impact Assessment, Brussels, November.

———. 2001c. The economic requirements of democracy, in *Encyclopedia of Democratic Thought*, ed. P. B. Clarke and J. Foweraker. London: Routledge.

———. 2002a. The evolution of the international human rights regime: political and economic determinants. Paper presented at the 98th Annual Meeting of the American Political Science Association, Boston, 29 August–1 September.

———. 2002b. Comparative politics and human rights, *Human Rights Quarterly* 24, no. 4:890–923.

———. 2003. *Issues and Methods in Comparative Politics: An Introduction*, 2nd ed. London: Routledge.

Landman, T., and J. Häusermann. 2003. Map-making and analysis of the main international initiatives on developing indicators on democracy and good governance. Report to the European Commission.

Lauren, P. G. 1998. *The Evolution of International Human Rights: Visions Seen.* Philadelphia: University of Pennsylvania Press.

Levy, J. 2002. War and peace, in *Handbook of International Relations*, ed. W. Carlsnaes, T. Risse, and B. Simmons, pp. 350–68. London: Sage.

Lewis-Beck, M. 1980. *Applied Regression: An Introduction.* London and Thousand Oaks, CA: Sage Publications.

Li, Q., and R. Reuveny. 2003. Economic globalization and democracy: an empirical analysis, *British Journal of Political Science* 33:29–54.

Lichbach, M. 1997. Social theory and comparative politics, in *Comparative Politics: Rationality, Culture, and Structure*, ed. M. Lichbach and A. Zuckerman, pp. 239–76. Cambridge: Cambridge University Press.

Lichbach, M., and A. Zuckerman, eds. 1997. *Comparative Politics: Rationality, Culture, and Structure.* Cambridge: Cambridge University Press.

Lijnzaad, L. 1995. *Reservations to UN-Human Rights Treaties: Ratify and Ruin?* Dordrecht: M. Nijhoff.

Lijphart, A. 1971. Comparative politics and comparative method, *American Political Science Review* 65, no. 3:682–93.

———. 1975. The comparable cases strategy in comparative research, *Comparative Political Studies* 8, no. 2:158–77.

———. 1999. *Patterns of Democracy: Government Forms and Performance in Thirty-Six Countries.* New Haven: Yale University Press.

Linz, J. J. 1964. An authoritarian regime: Spain, in *Mass Politics*, ed. E. Allardt and S. Rokkan. New York: The Free Press.

Linz, J. J., and A. Stepan. 1996. *Problems of Democratic Transition and Consolidation: South America, Southern Europe, and Post-Communist Europe.* Baltimore: Johns Hopkins University Press.

Lipset, S. M. 1959. Some social requisites from democracy: economic development and political legitimacy, *American Political Science Review* 53:69–105.

———. 1960. *Political Man.* London: Mercury Books.

———. 1994. The social requisites of democracy revisited, *American Sociological Review* 59 (February):1–22.

Loughlin, M. 2000. *Sword and Scales: An Examination of the Relationship Between Law and Politics.* Oxford and Portland: Hart.

Lustick, I. 1996. History, historiography, and political science: multiple historical records and the problem of selection bias, *American Political Science Review* 90, no. 3:605–18.

Lutz, E. L., and K. Sikkink. 2000. International human rights law and practice in Latin America, *International Organization* 54, no. 3:633–59.

Machiavelli, N. 1952. *The Prince.* New York: Mentor.

Macintyre, A. 1971. Is a science of comparative politics possible? in *Against the Self-Images of the Age*, pp. 260–79. London: Duckworth.

MacIntyre, A. 1981. *After Virtue: A Study in Moral Theory.* South Bend, IN: Notre Dame Press.

Macridis, R. C., and B. E. Brown, eds. 1990. *Comparative Politics*, 6th ed. Chicago: Dorsey Press.

Mair, P. 1996. Comparative politics: an overview, in *The New Handbook of Political Science*, ed. R. E. Goodin and H. Klingemann, pp. 309–35. Oxford: Oxford University Press.

Malanczuk, P. 1997. *Akehurst's Modern Introduction to International Law*, 7th rev. ed. London: Routledge.

Manzetti, L. 1993. *Institutions, Parties, and Coalitions in Argentine Politics.* Pittsburgh: University of Pittsburgh Press.

Mapel, D., and T. Nardin. 1992. Convergence and divergence in international ethics in *Traditions of International Ethics*, ed. T. Nardin and D. Mapel, pp. 296–322. Cambridge: Cambridge University Press.

March, J. G., and J. P. Olsen. 1984. The new institutionalism: organizational factors in political life, *American Political Science Review* 78:734–49.

———. 1998. The institutional dynamics of international political orders, *International Organization* 52, no. 4:943–69.

Marks, S. 2000. International law, democracy, and the end of history, in *Democratic Governance and International Law*, ed. G. H. Fox and B. R. Roth, pp. 532–66. Cambridge: Cambridge University Press.

Marshall, T. H. 1963. Citizenship and social class, in *Sociology at the Crossroads and Other Essays.* London: Heinemann.

Martin, L. L., and K. Sikkink. 1993. U.S. policy and human rights in Argentina and Guatemala, 1973–1980, in *Double-Edged Diplomacy: International Bargaining and Domestic Politics*, ed. P. B. Evans, H. K. Jacobson, and R. D. Putnam, pp. 330–62. Los Angeles: University of California Press.

Martin, L. L., and B. A. Simmons. 1998. Theories and empirical studies of international institutions, *International Organization* 52, no. 4:729–57.

Maxfield, S. 2002. International development, *Handbook of International Relations*, ed. W. Carlsnaes, T. Risse, and B. Simmons, pp. 462–79. London: Sage.

Mayer, P., V. Rittberger, and M. Zürn. 1997. Regime theory: state of the art and perspectives, in *Regime Theory and International Relations*, ed. V. Rittberger, pp. 391–430. Oxford: Clarendon Press.

McCormick, J. M., and N. J. Mitchell. 1997. Human rights violations, umbrella concepts, and empirical analysis, *World Politics* 49:510–25.

McDougal, M. S., H. D. Lasswell, and Lung-Chu Chen. 1980. *Human Rights and World Public Order: The Basic Policies of an International Law of Human Dignity.* New Haven, CT: Yale University Press.

Mearsheimer, J. J. 1994–1995. The false promise of international institutions, *International Security* 19, no. 3:5–49.

Mearsheimer, J. 2001. *The Tragedy of Great Power Politics.* New York: Norton.

Mendus, S. 1995. Human rights in political theory, *Political Studies* 43 (Special Issue):10–24.

Meyer, J. W., D. J. Frank, A. Hironaka, E. Schofer, and N. B. Tuma. 1997. The structuring of a world environmental regime, 1870–1990, *International Organization* 51, no. 4:623–29.

Meyer, W. H. 1996. Human rights and MNCs: theory vs. quantitative evidence, *Human Rights Quarterly* 18, no. 2:368–97.

———. 1998. *Human Rights and International Political Economy in Third World Nations: Multinational Corporations, Foreign Aid, and Repression.* Westport, CT.: Praeger.

———. 1999a. Confirming, infirming, and falsifying theories of human rights: reflections on Smith, Bolyard, and Ippolito through the lens of Lakatos, *Human Rights Quarterly* 21, no. 1:220–28.

———. 1999b. Human rights and international political economy in third world nations: multinational corporations, foreign aid, and repression, *Human Rights Quarterly* 21, no. 3:824–30.

Mill, J. S. 1843. *A System of Logic.* London: Longman.

Milner, H. V. 1998. Rationalizing politics: the emerging synthesis of international, American, and comparative politics, *International Organization* 52, no. 4:759–86.

Mitchell, N. J., and J. M. McCormick. 1988. Economic and political explanations of human rights violations, *World Politics* 40:476–98.

Mitchell, R. 2004. Quantitative analysis in international environmental politics: toward a theory of relative effectiveness in *Regime Consequences: Methodological Challenges and Research Strategies,* ed. A. Underdal and O. Young, pp 119–49. Dordrecht: Kluwer Academic Publishers.

Moon, B. E., and W. J. Dixon. 1985. Politics, the state, and basic human needs: a cross national study, *American Journal of Political Science* 29, no. 4:661–94.

———. 1992. Basic needs and growth: welfare trade-offs, *International Studies Quarterly* 36, no. 2:191–212.

Moore, S. F. 1978. *Law as Process: An Anthropological Approach.* London: Routledge.

Moravcsik, A. 1997. Taking preferences seriously: a liberal theory of international politics, *International Organization* 51, no. 4:513–53.

———. 2000. The origins of human rights regimes: democratic delegation in postwar Europe, *International Organization* 54 (spring):217–52.

Morgenthau, H. 1958. *Dilemma of Politics.* Chicago: University of Chicago Press.

Morgenthau, H. J. 1961. *Politics among Nations: The Struggle for Power and Peace,* 3rd ed. New York: Alfred A Knopf.

Muller, E. N., and M. A. Seligson. 1987. Inequality and insurgency, *American Political Science Review* 81, no. 2:425–51.

Munck, G. 2001. Game theory and comparative politics, *World Politics* 53(January):173–204.

Munck, G., and J. Verkuilen. 2002. Conceptualizing and measuring democracy: evaluating alternative ideals, *Comparative Political Studies* 35, no. 1:5–34.

Mutua, M. 2001. Review of *Theory and Reality in the International Protection of Human Rights*, by J. S. Watson. *American Journal of International Law* 95, no. 1:255–57.

Nardin, T., and D. R. Mapel. 1992. *Traditions of International Ethics*. Cambridge: Cambridge University Press.

Nielson, D. 2003. Supplying trade reform: political institutions and liberalization in middle-income presidential democracies, *American Journal of Political Science* 47, no. 3:470–91.

Nielson, D., and M. J. Tierney. 2003. Delegation to international organizations: agency theory and World Bank environmental reform, *International Organization* 57 (spring):241–76.

Norval, A. 1999. Review article: Truth and reconciliation: the birth of the present and the reworking of history, *Journal of Southern African Studies* 25, no. 3:499–519.

———. 2001. Reconstructing national identity and renegotiating memory: the TRC, in *States of Imagination: Ethnographic Explorations of the Postcolonial State*, ed. Thomas Blom Hansen and Finn Stepputat, pp. 182–202. Durham, NC, and London: Duke University Press.

O'Donnell, G. 1973. *Economic Modernization and Bureaucratic Authoritarianism*. Berkeley: Institute of International Studies.

———. 1999. *Counterpoints: Selected Essays on Authoritarianism and Democratization*. South Bend, IN: Notre Dame Press.

Orend, B. 2002. *Human Rights: Concept and Context*. Peterborough, Ontario: Broadview Press.

Orentlicher, D. F. 1991. The power of an idea: the impact of United States human rights policy, *Transnational Law and Contemporary Problems* 1, no. 1:43–80.

Paige, J. 1975. *Agrarian Revolution: Social Movements and Export Agriculture in the Underdeveloped World*. New York: The Free Press.

Park, H. 1987. Correlates of human rights: global tendencies, *Human Rights Quarterly* 9:405–13.

Parr, S. F. 2002. Indicators of human rights and human development: overlaps and differences, in *Matching Practice with Principles, Human Rights Impact Assessment: EU Opportunities*, ed. M. Radstaake and D. Bronkhorst, pp. 31–32. Utrecht, The Netherlands: Humanist Committee on Human Rights.

Pennings, P., H. Keman, and J. Kleinnijenhuis 1999. *Doing Research in Political Science: An Introduction to Comparative Methods and Statistics*. London: Sage.

Persico, J. E. 1994. *Nuremberg: Infamy on Trial.* New York: Penguin Books.

Peters, Guy. 1998. *Comparative Politics: Theory and Methods.* New York: New York University Press.

Petersmann, E. U. 2002. Time for a United Nations "global compact" for integrating human rights into the law of organizations: lessons from European integration, *European Journal of International Law* 13, no. 3: 621–50.

Philips, A. 1997. Preface, in *World Directory of Minorities*, ed. Minority Rights Group, pp. viii–xiii. London: Minority Rights Group International.

Poe, S. 1990. Human rights and foreign aid: a review of quantitative studies and suggestions for future research, *Human Rights Quarterly* 12:499–509.

Poe, S., and R. Sirirangsi. 1993. Human rights and U.S. economic aid to Africa. *International Interactions* 18, no. 4:1–14.

———. 1994. Human rights and U.S. economic aid during the Reagan years, *Social Science Quarterly* 75, no. 3:444–509.

Poe, S., and C. N. Tate. 1994. Repression of human rights to personal integrity in the 1980s: a global analysis, *American Political Science Review* 88:853–72.

Poe, S. C. 1990. Human rights and foreign aid: a review of quantitative studies and suggestions for future research, *Human Rights Quarterly* 12: 499–509.

———. 1991. Human rights and the allocation of U.S. military assistance, *Journal of Peace Research* 28:205–16.

———. 1992. Human rights and economic aid allocation, *American Journal of Political Science* 36:147–67.

Poe, S. C., and L. C. Keith. 2002. Personal integrity abuse during domestic crises. Paper prepared for the 98th Annual Meeting of the American Political Science Association, Boston.

Poe, S. C., and J. Meernik. 1995. U.S. military aid in the 1980s: a global analysis, *Journal of Peace Research* 32, no. 4:399–411.

Poe, S. C., and Sirirangsi. 1993. Human rights and U.S. economic aid to Africa, *International Interactions* 18, no. 4:1–14.

———. 1994. Human rights and economic aid. *Social Science Quarterly* 75, no. 3:494–509.

Poe, S. C., C. N. Tate, and L. C. Keith. 1999. Repression of the human right to personal integrity revisited: a global cross-national study covering the years 1976–1993, *International Studies Quarterly* 43:291–313.

Poe, S. C., D. Wendel-Blunt, and K. Ho. 1997. Global patterns in the achievement of women's human rights to equality, *Human Rights Quarterly* 19:813–35.

Prakash, A., and J. A. Hart. 1999. *Globalization and Governance.* London: Routledge.

Przeworski, A. 1985. Marxism and rational choice, *Politics and Society* 14, no. 4:379–409.

————. 1991. *Democracy and the Market.* Cambridge: Cambridge University Press.

Przeworski, A., M. E. Alvarez, J. A. Cheibub, and F. Limongi. 2000. *Democracy and Development: Political Institutions and Well-Being in the World, 1950–1990.* Cambridge: Cambridge University Press.

Przeworski, A., and F. Limongi. 1993. Political regimes and economic growth, *Journal of Economic Perspectives* 7, no. 3:51–69.

————. 1997. Modernization: theories and facts, *World Politics* 49 (January):155–83.

Przeworski, A., and H. Teune. 1970. *The Logic of Comparative Social Inquiry.* New York: Wiley.

Puchala, D. J., and R. F. Hopkins. 1983. International regimes: lessons from inductive analysis, in *International Regimes,* ed. S. Krasner, pp. 61–92. Ithaca and London: Cornell University Press.

Putnam, R. 1988. Diplomacy and domestic politics: the logic of two-level games, *International Organization* 42, no. 3:427–60.

————. 1993. Diplomacy and domestic politics: the logic of two-level games, in *Double-Edged Diplomacy: International Bargaining and Domestic Politics,* ed. P. B. Evans, H. K. Jacobson, and R. D. Putnam, pp. 431–68. Los Angeles: University of California Press.

Putnam, R. D. 1993. *Making Democracy Work: Civic Traditions in Modern Italy.* Princeton, NJ: Princeton University Press.

Radstaake, M., and D. Bronkhurst. 2002. *Matching Practice with Principles, Human Rights Impact Assessment: EU Opportunities.* Utrecht, The Netherlands: Humanist Committee on Human Rights.

Ragin, C. 1987. *The Comparative Method: Moving beyond Qualitative and Quantitative Strategies.* Berkeley: University of California Press.

————. 1994. Introduction to qualitative comparative analysis, in *The Comparative Political Economy of the Welfare State,* ed. T. Janoski and A. Hicks, pp. 299–320. Cambridge: Cambridge University Press.

————. 2000. *Fuzzy Set Social Science.* Chicago: University of Chicago Press.

Raustiala, K., and A. Slaughter. 2002. International law, international relations and compliance, in *Handbook of International Relations,* ed. W. Carlsnaes, T. Risse, and B. Simmons, pp. 538–58. London: Sage.

Rawls, J. 1993. The law of peoples, in *On Human Rights: The Oxford Amnesty Lectures,* ed. S. Shute and S. Hurley, pp. 42–82. New York: Basic Books.

Regan, P. 1995. U.S. economic aid and political repression, *Political Science Quarterly* 48, no. 3:613–28.

Reiff, D. 1999. The precarious triumph of human rights, *New York Times Magazine,* 8 August, 36–41.

Reiter, R. B., M. V. Zunzunegui, and J. Quiroga. 1992. Guidelines for field reporting of basic human rights violations, in *Human Rights and Statistics: Getting the Record Straight,* ed. T. B. Jabine and R. P. Claude, pp. 90–126. Philadelphia: University of Pennsylvania Press.

Renteln, A. D. 1990. *International Human Rights: Universalism Versus Relativism*. Newbury Park: Sage.

Ripsman, N. M. 2002. *Peacemaking by Democracies: The Effect of State Autonomy on the Post-World War Settlements*. University Park: Pennsylvania State University Press.

Risse, T. 2002. Transnational actors and world politics, in *Handbook of International Relations*, ed. W. Carlsnaes, T. Risse, and B. Simmons, pp. 255–74. London: Sage.

Risse, T., S. C. Ropp, and K. Sikkink. 1999. *The Power of Human Rights: International Norms and Domestic Change*. Cambridge: Cambridge University Press.

Rittberger, V. 1997. *Regime Theory and International Relations*. Oxford: Clarendon Press.

Robertson, A. H., and J. G. Merrills. 1996. *Human Rights in the World: An Introduction to the Study of the International Protection of Human Rights*, 4th ed. Manchester, England: University of Manchester Press.

Robertson, R. E. 1994. Measuring state compliance with the obligation to devote the "maximum available resources" to realising economic, social, and cultural rights, *Human Rights Quarterly* 16:693–714.

Roht-Arriaza, N. ed. 1995. *Impunity and Human Rights in International Law and Practice*. New York: Oxford University Press.

Roniger, L., and M. Sznajder. 1999. *The Legacy of Human Rights Violations in the Southern Cone: Argentina, Chile, and Uruguay*. Oxford: Oxford University Press.

Rorty, R. 1993. Human rights, rationality, and sentimentality, in *On Human Rights: The Oxford Amnesty Lectures*, ed. S. Shute and S. Hurley, pp. 112–34. New York: Basic Books.

Rosas, A. 1995. State sovereignty and human rights: towards a global constitutional project, *Political Studies* 43 (special issue): 61–78.

Rosato, S. 2003. The flawed logic of Democratic peace theory, *American Political Science Review* 97, no. 4:585–602.

Rosenau, J. N., and E. Czempiel, eds. 1992. *Governance without Government: Order and Change in World Politics*. Cambridge: Cambridge University Press.

Rosenau, P. M. 1992. *Post-Modernism and the Social Sciences: Insights, Inroads, and Intrusions*. Princeton, NJ: Princeton University Press.

Ross, M. H. 1997. Culture and identity in conparative political analysis, in *Comparative Politics: Rationality, Culture and Structure*. ed. M. Lichbach and A. Zuckerman. Cambridge: Cambridge University Press. 42–80.

Rubin, Barnett R., and Paula R. Newberg. 1980. Statistical analysis for implementing human rights policy, in *The Politics of Human Rights*, ed. P. R. Newburg, pp. 268–84. New York: New York University Press.

Rueschemeyer, D., E. H. Stephens, and J. Stephens. 1992. *Capitalist Development and Democracy*. Cambridge, England: Polity Press.

Ruggie, J. G. 1982. International regimes, transactions, and change: embedded liberalism in the postwar economic order, *International Organization* 36, no. 2:379–415.

————. 1998. What makes the world hang together? Neo-utilitarianism and the social constructivist challenge, *International Organization* 52, no. 4:855–85.

Russett, B., and J. O'Neal. 2001. *Triangulating Peace: Democracy, Interdependence and International Organizations.* New York: W. W. Norton.

Russett, B., J. R. O'Neal, and D. R. Davis. 1998. The third leg of the Kantian tripod for peace: international organizations and militarized disputes, 1950–85, *International Organization*, 52, no. 3:441–67.

Rustow, D. A., and K. P. Erickson, eds. 1991. *Comparative Political Dynamics: Global Research Perspectives.* New York: HarperCollins.

Sanders, D. 1995. Behavioural analysis, in *Theories and Methods in Political Science*, ed. D. Marsh and G. Stoker, pp. 58–75. London: Macmillan.

————. 1996. International relations: neo-realism and neo-liberalism, in *The New Handbook of Political Science*, ed. R. E. Goodin and H. Klingemann, pp. 428–45. Oxford: Oxford University Press.

Sanders, D., and H. Ward. 1994. Time-series techniques for repeated cross-section data, *Analysing Social and Political Change: A Casebook of Methods*, ed. R. Davies and A. Dale, pp. 201–23. Thousand Oaks, CA, and London: Sage Publications.

Sarkees, Meredith Reid. 2000. The correlates of war data on war: an update to 1997, *Conflict Management and Peace Science* 18, no. 1:123–44.

Sartori, G. 1970. Concept misinformation in comparative politics, *American Political Science Review* 64:1033–53

————. 1994. Compare why and how: comparing, miscomparing and the comparative method, in *Comparing Nations: Concepts, Strategies, Substance*, ed. M. Dogan and A. Kazancigil, pp. 14–34. London: Basil Blackwell.

Schabas, W. 1995a. Reservations to international human rights treaties, *Canadian Yearbook of International Law* 32:39–81.

————. 1995b. Reservations to the Convention on the Rights of the Child, 1995, *Human Rights Quarterly* 18:472–91.

————. 1995c. Is the United States still a party to the International Covenant on Civil and Political Rights? *Brooklyn Journal of International Law* 21:277–25.

————. 1997. Reservations to the Convention on the Elimination of all Forms of Discrimination Against Women and the Convention on the Rights of the Child, *William and Mary Journal of Women and the Law* 3:79–112.

Schmidt, B. C. 2002. On the history and historiography of international relations, in *Handbook of International Relations*, ed. W. Carlsnaes, T. Risse, and B. Simmons, pp. 3–32. London: Sage.

Schmitz, H. P., and K. Sikkink. 2002. International human rights, in *Handbook of International Relations*, ed. W. Carlsnaes, T. Risse, and B. Simmons, pp. 517–37. London: Sage.

Seligson, M. 1987. Development, democratization, and decay: Central America at the crossroads, in *Authoritarians and Democrats: Regime Transition in Latin America*, ed. J. Malloy and M. Seligson. Pittsburgh: University of Pittsburgh Press.

Shapiro, M., and A. Stone Sweet. 2002. *On Law, Politics, and Judicialization*. Oxford: Oxford University Press.

Sherman, E. F. 1994. The U.S. death penalty reservation to the International Covenant on Civil and Political Rights: exposing the limits of the flexible system governing treaty formation, *Texas International Law Journal* 29:69–93.

Sieder, R., ed. 1995. *Impunity in Latin America*. London: Institute for Latin American Studies.

Sikkink, K. 1998. Transnational politics, international relations theory, and human rights, *PS: Political Science and Politics* 31, no. 3:517–23.

Simmons, B. 2000. International law and state behaviour: commitment and compliance in international monetary affairs, *American Political Science Review* 94, no. 4:819–36.

Simmons, B., and L. L. Martin. 2002. International organizations and institutions, in *Handbook of International Relations*, ed. W. Carlsnaes, T. Risse, and B. Simmons, pp. 192–211. London: Sage.

Singer, J. D., and M. Small. 1972. *The Wages of War, 1816–1965: A Statistical Handbook*. New York: John Wiley.

———. 1994. *Correlates of War Project: International and Civil War Data, 1816–1992*. ICPSR 9905. Ann Arbor, MI: Inter-University Consortium for Political and Social Research.

Skaar, Elin. 1999. Truth commissions, trial or nothing? Policy options in democratic transitions, *Third World Quarterly* 20, no. 6:1109–1128.

Slaughter, A. 2000. Government networks: the heart of the liberal democratic order, in *Democratic Governance and International Law*, ed. G. H. Fox and B. R. Roth, pp. 199–238. Cambridge: Cambridge University Press.

Slaughter-Burley, A. 1993. International law and international relations theory: a dual agenda, *American Journal of International Law* 87, no. 2: 205–39.

Smith, J., R. Pagnucco, and G. A. Lopez. 1998. Globalizing human rights: the work of transnational human rights NGOs in the 1990s, *Human Rights Quarterly* 20, no. 2:379–412.

Snidal, D. 2002. Rational choice and international relations, in *Handbook of International Relations*, ed. W. Carlsnaes, T. Risse, and B. Simmons, pp. 73–94. London: Sage.

Spirer, H. 1990. Violations of human rights—how many? *American Journal of Economics and Sociology* 49:199–204.

Stanton, E. C. [1892] 2001. *Solitude of Self.* Ashfield, MA: Paris Press.

Steiner, H. J., and P. Alston. 1996. *International Human Rights in Context: Law, Politics, and Morals.* Oxford: Oxford University Press.

Steinmo, S., K. Thelen, and F. Longstreth, eds. 1992. *Structuring Politics: Historical Institutionalism in Comparative Analysis.* Cambridge: Cambridge University Press.

Stepan, A., and C. Skach. 1994. Presidentialism and parliamentarism in comparative perspective, in *The Failure of Presidential Democracy*, ed. J. Linz and A. Valenzuela, pp. 119–36. Baltimore: Johns Hopkins University Press.

Stimson, J. 1985. Regression in space and time: a statistical essay, *American Political Science Review* 29:914–47.

Stohl, M., D. Carleton, and S. Johnson. 1984. Human rights and U.S. foreign assistance, *Journal of Peace Research* 21, no. 3:215–26.

Stohl, M. D., D. Carleton, G. Lopez, and S. Samuels. 1986. State violations of human rights: issues and problems of measurement, *Human Rights Quarterly* 8:592–606.

Stokke, O. S. 2003. Boolean analysis, mechanisms, and the study of regime effectiveness, in *Regime Consequences: Methodological Challenges and Research Strategies*, ed. A. Underdal and O. R. Young. Dordrecht: Kluwer Academic.

Stone Sweet, A. 1999. Judicialization and the construction of governance, *Comparative Political Studies* 32, no. 2:147–84.

Strouse, J. C., and R. P. Claude. 1976. Empirical comparative rights research: some preliminary tests of development hypotheses, in *Comparative Human Rights*, ed. R. P. Claude, pp. 51–67. Baltimore and London: Johns Hopkins University Press.

Suksi, M. 1993. *Bringing in the People: A Comparison of Constitutional Forms and Practices of the Referendum.* Dordrecht: Nijhoff.

Thompson, K., and C. Giffard. 2002. *Reporting Killings as Human Rights Violations.* Colchester, England: Human Rights Centre, University of Essex.

Tickner, A. 2002. Feminist perspectives on international relations, in *Handbook of International Relations*, ed. W. Carlsnaes, T. Risse, and B. Simmons, pp. 275–91. London: Sage.

Timmerman, J. 2002. *Prisoner without a Name, Cell without a Number.* Madison: University of Wisconsin Press.

Union of International Organizations. 1995. *Yearbook of International Organizations 1994–1995*, Vols. 1–3. Munich: Union of International Organizations.

———. 2001. *Yearbook of International Organizations 2000–2001*, Vol. 3. Geneva: Saur.

United Nations Development Programme (UNDP). 1999. *Human Development Report 1999.* New York: Oxford University Press.

Vanhanen, T. 1997. *The Prospects of Democracy.* London: Routledge.

van Maarseveen, H., and G. van der Tang. 1978. *Written Constitutions: A Computerized Comparative Study.* New York: Oceana Publications.

Vincent, R. J. 1986. *Human Rights and International Relations.* Cambridge: Cambridge University Press.

Vogt, W. P. 1999. *Dictionary of Statistics and Methodology: A Non-technical Guide for the Social Sciences,* 2nd ed. London: Sage.

Wallensteen, P., and M. Sollenberg. 2001. Armed conflict, 1989–2000, *Journal of Peace Research* 38, no. 5:629–44.

Waltz, K. N. 1979. *Theory of International Politics.* New York: Random House.

Ward, M., and K. Gleditsch. 1998. Democratizing for peace, *American Political Science Review* 92, no. 1:51–61.

Watchirs, H. 2002. Review of methodologies measuring human rights implementation, *Journal of Law, Medicine, and Ethics* 30:716–33.

Watson, J. S. 1999. *Theory and Reality in the International Protection of Human Rights.* Ardsley, NY: Transnational Publishers.

Weede, E. 1992. Some simple calculations on democracy and war involvement, *Journal of Peace Research* 29:377–83.

Weir, S., and D. Beetham. 1998. *Political Power and Democratic Control in Britain: The Democratic Audit of the United Kingdom.* London: Routledge.

Weissbrodt, D., and M. L. Bartolomei. 1991. The effectiveness of international human rights pressures: the case of Argentina, 1976–1983, *Minnesota Law Review* 75:1009–35.

Welch, C. E., Jr. 2001. *NGOs and Human Rights: Promise and Performance.* Philadelphia: University of Pennsylvania Press.

Wendt, A. 1999. *Social Theory of International Politics.* Cambridge: Cambridge University Press.

Weston, B. H. 1989. Human rights, in *Human Rights in the World Community: Issues and Action,* ed. R. P. Claude and B. H. Weston, pp. 12–29. Philadelphia: University of Pennsylvania Press.

Whitehead, L. 1996a. Comparative politics: democratization studies, in *The New Handbook of Political Science,* ed. R. E. Goodin and H. Klingemann. Oxford: Oxford University Press.

———, ed. 1996b. *The International Dimensions of Democratization: Europe and the Americas.* Oxford: Oxford University Press.

———. 2002. *Democratization: Theory and Experience.* Oxford: Oxford University Press.

Wickham-Crowley, T. 1992. *Guerrillas and Revolution in Latin America.* Princeton, NJ: Princeton University Press.

Wiessner, S. 1999. Rights and status of indigenous peoples: a global comparative and international legal analysis, *Harvard Human Rights Journal* 12 (spring):57–128.

Wilson, R. 2001. *The Politics of Truth and Reconciliation on South Africa: Legitimizing the Post-Apartheid State.* Cambridge: Cambridge University Press.

Wilson, R. A., and J. P. Mitchell, eds. 2003. *Human Rights in Global Perspective: Anthropological Studies of Rights, Claims, and Entitlements.* London: Routledge.

Wolf, E. 1969. *Peasant Wars of the Twentieth Century.* New York: Harper and Row.

Wolfers, A. 1962. *Discord and Collaboration: Essays on International Politics.* Baltimore: Johns Hopkins University Press.

Wright, S. 2001. *International Human Rights, Decolonisation, and Globalisation: Becoming Human.* London: Routledge.

Young, O. R. 1980. International regimes: problems of concept formation, *World Politics* 32, no. 3:331–56.

———. 1992. The effectiveness of international institutions: hard cases and critical variables, in *Governance without Government: Order and Change in World Politics*, ed. J. N. Rosenau and E. Czempiel, pp. 160–94. Cambridge: Cambridge University Press.

———. 1999a. *Governance in World Affairs.* Ithaca: Cornell University Press.

———, ed. 1999b. *The Effectiveness of Environmental Regimes: Causal Connections and Behavioural Mechanisms.* Cambridge: MIT Press.

Youngers, C. 2003. *Violencia Política y Sociedad Civil en el Perú.* Lima: Instituto de los Estudios Peruanos.

Zacher, M. W. 1992. The decaying pillars of the Westphalian temple: implications for international order and governance, in *Governance without Government: Order and Change in World Politics*, ed. J. N. Rosenau and E. Czempiel, pp. 58–101. Cambridge: Cambridge University Press.

Zakaria, F. 2003. *The Future of Freedom: Illiberal Democracy at Home and Abroad.* New York and London: W. W. Norton.

Zanger, S. C. 2000a. A global analysis of the effect of regime changes on life integrity violations, 1977–1993, *Journal of Peace Research* 33.

———. 2000b. Good governance and European aid: the impact of political conditionality, *European Union Politics* 1, no. 3:293–317.

Zürn, M. 2002. From interdependence to globalization, in *Handbook of International Relations*, ed. W. Carlsnaes, T. Risse, and B. Simmons, pp. 235–54. London: Sage.

Index

Note: Figures are represented by italicized page numbers and the letter *f* (*25f*). Tables are represented by italicized page numbers and the letter *t* (*55t*).